P9-CDW-546

A12900 231196

DATE			

the known and the unknown

The KNOWN
and the
UNKNOWN

the iconography of
science fiction

Gary K. Wolfe

The Kent State University Press

Library of Congress Cataloging in Publication Data

Wolfe, Gary K   1946-
    The known and the unknown.

    Includes bibliographical references and index.
    1. Science fiction, American—History and criticism. 2. Science fiction, English—
History and criticism.
I. Title.
PS374.S35W6   823'.0876   79-88606
ISBN 0-87338-231-5

For Kary

contents

Preface   ix

Acknowledgments   xvi

PART ONE: IMAGE AND BELIEF IN SCIENCE FICTION

1. Icons of Wonder   3
*Myth and Speculation. . . A Historical Digression. . .
Science Fiction and the Cult of Rationality. . . The
Known and the Unknown. . . The Icons of Science
Fiction. . . The "Sense of Wonder". . . The Evolution of
New Icons*

2. The Image of the Barrier   30
*Barriers and Portals. . . The Barrier as Puzzle. . . The
Barrier and Cultural Isolation*

PART TWO: IMAGES OF ENVIRONMENT

3. Icon of the Spaceship   55
*The Rocket and the Hearth. . . The "Universe"
Tradition. . . The Spaceship Family. . . The Human
Spaceship*

4. Icon of the City   86
*The City as Babylon. . . Evolution of the Science Fiction
City. . . The Imperial City. . . The Technological
City. . . Arcology. . . The Space City*

5. Icon of the Wasteland   125
*The Transformed Landscape. . . The Evolution of the
New Order. . . The Rediscovery of Technology. . . The
Cycles of History*

PART THREE: IMAGES OF HUMANITY

6. Icon of the Robot   151
   Rebellious Machines. . . The Misused Tool. . . The
   Human Imperative. . . The Re-creation of Humanity

7. Icon of the Monster   184
   A Hierarchy of Monsters. . . Mineral Beings. . .
   Vegetable Beings. . . Animals. . . Aliens. . .
   Transformed Humans. . . Telepaths and Telekineticists

Afterword   225

Notes   231

Index   241

preface

This book is neither a history of science fiction nor a general introductory survey of the field. Several such books exist, some of them excellent, but one of the assumptions of the present study is that science fiction in general, and science-fiction criticism in particular, is no longer of such narrow interest that every new study of the field need take for its scope the totality of what science fiction means, or where it comes from, or how to teach it. Few popular genres have enjoyed as much detailed criticism, both by enthusiasts and scholars, as has science fiction, and few are of as much general interest today both in the classroom and in the popular imagination. Yet if the serious study of the genre is to move forward, it is necessary to realize that not every treatment of it need be definitive, that there is ample room for a variety of approaches to the genre, and that science fiction has grown to such complexity and breadth that more limited studies may be valuable.

This study, then, is deliberately limited in scope. It is an attempt to explore how a few images familiar to any science-fiction reader (and to most nonreaders as well) have developed into "icons," and how these icons are used within specific works, within the genre as a whole, and to some extent within the culture that the genre reflects. Since many of these icons antedate the genre, and since some of them have grown increasingly complex as recent writers have begun deliberately manipulating the genre's conventions, I have focused mainly on the "middle ground" of science fiction's development: the late 1930s to the early 1960s, when the bulk of works that led to the phenomenon we call science fiction were produced. It was during the period that science fiction began to move out of the pulp magazines and into book form that it began to exert a noticeable popular culture influence in such areas as film and television, and that many of the writers who now inhabit the pantheon of the genre established their reputations. Before this period, of course, lie centuries of fantastic writing, but here "science fiction" becomes a problematic notion, with a vast number of romantic and utopian works that might easily be admitted to the genre on a theoretical basis, but which probably had little direct influence on the more localized body of work produced by the somewhat inbred cadre of writers, fans, and readers that evolved during the pulp era and that remains a strong force in the field today. It is one thing to argue for the sake of legitimizing a once-maligned genre that Tommaso Campanella's *City of the Sun* contains science-fictional elements; it is quite another to demonstrate that it had any appreciable influence on such writers as Robert Heinlein or Clifford Simak. The earlier works I have had occasion to refer to in this book—such as those of Poe, Verne, and Wells—are generally works whose influence has indeed been felt in the vast network of modern science fiction. Similarly, when I have discussed more recent works, I have done so to demonstrate how these works partake of the kinds of issues I am exploring in regard to the larger body of work under discussion. Thus, although Samuel Delany's *Fall of the Towers* may seem one of his lesser works, I have included it more because of its clear relationships to earlier science fiction than for what it does that is new or different.

Some acute readers might object that by limiting the works under discussion to this general period, I have introduced a bias toward the so-called "Campbell era," that period during which John W. Campbell, Jr.'s, editorship of *Astounding Science Fiction* so heavily influenced the direction of the genre. Perhaps that is true; but it might also be argued that even if this study is so biased, Campbell was among the central figures in shaping the largest single body of science fiction during the era when it became science fiction—not the "scientifiction" of Hugo Gernsback, the "science fantasy" of A. Merritt, or the "space opera" of Edward E. Smith—and before it became the "speculative fiction" of more recent writers who seek—properly, I believe—to erase the barriers between this genre and the "mainstream." But whatever science fiction may be evolving into, whatever new directions the writers of the 1970s may be taking, whatever less restrictive definitions of the genre may be formulated, it is fatuous to believe that writers such as Heinlein, Williamson, or Sturgeon were not aware that they were writing something special during those long years when their only markets were magazines such as Campbell's, their only colleagues other writers who shared their peculiar images and conventions, their only visible readers that tightly-knit subculture known as "fandom." Science fiction may be a problem in genre studies today, but for a long time it was a clearly identifiable phenomenon of popular culture.

For these reasons also, I have with very few exceptions (Verne being the most notable) limited the works under discussion to American and British science fiction. There are certainly cultural differences between American and British science fiction, as there are between any comparable bodies of American and British literature, but in the case of science fiction I believe there has been an active interchange of ideas and concepts that has resulted in writers of both countries participating in the same "consensus cosmogony" or "consensus future history" that has been described by Donald Wollheim and James Gunn in their studies of the genre.[1] British science fiction may on the whole be more apocalyptic than American science fiction, and British writers may sometimes demonstrate a more acute awareness of the traditions of the novel, but ample evidence suggests that British writers learned a great deal from their American counterparts and incorporated into their fiction many of the icons that might have seemed peculiarly American. It is sometimes a bit jarring to read of Britain launching spaceships, as in Edmund Cooper's *Seed of Light*, when Britain has not, to my knowledge, ever shown much inclination to do such a thing and when even Jules Verne visualized a moon shot as a peculiarly American project; but when one realizes the extent to which British science-fiction writers enthusiastically shared the fantasies of their American counterparts, it becomes less of a shock.

Another reason for treating works of science fiction from these middle decades as a group has to do with the fans and early critics of science fiction. Harold Bloom has suggested that poets experience an "anxiety of influence," that, faced with an imposing tradition of past masterworks, they misread and try to supplant their forebears in order to declare their own identity (in *The Anxiety of Influence: A Theory of Poetry*, 1973). Much evidence suggests that science-fiction writers do the same on a much more limited canvas, and much of what has passed for criticism in the genre has been a kind of game of finding out who did what first—an interesting game, and a useful one, but a game nonetheless. Sam Moskowitz, who has long laid claim to being the "official historian" of science fiction, has, in essay after essay, book after book, meticulously traced standard science-fiction concepts back to their first appearance (such as the discovery that the first artificial earth satellite story was written by Edward Everett Hale).[2] While such bibliographical detective work may not tell as much about what a concept means or why it is important to the writers who use it, it nevertheless is useful in demonstrating that science-fiction writers can in some measure be defined as science-fiction writers by the extent to which they partake of the set-pieces of the field; writing a "first contact" story, or a "Universe"-type story, becomes somewhat like a pianist's adding Liszt or Scriabin to his repertoire, or—perhaps more to the point—like a mystery writer's undertaking a "locked room" murder mystery. Is it reasonable to assume that Brian Aldiss's *Starship* or Harry Harrison's *Captive Universe* would be the same had it not been for the earlier treatment of this same theme by Robert Heinlein in "Universe"? And even in cases in which science-fiction writers might never have read the specific works that they are attempting to supersede, such notions seem to filter down through the network of science fiction, making them aware that such a concept exists. One might even argue—though it would take greater familiarity with the subculture of science-fiction writers and fans than I possess to prove this—that such concepts are "in the air" even before their first appearance in a science-fiction story, that science-fiction notions are "culturally determined," just as A. L. Kroeber says inventions are: "that given a certain constellation and development of a culture, certain inventions must be made."[3] Similarly, certain developments in science fiction seem almost inevitable. Even had it not been for Philip José Farmer and Theodore Sturgeon, the theme of sexual love would likely have appeared in the genre sometime in the 1950s; even without the "New Wave" of the 1960s, science fiction would have discovered narrative and stylistic experimentation probably within a few years of the actual "New Wave" experiments. That such a claim could be made seems to me further evidence of the essential interrelatedness of the science fiction of this era.

To some extent, then, I am regarding science fiction as a popular aesthetic movement and not just a body of works of fiction on similar themes. The marvelous and sometimes intimidating institution of "fandom," with its conventions, awards, newsletters, fanzines, and feuds, has done much to consolidate this aspect of science fiction while at the same time possibly constraining the genre from developing to its full potential. The "consensus" of which Wollheim and Gunn speak is a consensus of fans as much as writers, and it has on occasion exerted a powerful cautionary feedback to authors seeking to stretch the boundaries of the genre. Whatever theoretical definitions we may arrive at for science fiction, we have the continuing influence of a fandom that awards or withholds its imprimatur largely according to the extent to which works conform to the basic assumptions of the genre, and when I speak of "mainstream" science fiction, I am referring to works that have been awarded this unofficial seal of approval. By focusing on this collective body of mainstream science fiction, I have included some discussion of works that are by no means major fictions, and other works of film and art that might properly be excluded from a more narrowly literary survey. No doubt many science fiction advocates will take umbrage at the very mention of, say, Jack Arnold's monster movies in a discussion that also includes Olaf Stapledon, but a few of those advocates will not at once recognize their own familiarity with such movies. Despite the contempt fans may feel for the crude reduction of science-fiction concepts to special effects and melodramatic formulas, I will maintain that many science-fiction films, despite the lack of involvement of "real" science-fiction writers, are in fact structured by the same concerns that structure much of the literature, and sometimes even succeed in reaching deeper centers of consciousness in a wider audience than the literature does. Similarly, I make occasional references to science-fiction art, which consists mostly of magazine illustration and which, to judge from letter columns in the pulp magazines of the 1930s and 1940s, played almost as large a role in the development of a science-fiction sensibility during that period as did the stories themselves.

The book is organized not according to historical chronology, nor to different authorial styles, nor to some hidden definition of what science fiction is. The quest for a universally applicable definition of the genre has become something of a Grail quest for science-fiction readers and critics, and I suspect it is quite hopeless, diverting though it may be. Thus, although I have at several points tried to identify characteristics that are common to much of the genre—that it tends to speculation and generally believes in the "knowability" of the universe, that it tries to achieve a "sense of wonder" through a juxtaposition of the known and the unknown, that it is often structured around symbolic barriers to knowledge—I do not claim that these characteristics, either singly or as a group, are at all times sufficient to qualify one work as science fiction and another work as non-science-fiction. In all probability, science fiction will ultimately have to be characterized by the questions it raises rather than by the answers it offers. If we claim that science fiction teaches faith in technology, for example, we are immediately confronted by a large group of works, clearly science fiction in intent and audience reception, that are severely critical of technology. But if we say that science fiction asks what the role of technology is in human affairs, both groups of works fall into place around this question. (Of course, we then have to deal with the large number of non-science-fiction works that also address the question.) Although I discuss a number of such questions in this book, I have employed a rather simple principle in deciding if a work qualifies for discussion as science fiction: if a book or story or film was conceived as science fiction, presented as science fiction, and received by its audience as science fiction, it was fair game for discussion, even though the principle of selection allowed the inclusion of a few semi-fantasy works (such as A. Merritt's *The Metal Monster* or Theodore Sturgeon's "It") that contributed to the evolution of the specific icon under discussion.

The study is arranged in three large parts. The first two chapters lay out a number of broad issues that underlie the iconography of science fiction and explore an image that is so ubiquitous in the genre that it transcends the label "icon"—the image of the barrier between known and unknown. Chapters Three through Five explore specific icons that science fiction has evolved concerning artificial or unnatural environments: the spaceship, which represents entry into the unknown; the city, which represents subjugation of the unknown; and the wasteland, which represents the reemergence of the unknown. Finally, Chapters Six and Seven shift the focus from images of the environment to images of humanity itself, first as reflected in technology through the icon of the robot, and then as reflected in the images of transformation that are represented by science fiction's various treatments of monsters, aliens, and transformed humans. Obviously, many of these icons overlap and merge in certain works. The alien being becomes the robot, the robot becomes the spaceship, the spaceship becomes the city, the city becomes the wasteland: such transformations and combinations of the favorite images of the genre become like variations on a theme, with writers working from a relatively limited number of consensual images to create a vast and complex body of fiction that nevertheless often rests upon the assumption of reader familiarity with the fundamental icons of the genre.

By classifying these various icons and discussing the ways in which they generate "wonder" and reflect some of the basic beliefs that underlie science fiction, I am not trying to arrive at a definitive taxonomy of science-fiction works; the genre is too complex to allow for such a straight forward formulaic analysis. Thus I may occasionally focus on a monster image in a text that also abounds in other icons, such as spaceships or cities. In such cases, my intent is not to reduce the text under discussion to a simplistic expression of this or that icon, but rather to draw from it some of the qualities it shares in common with other works that employ this icon, and to explore how the author may draw on and modify a common mythology in a context that may include other themes and motifs as well.

Finally, a note on the editions used: a well-known problem in the study of science fiction and other forms of popular literature is that not many standard library editions exist. Although a number of publishers have begun to correct this situation by issuing hardbound library editions of major works, most of these editions have not yet found their way into most libraries, and in any event, such a solution does not seem likely in the near future for any but the major works in the genre. Thus we are left with the marketing vicissitudes of the paperback houses to determine which works are likely to be available at a given time—a situation that often changes from month to month. Where possible, I have tried to use generally available paperback editions on the assumption that these editions are frequently reprinted. When this was not possible, or when a paper edition was not available at the time of writing, I have used hardbound editions that are likely to be available in libraries. Thus, for John Wyndham's *Re-Birth,* I have used the edition reprinted in Anthony Boucher's *A Treasury of Great Science Fiction,* since the Boucher anthology is more likely to be available through libraries than the original hardbound novel. And in some cases, I have had no recourse but to use whatever edition is in my own library, since many interesting science-fiction titles unfortunately disappear from all but private libraries within a few months of their original publication.

Gary K. Wolfe

Roosevelt University
May, 1979

acknowledgments

There are many people without whom this book might never have been written, and were I to be thorough in acknowledging all of them I should probably have to begin with used book merchants and magazine store owners in small towns in Missouri. But more to the point, perhaps, are the teachers I have had who encouraged me in the belief that science fiction is a field worth thinking about, and I would like to thank them first. Many years ago, at the University of Kansas, James Gunn supported me in my first serious researches into this field, and his own considerable accomplishments, before and since, have been a continuing source of encouragement. Later, at the University of Chicago— where I was not at all sure I would be able to get away with this sort of thing—John Cawelti offered enthusiastic support and taught me much of what I know about the analysis of popular culture of all kinds. I later discovered that other instructors, too, would take an interest in this strange field, especially Michael Murrin, Jerome McGann, and Paul Herring.

Some of the ideas in this book may be traced to an article of mine that Thomas Clareson published in *Extrapolation* in 1972 ("The Limits of Science Fiction," *Extrapolation,* 14: 1, 39-48). Tom also included an earlier version of part of Chapter Four in his 1977 Kent State University Press book *Many Futures, Many Worlds,* and his criticism of that earlier manuscript did much to help me think out the issues in this book. More than anyone else, he taught me not to apologize for writing about science fiction. Since then, I have talked and corresponded with other scholars in the field, and several of them—notably Thomas Wymer and David Samuelson—may find fragments of their own insights in this book, I hope not too seriously distorted.

Of my colleagues and students at Roosevelt University, Daniel Headrick provided me with some useful leads from his own researches into the history of technology. Steve Armentrout, my research assistant, read an early version of the manuscript, made many helpful suggestions, tracked down references, and uncovered some stories I had not previously been aware of. Roberta Fireman patiently typed parts of the manuscript.

I owe also a debt of gratitude to my editors at Kent State University Press, Michael Di Battista and Martha Gibbons. Mike first expressed interest in a book-length study, and insightfully shepherded the book through its early revisions; much of the present structure of the book was his idea. Martha copyedited the final manuscript, improving the style and attending to a myriad of details.

Finally, I should like to thank three people whose faith in the book has been the most enduring, and who repeatedly encouraged and even badgered me to get it done. Carol Williams, colleague, frequent collaborator, and always friend, took time to read and comment on part of the manuscript despite her lack of familiarity with the subject matter. Ed Gerson, with whom over the years I have had many long and enlightening conversations about science fiction and popular culture, has helped to shape the book in ways he may not be fully aware of. And my wife Kary, who is also my best editor and sounding board, provided ideas, criticism, and a great deal of patience. What I have learned from these people goes far begond the scope of this book.

A portion of Chapter Three appeared, in slightly different form, in *Selected Proceedings of the 1978 Science Fiction Research Association National Conference,* edited by Thomas J. Remington (Cedar Falls: University of Northern Iowa, 1979).

image and belief in science fiction

1
icons of wonder

Some of you have asked why we should set out for a goal that lies we know
not how far away or that might not even exist. I will tell you that we are
setting sail because the Unknown exists and we would make it the Known.
That's all!

Richard Francis Burton,
in Philip José Farmer's *To Your Scattered Bodies Go* (1971)

MYTH AND SPECULATION

In Dahomey, according to Pierre Grimal, a person facing a crisis
consults a sorcerer to discover what the future holds. The sorcerer
"draws the Fa"—a form of divination that involves "reading" fruit pits
scattered on a table—thus invoking certain gods or demons and their
associated myths. Although the connections between these myths and
the immediate problem may seem at first tenuous, a link is eventually
forged, producing "a certain state of mind in the consulter, which puts
an end to uncertainty and allows him to take action."[1] In this way, the
myths of the society are made useful, becoming the bases for programs
of action rather than mere narratives. Ethnologists have long been
aware of this practical function of myth, but it has been widely ignored
in most discussions of myth as a cultural model for literature, and
especially in discussions of science fiction, despite recurring claims that
science fiction is or can be a "modern mythology," born of our
technological environment and best suited of all popular genres to aid us
in coping with it. Unexamined as the claims for a special relationship
between science fiction and myth may be, I believe they are worth
exploring, not just because of the surface similarities of heroic narratives
and cosmic imagery, but because I suspect that many who read science
fiction, or enjoy it in the movies or on television, invest a certain part of
their own fate in what it has to say. It provides them with mythic

reflections of themselves and of their potential environments, and shows them what courses of action are possible both on a personal and cosmic scale. As with the magical Fa, there is far more to be seen than merely the fruit pits on the table.

Examples of such a personal response to science fiction can be found at all levels of society, from the numerous astronauts and engineers who trace their career decisions to an adolescent interest in the genre to members of various fringe cultures in the 1960s who found in such works as Robert Heinlein's *Stranger in a Strange Land,* Arthur C. Clarke's *Childhood's End,* or Frank Herbert's *Dune* validations of their own beliefs and behavior—even when these beliefs proved bizarre or dangerous, as was the case with Ken Kesey's Merry Pranksters or the Manson family. Whether science fiction operates on so intensely personal a level with most of its readers, it fulfills a cultural function not unlike that of the Dahomeyan sorcerer: it provides technological society with a ritual methodology for action. In its simplest formulation, this methodology is the scientific method of systematic induction. Scientific rationalism has apparently "worked" so often in the past that we are led to believe that it can be applied to almost any situation, whether it be vast historical movements (as in Isaac Asimov's *Foundation* trilogy) or the minute details of human behavior (as in Frank Herbert's *Dune* stories). Such a belief is not unlike the belief in myth described by Mircea Eliade:

> Myth assures man that what he is about to do *has already been* done, in other words, it helps him to overcome doubts as to the result of his undertaking. There is no reason to hesitate before setting out on a sea voyage, because the mythical hero has already made it in a fabulous Time. All that is needed is to follow his example. Similarly, there is no reason to fear settling in an unknown, wild territory, because one knows what one has to do. One has merely to repeat the cosmogonic ritual, whereupon the unknown territory (="Chaos") is transformed into "Cosmos," becomes an *imago mundi* and hence a ritually legitimized "habitation." The existence of an exemplary model does not fetter creative innovation. The possibilities for applying the mythical model are endless.[2]

One can read "science" for "myth" in the above passage, and "scientific method" for "cosmogonic ritual," and arrive at something fairly close to a description of what much "mainstream" science fiction does. *The transformation of Chaos into Cosmos, of the unknown into the known, is the central action of a great many works of science fiction.*

Science fiction, of course, is not the only purveyor of myth in our culture; other genres of popular fiction also serve this function in various ways, and science fiction's own sister genre of fantasy is perhaps the clearest direct descendant of primitive myth among all narrative genres. But what science fiction does that is uniquely suited to a technological society is to explore the mythical aspects of reason itself, specifically of scientific reasoning. Science, one might well argue, is the real myth of our culture, and science fiction is merely the codification and expression of beliefs in that myth. Science-fiction writers are the sorcerers and divines who interpret and order those culturally accepted beliefs that in our society so often revolve around science and the scientific method. Like the Dahomey sorcerer, they show us how our beliefs can be applied to resolve specific cultural problems and enable us to take action, but they do not create those beliefs any more than the primitive sorcerer creates the gods whose works he interprets. As Ian Barbour writes, "Myth sanctions the existing social order and justifies its status system and power structure, providing a rationale for social and political institutions."[3]

But myth is more than a political tool. "It is the object of myth, as of science," writes Grimal, "to explain the world, to make its phenomena intelligible. Like science too, its purpose is to supply man with a means of influencing the universe, of making sure of spiritual and material possession of it."[4] Without resorting to the reductive nineteenth-century view of myth as a primitive attempt at science, we can observe a number of ways in which science, as expressed through the medium of science fiction, becomes a modern paradigm of myth. One of the most significant of such ways is the function of *speculation*, long a key term in describing what science fiction does. First suggested by Robert Heinlein in 1947,[5] the term "speculative fiction" as an alternative to "science fiction" gained considerable currency during the "New Wave" movement of the 1960s, and is still the preferred term for many science-fiction writers. The nature of speculative thought and its importance to mythmaking has been well described by Henri Frankfort in his study of the myths of the ancient Near East:

> Speculation—as the etymology of the word shows—is an intuitive, an almost visionary, mode of apprehension. This does not mean, of course that it is mere irresponsible meandering of the mind, which ignores reality or seeks to escape from its problems. Speculative thought transcends experience, but only because it attempts to explain, to unify, to order experience. It achieves this end by means of hypotheses. If we use the word in its original sense, then we may say that speculative thought attempts to *underpin* the chaos of experience so that it may reveal the features of a structure—order, coherence, and meaning.

5

> Speculative thought is therefore distinct from mere idle speculation in that it never breaks entirely away from experience. It may be 'once removed' from the problems of experience, but is is also concerned with them in that it tries to explain them.
>
> In our own time speculative thought finds its scope more severely limited than it has been at any other period. For we possess in science another instrument for the interpretation of experience, one that has achieved marvels and retains its full fascination. We do not allow speculative thought, under any circumstances, to encroach upon the sacred precincts of science.[6]

Scientists may justifiably take exception to Frankfort's last point—his own earlier use of the term "hypotheses" belies it—but it seems evident that one reason for the popularity of science fiction is the felt need for a body of comprehensible speculative thought in the face of the manifold complexities and specializations of modern science. Science fiction deliberately uses the terms and structures of scientific thought to create mythic patterns, and the belief that underlies these patterns is a belief not so much in supernatural beings as in the almost supernatural power of rationality itself.

A HISTORICAL DIGRESSION: MOSTLY ON POE

Evidence of this gradual mythification of reason can be detected in embryonic form in some of the earliest direct precursors of modern science fiction. Brian Aldiss, for example, sees the sources of the genre in the Gothic novel, and specifically cites *Frankenstein* as the Gothic model of science fiction.[7] But even before Mary Shelley sent her eminently reasonable monster forth on the landscape, we see the supernatural universe giving way to the rational universe in the works of Ann Radcliffe, who, despite her carefully orchestrated interplay of immanent landscapes and shady characters—the full complement of Gothic trappings—was careful to provide rational explanations for the supernatural events in her narratives. Although she has often been taken to task for this, as Walter Allen notes, "she had merely anticipated the basis of logic without which the thriller cannot exist."[8] The hideous unknown in her novels is always brought safely into the known, leaving us with a landscape infused not with chaotic powers that transcend human understanding, but only with the fears and apprehensions of the real characters who inhabit it. The marvelous made mechanical is also evident in Mary Shelley's *Frankenstein: or, the Modern Prometheus* (1818), which combines Promethean myth with contemporary chemistry and surgery. Significantly, as Aldiss points out, Victor

Frankenstein chooses to conduct his experiments not only on the basis of the hermetic arts of alchemy, but also on the basis of the rational science of Erasmus Darwin and Luigi Galvani.[9] Reason becomes the agent that unveils the unknown; the mystery—in this case the mystery of the creation of life—is revealed as susceptible to rational exegesis.

To an even greater extent, Edgar Allan Poe delighted in constructing wildly irrational situations and characters and then demonstrating to the reader the underlying logical or scientific sources of this construct. His interest in hoaxes may have been a reflection of his interest in the ways science and mechanics could provide a basis for belief and myth; the value of hoaxes lay in their explanation more than anything else. For Poe, as for many later science-fiction writers, rationality became an end in itself—almost divorced from considerations of abstract morality. The *why* of events was less important than the *how*—how the mechanical chess player hoax was brought off, how one might reach the moon in a balloon, how the most irrational behavior might be accounted for. For this reason, Poe's often cited "proto-science fiction" works such as "Mellonta Tauta" or "The Narrative of Arthur Gordon Pym" are in some ways less revealing of the history of the genre than are his puzzles and tales of ratiocination.

An example may be found in as simple a popular story as "The Gold Bug" (1843). Ostensibly, the story deals with William LeGrand, a typically mysterious and romantic Poe protagonist who, through a process of what seems to be almost visionary divination, discovers a priceless treasure hidden by Captain Kidd. The first half of the story is riddled with supernatural overtones: LeGrand discovers a mysterious golden beetle and is bitten by it. His servant Jupiter fears the bite may have been poisonous, since LeGrand begins to behave in an apparently irrational manner. He becomes reclusive, obsessed with the gold bug and what mysteries it might conceal, and he finally persuades Jupiter and the narrator of the story (who has become concerned after hearing Jupiter's account of the change in LeGrand's behavior) to accompany him to a desolate stretch of forest where, after much mystic ritual (such as passing the gold bug on a string through the eye of a skull nailed to a tree) and much digging, they uncover the treasure. At this point in the story the reader might well be puzzled: what has appeared to be chaotic, irrational behavior has led to a positive reward. What few readers remember about the story, however, is that nearly the entire second half of it is given over to LeGrand's elaborate explanation of the careful reasoning processes that really lay behind the discovery of the treasure. What we had been led to regard as irrational was in fact superrational: a process of constructing hypotheses, decoding ciphers, and calculating distances that to Jupiter *appeared,* from his credulous point of view, to be insane. In the end, we are satisfied with the ingenious explanations that LeGrand gives for his behavior; the latent chaos in the story has been ordered, not by any supernatural agency, but by simple rationality. In a real sense, the climax of the story is less the discovery of the treasure than the discovery by the reader of the ordering *principle* that led to the finding of the treasure; the satisfaction the story offers comes less from its mystery than from its explanation of that mystery. This is the pattern of virtually all the Dupin stories, and indeed of many later mystery stories such as those of Conan Doyle—who, not coincidentally, was another early master of science fiction. In a curious way, it is also the pattern of much modern scientific thought. The search for a steady state model of the universe, for example, can never lead to the kind of eschatological comfort that religion once offered, but it may eventually lead to the discovery of a *process* by which any given phenomenon might be explained. This process—reason itself—has become the goal. On a cosmic scale, we no longer seriously seek to know who the culprit was or why he did it; we only ask how it was done.

SCIENCE FICTION AND THE CULT OF RATIONALITY

More than any other modern genre, science fiction provides a narrative realization of this new dogma of reason for reason's sake. One of its essential structures is a codification of the scientific method itself, a kind of systematized speculation. Although it is today primarily in the "hard science" school of science-fiction writers that we can most easily perceive the scientific methodology underlying the narrative structure, most science-fiction writers to some degree partake of this dogma, and it is certainly at the basis of the "consensus future history" that James Gunn sees as having developed out of the massive core of modern science fiction produced during the 1940s and 1950s.[10] During this heyday, one of the genre's leading writers expressed the new dogma quite directly: in an address at the University of Chicago in 1958, Robert Heinlein claimed that science fiction alone of all literary genres takes into account the scientific method in structuring narratives. Other fiction, he said, only shows awareness of how the method has already produced effects. "It is a static attitude, an assumption that what is now forever shall be. . . .The mature speculative novel is the only form of fiction which stands even a chance of interpreting the spirit of our times."[11]

8

The attitude expressed by Heinlein has been a dominant theme in the various defenses of the genre that have been written in the last twenty years or so, and it is reflected in the critical writing both of other science-fiction writers and of academic critics and scholars. Sometimes the defense is accompanied by an all-out attack on something called the "mainstream," a rather vaguely defined term that seems to refer to everything that isn't science fiction, and hence could conceivably range from Aristotle's *Poetics* to Erich Segal's *Love Story*. Isaac Asimov, in an article titled "When Aristotle Fails, Try Science Fiction," characterizes this "mainstream" as "tasteless pap" that is no longer relevant to the demands and values of a technological society.[12] Robert Barthell, an academic critic of science fiction, has compared "aesthetic and humanistic" goals to the decorations on early machinery, decorations that disappeared with the full-fledged advent of the technological society.[13] It should be noted that not all science-fiction advocates share this view. Ursula Le Guin, for example, bemoans the persistent notion of the "mainstream" as something apart from science fiction: "Nobody but Americans know what mainstream even means," she observed in an interview a few years ago, arguing that European literature does not "ghettoize" science fiction in the way American literature does—or the way American science fiction does.[14] And there is growing evidence that science fiction is moving out of this largely self-imposed ghetto, especially on college campuses. But the attitude remains: in an editorial for the fiftieth anniversary of *Amazing Stories*, Ted White expressed reservations about the wider acceptance of science fiction, noting with irony that as science fiction begins to attain the wider audience and higher standards it deserves, it begins to lose its "clubby," consensus atmosphere.[15] Once the mythology of the entire culture catches up with the mythology of science fiction, science fiction is no longer something special, no longer a secret society only for the initiated.

But as science fiction continues to move into this wider arena and becomes an expression of the goals and values of larger numbers of people, it also becomes subject to a kind of ideological criticism that may be far more serious than the familiar literary attacks on the genre for failing to produce works of lasting aesthetic merit. Such criticism goes directly to the heart of what Heinlein, Asimov, and others seem to regard as the redeeming strength of the genre: its faith in the scientific method and its assumption that technology must somehow be made the basis for fiction. Such ideological criticism is still comparatively rare in science-fiction circles, despite efforts of leading writers such as Stanislaw Lem to generate a dialogue. Lem has characterized the

9

rationalistic ideology of Asimov and Heinlein as portraying a "totally false, domesticated universe" in the construction of which "the sins of individual authors have always been relatively small" because of the very same consensus among writers of which Gunn speaks. Lem calls this consensus "a gradual process of self-organization, and therefore all together are responsible for the final deformation—and nobody."[16]

One of the earliest ideological critics of science fiction came from outside its subculture altogether, and unfortunately displays only a limited familiarity with it. Still, it is surprising how little science-fiction writers and critics have addressed themselves to the issues raised by Lewis Mumford in *The Pentagon of Power* (1970). Mumford's critique is not directed so much at the literature of science fiction as at the myth that he believes science fiction to embody, the "myth of the machine" that gives the overall title to the two-volume work comprising *The Pentagon of Power* and its predecessor, *Technics and Human Development* (1967). It would at the outset be a simple matter to try to rebut Mumford by pointing out that because of the rather shallow view of the genre he displays, he has failed to take into consideration the many science-fiction works that do not exhibit the simplistic faith in mechanical progress with which he characterizes the genre (although it is worth noting that these same works are also frequently overlooked or ignored by formulations such as Heinlein's and Asimov's and rejected by a substantial number of science-fiction readers who regard them as too "unscientific" or "literary"). What is most interesting about Mumford's critique, however, is that the focus of his attack is precisely on those qualities of science fiction that its defenders have so often pointed to as its strengths: its optimism, its belief in the methods of science, its vision of infinite mechanical progress.

According to Mumford, such advances as the invention of glass lenses and the subsequent development of the telescope and microscope led to a reification of what had hitherto been supernatural concepts such as infinity, eternity, and even immortality. By making such concepts quantifiable, science "became the only trustworthy source of authentic and reputable knowledge," a new religion whose "most devout worshippers still do not realize that it is in fact a religion."[17] All phenomena, according to this new religion, must eventually be made measurable, predictable, controllable. The machine became the central metaphor for the universe and the dominant power impulse of the new world. He writes of the tendency of such early science-fiction works as Johannes Kepler's *Somnium* and H. G. Wells's *The Time Machine* to end in visions of "shapeless monsters" and "kakotopias," and uses this as evidence for what he calls "the essentially archaic and regressive nature of the science-fiction mind."[18] "The true criterion of science fiction," he says, "is that the perfection it seeks rests exclusively within the realm of conceivable scientific knowledge and technical invention; and that there is no attempt by most writers to show that this has any viable connection whatever with human welfare or further human development."[19]

Mumford's attitude should not seem new to science-fiction readers: the theme of unrestrained technology, and its corollary of "things man was not meant to know," are especially evident in anti-utopian fictions and in treatments of science-fiction themes in film. As early as 1927 (the same year that Fritz Lang brought one of the first, and still one of the best, cinematic cautionary tales of technology to the screen with *Metropolis*), Julian Huxley, in his only science-fiction story, had his narrator comment that "it is the merest cant and twaddle to go on asserting, as most of our press and people continue to do, that increase of scientific knowledge and power must in itself be good."[20] Like Huxley, Mumford believes that science fiction reflects a widespread cultural belief, and while he perhaps naïvely assumes that science fiction that is critical of technology is inevitably the result of blundering authors trapped by their own mechanistic imaginings, his concluding argument, in which he ironically sides with the defenders of the genre in arguing that it should be taken seriously, is worth noting:

> So far from dismissing these confident probings of the future as empty fantasy, I hold that we have an obligation to take them seriously—not, as so many of the science-fiction writers themselves believe, so that we may push at a more furious pace toward their projected futures, but so that we may overcome these compulsions and plot a radically different destination, more compatible with the nature of organic development and the needs of the human personality.[21]

Certainly such a thesis is as one-sided in its way as Asimov's and Heinlein's theses are in theirs, and certainly one can think of many recent science-fiction works that do "plot a radically different destination" from that which Mumford fears, but I believe the issues he raises are fundamental to an understanding of the growth of science fiction. In the end, Mumford invests the genre with a far greater level of social significance than do many of its most ardent admirers (though I doubt that during the many years in which these admirers yearned for someone to take science fiction seriously they had in mind a response that would view science fiction as a threat to our very survival!). Surely he is guilty of overgeneralizations about the genre, but so are the genre's

11

own writers who seek to define it narrowly in terms of scientific induction or mechanistic extrapolation; surely he assumes a greater consensus of belief among writers than actually exists, but such a consensus is also at the heart of the belief systems described by Gunn in *Alternate Worlds* and Wollheim in *The Universe Makers.* And surely the issues he raises are in his own mind issues of which science fiction is only a symptom. But they are issues that are important to science fiction, for they reveal a level of popular consciousness that the genre has always been close to, a set of values that can best be detected in that large body of work from the 1940s and 1950s out of which our modern notions of science fiction evolved.

Mumford is of course not the only critic of technology whose concerns come close to the heart of science fiction, though he is one of the few who have identified science fiction as an important expression of the values he seeks to attack. Siegfried Giedion, in *Mechanization Takes Command* (1948), presents a detailed view of how nineteenth-century technology gradually altered human behavior by redefining its needs; although avowedly an objective survey rather than a polemic, it details an impact of the machine on human affairs not unlike that detailed by Mumford. More to Mumford's point, however—and far beyond it—is Jacques Ellul's *The Technological Society (La Technique)* (1954), which views virtually all of modern civilization as a function of what he calls "technique": "any complex of standardized means for attaining a predetermined result. Thus, it converts spontaneous and unreflective behavior into behavior that is deliberate and rationalized."[22] Technique, writes Ellul, "has arrived at such a point in its evolution that it is being transformed and is progressing almost without decisive intervention by man."[23] Furthermore, it is by nature totalitarian and cannot be stopped because "it is a whole civilization in itself."[24] Had Ellul been familiar with the American science fiction of the time in which he was writing, he might have seen in much of it the technique he was describing; he might have seen a literature that often seemed to view technological evolution as a force as self-determining and powerful as that of organic evolution.

Victor Ferkiss, in *Technological Man* (1969), surveyed Ellul's work among others and concluded that the growing dependence of man on machines might be "antievolutionary" (p. 255). More recently, Theodore Roszak has sought a visionary transcendence of what he views as the "wasteland" generated by an undisciplined technological imperative, in *Where the Wasteland Ends* (1972); and Michael Polanyi has called for a rediscovery of the personal knowledge implicit in myth and religion as a counterbalance to a vision of science and technology that "has become the greatest source of dangerous fallacies today."[25] Langdon Winner, in *Autonomous Technology* (1977), subtitled "Technics-out-of-Control as a Theme in Political Thought," provides a convenient overview of many of the sociopolitical apprehensions toward technology that have been expressed by these and other writers, and joins them in expressing a fear that humanity may face "a woefully permanent bondage to the power of its own inventions" if something is not done.[26] All of these writers address issues that might well be taken to heart by those who seek to explore the meaning of science fiction, and yet the real dialogue between the humanities and technology that science fiction offers the potential of stimulating remains unrealized from both sides. With few exceptions, the technological critics seem barely aware that science fiction exists, much less that it might reveal a complex codification of many of the beliefs and values of an increasingly technological culture; and for their part, science-fiction writers have only recently begun to be aware that the issues they are writing about are not their exclusive province, and are in fact the substance of a growing intellectual debate in which many viewpoints deserve to be heard.

THE "GROWING EDGE": THE KNOWN AND THE UNKNOWN

Whether the implicit criticisms of science fiction in the works of the writers I have mentioned are overstated in terms of modern science fiction, it is true that much of the genre teaches, as R. Gordon Kelley notes, that "the rational intelligence can preserve the future and make it a better, fuller life for all men," that evil is "likely to be mechanically conceived and hence capable of scientific solution."[27] It teaches this not only through the didactic speeches of its characters and the public statements of its authors, but also and more importantly through the structures and patterns of imagery of the narratives themselves. It has sometimes been said that there is not much real evil in science-fiction stories, and that what there is is often presented in terms of stasis—the "evil" forces being those that prevent man from realizing his true technological potential, from rediscovering the forgotten mission of the spaceship he inhabits, from liberating himself from earth and going into space, from accepting the utopia that automation promises. Technological destiny is manifest, and it will eventually lead, according to Donald Wollheim, to a final direct confrontation with God.[28] By then, presumably, man's technology will enable him to say, along with the protagonist who chooses to war with God in Lester del Rey's "For I Am a Jealous People!" (1954), "'He has found a worthy opponent.'"[29] This

13

myth—a central one in science fiction during its developmental years—depicts a complete mastery of the universe through knowledge, and it is a myth expressed in earlier generations by scientists themselves. Michael Polanyi writes of Pierre Laplace's formulation of such an ideal:

> Laplace's ideal of embodying all knowledge of the universe in an exact topography of all its atoms remains at the heart of the fallacies flowing from science today. Laplace affirmed that if we knew at one moment of time the exact positions and velocities of every particle of matter in the universe, as well as the forces acting between the particles, we could compute the positions and velocities of the same particles at any other date, whether past or future. To a mind thus equipped, all things to come and all things past would stand equally revealed.[30]

One can see in much science fiction a movement toward such a goal, toward liberation from time as well as space, and the assimilation of all possible knowledge into the framework of a cumulative body of science and technology whose destiny is manifest.

Thomas Kuhn has brilliantly argued that such a cumulative view of science is misleading, however popular it may be among scientists themselves: "Cumulative acquisition of unanticipated novelties proves to be an almost non-existent exception to the rule of scientific development. The man who takes historic fact seriously must suspect that science does not tend toward the ideal that our image of its cumulativeness has suggested."[31] He mentions the common metaphor of science as a growing structure with scientists adding new bricks to the overall edifice through the discovery of new laws, facts, and theories. "But that is not the way a science develops. Many of the puzzles of contemporary normal science did not exist until after the most recent scientific revolution."[32] In place of this cumulative vision of science, Kuhn suggests a model of succeeding paradigms, in which new scientific visions gradually supplant the old ones after the old ones are weakened by the discovery of anomalies. Science fiction has on occasion posited a different paradigm for science (one thinks of A. E. van Vogt's "non-Aristotelian logic," for example), but for the most part it accepts the dominant paradigms of contemporary science and projects them linearly in time and space. This results in a radical discontinuity between the science fiction of the past and that of the present, and creates problems for the scholar or anthologist who seeks to trace a purely literary line of descent for the genre.

What lies outside the dominant paradigm is not evil in any sense that we have come to accept that term on the basis of other literary forms; it is simply that which has not yet been assimilated—the unknown. And one way of accounting for what seemed to be the absence of a strong moral sense in the science fiction of the 1940s and 1950s may be to look at the traditional opposition of good and evil as being transformed into the more "objective" opposition of known and unknown. In science fiction it is less important to conquer the villain than to conquer the unknown, and the importance of this conquest is what the ideological structure of many science-fiction narratives teaches. The unknown is an overwhelming presence in science fiction, and it is the transformation of the unknown into the known, usually by breaching a symbolic barrier that separates the two, that I believe characterizes much of the narrative action of the popular science fiction of the 1940s and 1950s and accounts for its conventions and formulae. John Huntington goes so far as to suggest that these conventions reflect Kuhn's paradigms within which normal science operates: "In fact, insofar as the addict takes pleasure in exploring the 'unknown' in the context of the 'known,' that is within the frame defined by the conventions, he is recapitulating in significant ways the activity of normal scientists."[33] Conventions, in other words, provide science-fiction writers with a means of setting up barriers to the unknown and then breaching them—moving beyond normal science— while still maintaining logical control over the extrapolations through which the narrative moves.

Reason—often the scientific method itself—is usually the hero's weapon in breaching such a barrier, and his reward may be the salvation of the universe; he is rewarded for a scientific action as though it were a moral one. But his victory is never absolute, and every partial conquest of the unknown sets up another opposition and another barrier. This is the source of one of the central ironies of science fiction: for all its demythification of the cosmos into quantifiable concepts, it only succeeds in creating new arenas for myth. A branch of fiction that often boasts of its genesis in rationality, it has become more closely associated with the secret centers of consciousness represented by myth than any other popular genre. Myth, of course, cannot ever really be dissolved by reason, perhaps because myth itself is a kind of reason; as the Jungian analyst June Singer writes:

As knowledge proceeds with spiraling movement to penetrate the vast universe of black mystery, one is continually astounded to discover that at the outer limit of awareness where science interfaces with the unknown, there is nothing but a growing edge, where knowledge and ignorance meet. The more one learns, the more one discovers the increasing magnitude of the unknown, as anyone who has tried to do "exhaustive" research knows very well![34]

In other words, the movement from unknown to known is not linear but dialectical, and in succeeding chapters I will try to demonstrate how science fiction reflects this.

This abiding concern in science fiction with the dialectic of known and unknown has not only evolved a structural pattern that is common to many science-fiction works; it has also resulted in the development over the years of a number of recurrent iconic images that contain in themselves the dynamic tensions between known and unknown around which their narratives are likely to be structured. Foremost among these, and tending to incorporate all the rest, is the image of the barrier, which I shall discuss in the next chapter. But more familiar to even the casual reader of science fiction are the images that mediated between known and unknown, the recognizable "props" of the genre such as mutations, alien beings, spaceships, cities, robots, the wasteland. Such props, it may seem, should have been done to death long ago; there is not one among them that we cannot find already well-developed in science fiction prior to 1940. Why, then, do such images exert such a powerful and continuing hold on the science-fiction imagination (and indeed on the popular imagination in general, which has begun to turn more and more to science fiction images with such films as *Star Wars* and *Close Encounters of the Third Kind* and the veritable industries that have sprung up in the wake of these films)? Is it that the genre is indeed so narrow in scope that it must return over and over to the same images? Is it that science-fiction writers, constrained for so long by the formula-minded audiences and editors of a genre that began as pulp fiction, simply cannot free themselves from a standard repertoire of convention-al images? These factors may indeed play a part, but I would argue that such images as these transcend the familiar popular literature notions of conventions and stereotypes. They are in fact icons, as representative of the fundamental beliefs and values that the genre explores as the icons of Christ were representative of the fundamental beliefs and values of the religion of the early Christians.

THE ICONS OF SCIENCE FICTION

Like a stereotype or a convention, an icon is something we are willing to accept because of our familiarity with the genre, but unlike ordinary conventions, an icon often retains its power even when isolated from the context of conventional narrative structures. Certainly, the spaceship in a Buck Rogers movie serial is not as suggestive of meaning as, for example, the spaceship in a story such as Sturgeon's "Bulkhead" or Heinlein's "Universe"; nor is Hugo Gernsback's simplistic projection of a future New York in *Ralph 124C 41+* as revealing as Fritz Lang's *Metropolis*—yet all of these are model environments that partake of the aura of mystery or magic that many science-fiction writers and readers characterize as "the sense of wonder." To some extent, even real spacecraft such as Skylab or the space shuttle Enterprise, divorced from fictional contexts altogether, participate in this mystique.

A number of factors tend to give these icons a special meaning within the context of science fiction, however, and particularly in what we might call the "science-fiction culture" of readers, writers, and fans, whose involvement in the genre seems far more deep and complex than that of the casual reader. Essentially, these factors are that (1) the icon connotes the opposition between the known and the unknown, and thus serves as a structural pivot for the work of which it is a part; (2) the icon represents not a mimetic, but what has been called a "subjunctive" reality, portraying hypothetical environments and beings rather than imitations of real ones, and thus encompassing by its very mode of meaning a fundamental sensibility of the genre; and (3) the meaning of icons involves psychological and cultural levels as well as fictive and aesthetic ones, so that the emotional power of a particular icon does not derive exclusively from the aesthetic structure of which it is a part. Taken together, these factors go a long way toward explaining why the icon is an embodiment of the "sense of wonder" that is so often described as essential to the emotional effect of science fiction.

First, the icon gains special power by its embodiment of the opposition of known and unknown. For example, the spaceship is an image that functions in a number of ways both to separate the known from the unknown and to bring them together. A hollow metal shell, the rocket may be the instrument for carrying representatives of the known world into the unknown, with the hull of the ship becoming the symbolic barrier that separates the known world (often portrayed as a microcosmic society within the rocket itself) from the unknown chaos of space or an alien planet. Conversely, the rocket may bring aliens to earth, introducing a part of the unknown into the known world—again with the hull of the ship setting up a barrier between the two. Another image, the mutant, partakes of both known and unknown in that it is like us in many ways, but is also different and strange: perhaps it is physically deformed, perhaps it can read our minds, or perhaps it possesses other powers of which we can be only dimly aware. It is thus an

17

image of a borderline state between known and unknown, a being transformed from a familiar state into a mysterious one. The time machine is a product of familiar technology (or pseudo-technology) in that it is a *vehicle,* a means of getting from one place to another. But it takes us from our known world into an unknown world of future or past, separated from us by what some science-fiction films and stories have called the "time barrier." Unlike more familiar vehicles, the time machine always has a destination that is at least partly unknown; we can never be sure exactly where it is going or what will happen there. The wasteland, perhaps the product of a nuclear war or a natural catastrophe, is the known environment transformed into the unknown; we are not sure of what lives there or just how different it is from our own world, but it is usually a part of what was once that same world, though now cut off by a barrier of radiation or social sanctions. It is the environmental equivalent of the mutant. Over time, these and other icons have evolved into a kind of symbolic shorthand for the genre, and readers have learned to recognize in them a vast potential for working out themes and narratives; hence heavy science-fiction readers customarily speak of a "post-holocaust yarn" or a "first-contact story" to indicate the various subgenres and formulas that science fiction has evolved to go along with its familiar icons.

A second reason for the special meaning of icons in science fiction is the "subjunctive reality" that the icon represents. This term was proposed by Samuel Delany, who defines it as "the tension on the thread of meaning that runs between word and object."[35] According to Delany, science fiction differs from fantasy in that fantasy deals with the impossible and from realistic fiction in that such fiction deals with what could have happened. Science fiction, instead, deals with what has not happened: that which is neither impossible nor verifiably possible. The only rule governing our response to science fiction, says Delany, is that its actions and images must be "in accord with what we know of the physically explainable universe." Joanna Russ, responding to Delany, goes further in delineating the access of science fiction to reality: "Its connection with actuality, with possibility, is one of its chief pleasures. Whenever some scientific or technological advance becomes known, sf writers search the literature to find out who predicted it and when and how close he got; apparently *what has not happened* and *what could not have happened* (or *what cannot happen*) are not the same."[36] This notion of subjunctivity is an important aspect of the icons of science fiction. Such icons represent neither a purely fantastic vision (what could not have happened) nor a purely realistic one (what could have happened). Instead, they invoke a tension between reality and fantasy, a potential that is neither purely of the known nor of the unknown. The robot, for example, partakes of the known in a number of ways: its genesis lies in the technology of toolmaking and the sociology of slave labor; its place in society is predetermined by the existing class system; its physical appearance is usually derived from the familiar image of the human body. But it also partakes of the unknown: its intelligence is unlike our own, its motivations (if it has any) are unclear, the results of its coming into existence are unpredictable. The city is also familiar to most readers—one of the most familiar environments in modern realistic literature, in fact—but it is also a technological habitat so complex that it contains the unknown as well as the known, and one is never sure of what mysteries a city might contain once it grows to megalopolitan proportions. "Subjunctivity" may be an awkward term to describe the immanence of the unknown in science fiction icons, but it is one that accurately reflects the sense of foreboding that such images represent.

A third reason for the power of icons is the complex levels of meaning that such images embody. In terms of personal psychology, these icons may function in ways reminiscent of Jungian archetypes or Freudian symbols, and it is surprising how little real attention has been paid to science fiction by psychologists, though Jung himself once offered a commentary on some of the key icons in science fiction and specifically on two novels that embody these icons. Jung sees in the spaceship, as embodied in the image of the UFO, a mandala, an "individuation symbol" that offers a promise of unity in a world torn with discord and unimaginable complexity—"an archetype that has always expressed order, deliverance, salvation, and wholeness."[37] (The recent film, *Close Encounters of the Third Kind,* seems to directly reflect Jung's interpretation of the UFO phenomenon.) In discussing Fred Hoyle's novel *The Black Cloud* (1957), which describes an alien being in the form of a sentient cloud that threatens to destroy the earth, Jung sees a confrontation of the conscious and the unconscious, a "psychic collision" portrayed on a cosmic scale, with the result that the attempt by the conscious mind (represented by scientists who seek to communicate with the cloud) fails to assimilate the unconscious (the mind of the cloud). "The scientific pioneers, the spokesmen of the *avant-garde,* prove too weak or too immature to receive the message from the unconscious. It remains to be seen whether this melancholy outcome is a prophecy or a subjective confession."[38] The transformed children of John Wyndham's *The Midwich Cuckoos* (1957) are seen by Jung in a similar light: their telepathic union represents a *"participation mystique, or unconscious identity, that precludes individual differentiation and development."*[39] In other words, they pose a threat to the individuation process that is such an important part of Jungian psychology. It is not difficult to see Jungian concepts at work in other icons of science fiction as well. The city is in Jung's own terms a mother-symbol, nourishing, confining, finally repressing; and the spaceship certainly partakes of the "vessel-images" that Jung often sees as symbolic of the womb. The robot, too, may be viewed as a kind of Jungian doppelgänger, a shadow-image of the personality of man.

More traditional Freudian symbolism might also be at work in these icons. It is perhaps too simplistic to regard the spaceship as a phallic symbol (and I will later attempt to show that its usual meaning in science fiction is quite the opposite), but a few writers have indeed developed it as such. Charles Eric Maine (David McIlwaine), describing an all-woman civilization (*World Without Men,* 1958), argued that such a society would not develop space travel as enthusiastically as a male-dominated society because of the essentially phallic nature of such a quest. And in a recent novel by Larry Niven (*World Out of Time,* 1976), the protagonist certainly seems to regard his spaceship as phallic: "This enormous, phallic, germinal flying thing of metal and fire! Carrying the seeds of life for worlds that had never known life, he roared around the sun and out. The thrust dropped a bit then. . . ."[40] The ship gives him a sense of "enormous masculine power," and he even names it *Don Juan* "for its phallic overtones,"[41] but much of the other imagery concerning the ship seems to describe it as a womb rather than a phallus (the control room is called the "Womb Room," for example). Imagery suggestive of the womb is prominent not only in science fiction that deals with spaceships, but in science fiction that deals with cities as well. And in a few works of science fiction, such as the film *Forbidden Planet* (1956) with its "monsters from the Id," the whole structure of the narrative involves a dramatization of Freudian concepts (in this case, a post-Freudian rendering of Shakespeare's *The Tempest*). Asimov's robots are allowed to function only with the imposition of a repressive superego (the "laws of robotics"), while Cordwainer Smith's flamboyant outer-space dragons are associated with "the primordial id itself, the volcanic source of life."[42] And the Freudian notion of racial memory (mentioned in *Moses and Monotheism*) is associated both with the alien Overlords of Clarke's *Childhood's End* (1953) and the robots in Jack Williamson's *The Humanoids* (1949).

20

These icons are also highly suggestive on a broader cultural level. Among the subculture of science-fiction aficionados in particular and to a' lesser extent in American popular culture in general, they are images whose power often transcends their functions as fictive devices, becoming direct expressions of the fears and values of society. At the simplest level, we can see this operating in the cycle of monster movies that appeared in the 1950s: after viewing enough of these films, we gradually come to view the monster as a convention of our cultural life, almost detached from the movie of which it is a part. If the monster succeeds in generating the awe and terror that we have come to expect of it, the movie more or less succeeds on these most basic terms; if the monster does not fulfill that role adequately, the weaknesses of other aspects of the film become all too apparent, and it fails. When the television series *The Outer Limits* began to lose viewers in the 1960s, the producers responded by requiring scripts to feature a different monster each week—hoping that viewers would tune in to see the monster even if they did not care for the stories or characters (it didn't work). A similar fate befell another science-fiction series, *Voyage to the Bottom of the Sea*. The importance of the monster above and beyond its narrative context is also demonstrated by Forrest Ackerman's long-running magazine, *Famous Monsters of Filmland,* which has captivated two generations of adolescents by running articles and pictorial features on monsters and other special-effects paraphernalia and all but ignoring the narratives in which they appear. Indeed, it is not difficult to defend the proposition that the man in the rubber suit, the costume department's version of the creature from the Black Lagoon, is as significant a work of American popular art of the 1950s as the film in which he starred.

The spaceship, too, as we have already noted, is an icon that has detached itself from the necessity of any narrative context in order to have cultural significance. When the first free-flight test of the American space shuttle *Enterprise* (named after a science-fiction creation) took place in 1978, the vehicle merely gliding to earth warranted the live coverage of three television networks and all major news agencies. Since the beginning of President John F. Kennedy's space program in the early 1960s, the spaceship has been one of the quintessential images of American technology, and surely this meaning is not lost on the science-fiction writers who continue to use it. Similarly, robots function as a cultural image not only for the manner in which they remind us of the social institution of slavery, but for the fears of technology and automation that have characterized our life since Norbert Wiener first began to articulate them in the late 1940s. And the various images in science fiction that have been employed in connection with nuclear weaponry, such as the nuclear wasteland and the genetic mutant, are images that have dwelt at the back of the popular consciousness, quite apart from science fiction, since Hiroshima. Science fiction may still be the only creative genre to explore fully the implications of such icons, but the icons would in most cases be there even if science fiction did not exist.

But it is at the structural level, within particular works of science fiction, that the most consistent meaning of these icons becomes apparent. In a science-fiction film, a whole pattern of meaning may be structured around the visual style of the monster, robot, or city; can one imagine what *Metropolis* would be like without its angular buildings or its chromium robot, or what *2001* might be without the severe, clean lines of the spacecraft, reflected on a darker level in the precisely machined appearance of the famous monolith? More important than this visual meaning is the meaning of these icons to the structure of ideas in science-fiction narratives. On the most immediate level, they may function as merely a problem to be solved in order for the plot to progress: the scientists must find a way to stop the monster; the young hero must escape the stifling atmosphere of the technological city; the detective must discover how a robot or computer might violate its program to commit a crime. But by solving these problems, the protagonist reveals a deeper structure, in which the icon is again the pivotal image. As in *2001*, or in the Arthur C. Clarke story "The Sentinel" that suggested that film, the icon ceases to be merely a puzzle and becomes the gateway to a whole universe of unknown possibilities. The story makes the meaning of the monolith much clearer than the film does, for the story ends when the scientists have broken open the pyramid (which became a monolith in the film), its signals have ceased, and all that is left is to wait for the unknown to be made manifest. "I can never look now at the Milky Way without wondering from which of those banked clouds of stars the emissaries are coming," muses the narrator at the end of the story.[43] The solution to the initial problem—the purpose of the pyramid—reveals only a much deeper problem of how to cope with the much larger unknown that may soon be made manifest. The focus of the story is less on finding the icon and prying it open than on the unstated consequences of this act, and these consequences indeed become a narrative focus in Kubrick's film. The icon represents the synthesis of opposing forces in the science-fiction narrative; it stands at the interface between the fundamental opposition of known and unknown, and it is this level of iconic meaning that I will explore further in succeeding chapters.

Because of the key position of these icons in works of science fiction, they have gradually come to be symbolic also of the "sense of wonder" that the genre is supposed to generate. One sees references to this "sense of wonder" in critical essays about science fiction, dustjacket blurbs, film ads, even book titles. The term is most often used to describe the peculiar power of science fiction to generate a feeling of awe and perhaps a slightly elevated state of awareness in the reader or viewer, but few attempts have been made to elucidate exactly what "wonder" is or what its sources are. Reginald Bretnor simply describes it as an "elusive quality" and adds that "science fiction tries to induce a sense of wonder about the physical universe and man's own interior private universe."[44] Sam Lundwall, a Swedish critic, suggests that it has something to do with reader motivation: "Exactly what this Something is, no one has succeeded in finding out, even though the phenomenon has been given a name: Sense of Wonder. If you have Sense of Wonder, then you can appreciate science fiction."[45] Stanislaw Lem, perhaps the most rigorous of modern European critics of science fiction, dismisses the phenomenon as akin to "the tricks of a stage magician." "As popular fiction, SF must pose artificial problems and offer their easy solution."[46] Franz Rottensteiner attempts to be a bit more specific; the sense of wonder, he writes, is "a deep longing for the different, for 'otherness,' for a departure from the familiar norm, a desire to experience (if only in the mind) something unheard of," or "an ability to accept the radically different with an open mind, or to look at the familiar with a fresh eye, transforming it, as it were, into something strange and wonderful."[47] Rottensteiner sees this feeling or ability as related to the *thaumazein* of classical philosophy and manifested in the systematic doubt of the scientific method in more sophisticated science fiction. Rottensteiner's idea is worth exploring: science fiction's sense of wonder is indeed related to Plato's dictum that philosophy begins with wonder or Aquinas's observation that wonder is the principle of philosophy, but the scientific doubt that accompanies such wonder in much science fiction is less a manifestation of it than a principle working in dialectical opposition to it. Science-fiction narratives often undermine the very sense of wonder that they attempt to generate by appropriating ever

23

greater marvels into contexts of simplistic rationality and one-dimensional character development.

Cornelis Verhoeven, in a little book entitled *The Philosophy of Wonder,* begins with Plato and Socrates and quickly moves to a meditation on the meaning of wonder in philosophy. Many of his insights, I believe, might well be viewed in the light of science fiction's use of wonder. Wonder, he writes, is not easily definable because "it changes character as it changes direction," but it is less a feeling or emotion than a "disposition" toward feeling or emotion. "In wonder we experience ourselves on the basis of a confrontation with a reality."[48] There is indeed a sense of "otherness" involved, as Rottensteiner noted, but it is an otherness tempered with a heightened self-awareness and an uncertainty as to the nature of that otherness.

> Wonder is a certainty which has only just been established and has not yet lost the expectation of seeing its opposite appear. This does not exclude the knowledge of that which is incited by wonder. On the contrary: the more we know about something the more we realize that this knowledge is never exhaustive. Knowledge may nourish wonder since it can postulate the possibility that things may be different than they are. . . . Wonder that a thing is so is motivated by the possibility that it might be different. This movement is endless since this "difference" remains completely undefined. [P. 27]

We begin to see emerging a dialectic not unlike our earlier dialectic between known and unknown. "Philosophy is an enemy of wonder" (pp. 35-36), says Verhoeven, and "there is a constant dialectic in progress between pure wonder and its assimilation in reasoning and systems" (p. 39). Later he restates this as "the dialectic between the usual and unusual which gives wonder its prestige" (p. 40). All of this leads to a conclusion that the sense of wonder in science fiction may well be a sense of the tension set up between the familiar and the unfamiliar, the known and the unknown. In experiencing the sense of wonder, we experience a feeling of endless possibility, like standing at the edge of a vast abyss that is close enough to us to be real, yet great enough to be unfathomable. There is a sense, in the best science-fiction works, of being set in intellectual motion, of being led down a chain of potentialities with seemingly endless ramifications and endless mysteries.

We might look briefly at how this dialectic of wonder is set up in the opening sentences of a representative science-fiction story. I have chosen Isaac Asimov's "Nightfall" (1941) because it has been cited by many as one of the genre's finest stories and because it seems appropriate, since it is a story that concerns itself directly with the sense of wonder, and the terrifying power wonder can have.[49] The story actually begins with a quotation from Emerson: "If the stars should appear one night in a thousand years, how would men believe and adore, and preserve for many generations the remembrance of the city of God!" (p. 112). For a veteran science-fiction reader, this quotation together with the story's title might well give away the whole story: it has something to do with the coming of night, and something to do with the stars appearing only once in a thousand years. The latter notion already begins to build up a tension between the familiar and the unknown: "the stars at night" is among the most familiar images imaginable, and yet by coupling this with a time scheme that is unknowable to our personal experience—a thousand years—and by forcing us to regard it not as a commonplace occurrence but as something rare and virtually unknown, Asimov has set up the fundamental tension of the story before he himself has even written a word.

Asimov's first sentence creates another sort of tension by its stylistic contrast with the poetic Emerson meditation that preceded it: "Aton 77, director of Saro University, thrust out a belligerent lower lip and glared at the young newspaperman in a hot fury"—a one-sentence paragraph that certainly offers little in the way of meaningful exposition, but that gives an added perspective to our sense of wonder. Asimov is telling us immediately that he will, in this story, somehow transform the mystical ideas introduced by the Emerson quotation into a bluntly realistic, even a mundane context, that he will take this Emersonian vision and make it a potential part of everyday life. But the everyday life he introduces us to is not quite familiar, either, and further tensions are set up: though we know what a university is and what a newspaperman is and we recognize the characteristic human actions of Aton 77, what on earth does that name mean? And where is Saro University? An element of the unknown is thus introduced even into this first sentence—not a major element, not at all awe-inspiring in the sense that we usually expect wonder to be, but large enough to convey to us that this character probably is not a part of our own society. Had Aton 77 been called "George Smith," there would be no problem, for we could accept the fact that we simply didn't know enough universities to be aware of the existence of one called Saro; but the name Aton 77 allows no such easy dismissal, and by the simple act of replacing this one tiny unit of the known with a name whose origin and social context must be unknown to us, Asimov starts the wheels turning. If such a name is not likely to exist in our familiar world, then the world of this story must be an unfamiliar one in some respect, but in what respect? The precipice is opened: are we in the future, the past, on

25

another planet, or perhaps in a world that is made unusual only because of the presence of a character called Aton 77? (This latter surmise is quickly disposed of by the first word of the second sentence, which introduces us to a character named Theremon 762.)

The tension between the known and the unknown continues to build, as Asimov describes in greater detail the confrontation between this strangely named character and the reporter sent to interview him. As the interview—such a familiar event to all of us—strengthens our sense of the known, Asimov periodically drops in allusions and unexplained references that increase our sense of the unknown: more strange names, references to astronomy, and finally —in a sentence that brings this growing tension to a temporary peak and consolidates the sense of wonder that this tension represents—a reference to "Gamma, the brightest of the planet's six suns," followed in quick succession by Aton's thought that "he would never see it again as a sane man" (p. 113). After a relatively gentle beginning, Asimov is pulling us to the edge of the precipice. The unknown is brought out in full force in two quick punches that clearly establish we are on another planet (the physical unknown) and that madness is in the offing (the psychological unknown). Endless possibilities open up before us, restrained only by our knowledge that these characters are at least familiar enough to share our behavior patterns, such as belligerence, and our institutions, such as science and journalism. The one pattern of imagery pulls us toward fantasy, the other toward reality, and at this moment in the story, I believe, a kind of equilibrium is established between the two. The dialectic is laid out, not only clearly establishing the sense of wonder on which the rest of the story will build, but also setting in motion the ideological movement of that story.

The introduction of the multiple suns in this passage is the closest Asimov comes to employing a traditional icon, and his opening for "Nightfall" serves to demonstrate that the "sense of wonder" might be a function of style as well as of imagery. But it is only with the introduction of this obviously alien planet that the dissociation characteristic of wonder becomes striking. It is likely that Asimov was aware of this, and deliberately withheld this revelation until the second page of the story. It assures the reader that the wonder implied by these early passages will indeed conform to the conventions of the genre, and not—as might happen in a work by Vladimir Nabokov or John Cowper Powys—function as a more demanding (and hence for many readers less satisfying) literary device. Such a pattern of narrative opening is so common in science fiction as to be virtually formulaic: a short scene of conventional action, followed by the introduction of a familiar icon that links the story with the rest of the genre. Jack Williamson's *The Humanoids,* for another example, begins with a short dramatic scene between a ragged little girl and a guard at an observatory called Starmont; then, seven pages into the book, we are confronted with this sentence: "For Starmont was not on Earth, nor Jane Carter's language English; even her name is here translated from less familiar syllables."[50] We are thus at once removed from the preceding action, which we have assumed took place in familiar earthly settings, and are assured that the work will indeed conform to what we have come to expect of science fiction. Alfred Bester's *The Stars My Destination* (1956) opens with a short paragraph that parodies Dickens's opening to *A Tale of Two Cities,* preceded by a few familiar lines from Blake for an epigraph—allusions that set up thoroughly familiar associations that are immediately contravened by the very first sentence of the second paragraph: "All the habitable worlds of the solar system were occupied."[51] Robert Heinlein's *Stranger in a Strange Land* (1961) offers the reversal even more quickly; the opening line starts with the conventional "Once upon a time" followed by "there was a Martian."[52] At once we are removed from the fairyland of the conventional opening phrase and placed in a science-fiction universe by the introduction of the single word 'Martian.' Examples might go on endlessly, but in all cases the intention is the same: to consolidate the "sense of wonder" and offer readers some word or image that will assure them that what they are reading is in some way connected to the vast body of other science-fiction works.

THE EVOLUTION OF NEW ICONS

The use of conventional symbols or icons is one of the most convenient methods for science-fiction writers to make this connection, for they embody not only the dialectic of known and unknown but also the germ of recognizable formulas. They are a message in code to the initiated reader and an emblem of dissociation to the uninitiated. But such conventional icons are limited in number, and while it is these conventional icons that will provide the focus for the rest of this book, some mention might be made of the efforts of recent science-fiction writers to develop a second kind of icon—the "device" that is unique to a particular author or work, but that embodies the antinomies and values of science fiction as clearly for a specific work as the more conventional icons do for the genre as a whole. Such devices have also come to be recognized as emblematic of the "sense of wonder" to veteran science-

27

fiction readers, and the success or failure of an author in making such a device truly awe-inspiring becomes a major factor in the success or failure of his work before a science-fiction audience.

There are many examples of such devices; some of them have even been passed around among authors in the genre, while others have lost their iconic meaning because of the simple fact that they "came true," i.e., were invented and thus introduced into the "real world." A good example of the latter is television, which certainly must have conveyed a "sense of wonder" to readers of such works as H. G. Wells's "The Crystal Egg," Mark Twain's "From *The London Times* of 1904," or Hugo Gernsback's *Ralph 124C 41+*. The notion of images seen at a distance through electrical or magical means had been a long-standing feature of early science fiction, dating back at least to Francis Bacon's *The New Atlantis* (1627); but once it became a reality, it ceased to be an object of much wonder. (The spaceship, one might argue, has also become a reality, but it is not yet a part of the daily reality for most people the way television is.) But science fiction has not quite abandoned television altogether, and one still encounters stories of TV sets that show the past or the future. Even Piers Anthony's *Macroscope* (1969) might be read partially as an attempt to revivify the iconic value of the television screen. But in order to do this, Anthony had to elevate television to truly cosmic proportions: his "macroscope" allows us to see all space and time, thus opening up the entire cosmos to man's perusal. *Macroscope* is one of the more striking attempts to create a science-fiction "device" that serves the function of an icon.

Another device that seems to be growing into a convention is the artificial world. Artificial environments such as cities, spaceships, and space stations are common enough in the genre, but three recent works have attempted to expand the proportions of the created universe in such a way as to revive the sense of wonder by portraying artificial objects of truly cosmic proportions. Larry Niven's *Ringworld* (1970) is built around the notion of an artificial world in the shape of a ring that encircles a star at a distance roughly comparable to earth's orbit; in a sense, the novel reifies the commonplace abstraction "orbit" into an iconic object. Bob Shaw's *Orbitsville* (1975) carries the concept a step further by describing an artificial hollow sphere three hundred million kilometers in diameter which encloses a sun, and which on its interior surface provides a virtually infinite amount of habitable space for settlers. The "Dyson Sphere," as it is called, is also the basis for other science-fiction stories. *Orbitsville* is similar to the artificial space habitat of Arthur C. Clarke's *Rendezvous with Rama* (1973) carried to spectacular proportions, and these three works together suggest that such a habitat may be evolving into a new icon, one that is given further credence by recent serious proposals to construct a *Rama*-like habitat in space. It is significant that in all three novels, however, the artificial world is the product of an unknown alien civilization that had apparently abandoned it or died out, thus adding the impact of the deserted-world motif to the simple wonder of the technical achievement itself. In this single image, these writers have been able to suggest several of the favorite themes of science fiction: the alien civilization, the potentially infinite power of technology to restructure whole solar systems, the idea of utopia, interplanetary exploration, and the spaceship, with its inside-outside opposition reflected in the internal worlds portrayed in these novels. All of these themes in turn suggest the opposition of known and unknown.

Other such devices appear regularly in the genre. Bob Shaw himself, in an earlier work (*Other Days, Other Eyes*, 1972), posited the idea of "slow glass," which slows down light and thus offers a view into the recent past. Philip José Farmer's *Riverworld* books are based on the device of a multi-million-mile-long river along the shores of which virtually the entire human race from all periods of history has been resurrected. Novels by Philip K. Dick, Ian Watson, Diana and Meir Gillon, and others have concerned the effects of remarkable drugs on behavior and society. Brian Aldiss's *The Primal Urge* (1961) is about a device implanted into everyone's forehead which lights up when that person is sexually aroused. Ursula Le Guin has made the "ansible," a contraption for instant interstellar communication, a recurring feature in a number of her works. Again, examples might be multiplied endlessly. But none of these devices has attained quite the universal acceptance of such images as the spaceship, the robot, the city, the mutant, the wasteland, or the time machine, and it is these icons that I believe need to be explored first. But before doing so, we should look at an image that because of its very abstractness seems to encompass all the others—the image of the barrier itself, that separates known from unknown.

2

the image of the barrier

Something there is that doesn't love a wall.

Robert Frost

BARRIERS AND PORTALS

At some elementary level, the notion of a barrier is really an essential feature of most narrative plot construction: suspense is generated by the presence of some obstacle that must be overcome in order for a narrative to be brought to a satisfactory resolution. Furthermore, in twentieth-century literature in particular, specifically in the literature of existentialism, we find the barrier brought into focus as not merely a narrative device, but as a recurring image of alienation and isolation. Perhaps the archetype of this use of the barrier is Kafka's parable of the Law in *The Trial* (1925), in which a man finds the gateway to the Law guarded by a fierce doorkeeper who for years intimidates the man and prevents his admittance until, in the last moments of the man's life, the doorkeeper explains that the gate was made only for this one man, and no one else might ever be admitted through it. Kafka's parable is hardly science fiction, but it does suggest the need for action in a universe that does not willingly offer up its rewards, and this need for action is also what often underlies science fiction's use of the image of the barrier. Unlike other genres of modern literature that internalize the barrier, making it a function of character or the object of a parable, however, science fiction until comparatively recent years has not been much concerned with character or with literary devices, and the constrictions of its ancestral pulp narrative style have demanded that what inner conflicts exist be portrayed in easily accessible images and actions. Like the science-fiction film, with its overdependence on "special effects" (or "SFX," as fan lingo would have it), science fiction at large has tended to strive for the dramatically visual at the expense of the thematically subtle. Conflicts tend to be expressed in terms of galactic war, invasion, revolution, and the barriers around which these conflicts operate tend to be reified and focused into specific, concrete images.

Many of these images, of course, are the icons that I will discuss in later chapters. The spaceship, the city, and the wasteland all present images of barriers that separate the human community from an unknown and hostile environment; the robot and the monster somewhat more subtly challenge the limits of our definition of man. But apart from these icons, science fiction has produced a number of works that focus primarily on actual barrier images. Often such an image will simply be termed "the Barrier," as in such stories as Damon Knight's *Beyond the Barrier* (1965), Henry Kuttner's "Jesting Pilot" (1947), or Anthony Boucher's "Barrier" (1942). On occasion, such barriers may be more metaphorical, as in Judith Merril's "Barrier of Dread" (1950), in which the "barrier" is one that might well generate dread in the cosmos of science fiction: in the distant future, a constantly expanding human civilization finds that the universe is not infinite, and that in order to survive, humanity must reorganize its economics, science, and pattern of life to achieve a balanced ecology. Eric Frank Russell's "Sinister Barrier" (1939) is likewise metaphorical; the barrier here is one of consciousness that prevents man from becoming aware that he is merely the chattel of a superior race of invisible beings who feed on human suffering. Russell's barrier is every bit as sinister as Merril's is dreadful, because it implies that humanity is not in control of its destiny—a notion anathematic to the spirit of most science fiction.

Barrier images of one sort or another are common enough in science fiction that we need look no further than a representative anthology, Robert Silverberg's *The Science Fiction Hall of Fame,* for more examples. Theodore Sturgeon's 1941 "Microcosmic God," which concerns a scientist who develops a miniature race of humans, the Neoterics, on an island—itself cut off by the barrier of ocean around it—ends with the Neoterics, because of their accelerated life cycle, developing a technology far superior to man's and cutting themselves off from the outside world by means of an impenetrable gray force field. The closing lines of the story are, "The important thing is that the great gray shell will bear watching. Men die, but races live. Some day the Neoterics, after innumerable generations of inconceivable advancement, will take down their shield and come forth. When I think of that I feel frightened."[1] The world of the Neoterics, with its mysteriously advanced technology, becomes an image of the unknown, and their force field the barrier that separates known from unknown.

Clifford Simak's "Huddling Place" (1944), one of his series of "City" stories, focuses on the rather mundane image of the walls of a room. Webster, the central character, suffers from an inordinate agoraphobia which prevents him from following most of the rest of the human race into space, even though he is the only one who can perform a life-saving operation on a great philosopher on Mars. At the end of this story, Webster feels "the walls of the room closing in about him, a trap that would never let him go" (Silverberg, p. 224). I doubt that this story is really about simple agoraphobia, however; Webster's attachment to his room, and by extension his attachment to the environment of earth, seems to me fundamentally a fear of the unknown that is such a familiar part of science fiction's effect. The walls of Webster's room separate him not only from the outside of his house, but from the whole universe and the rest of the human race; as such, they too are barriers to the unknown.

Frederic Brown's "Arena" (1944), which I shall discuss in more detail shortly, concerns a battle for supremacy of the universe fought across an invisible but very real force barrier that separates the human protagonist from the alien antagonist. James Blish's "Surface Tension" (1952), which is discussed in Chapter Seven, concerns a microscopically small civilization whose principle technological goal is breaking through the barrier represented by the surface tension of the pool of water in which they live, into the great unknown of "outer space." Other stories in the anthology feature barrier images to lesser degrees, but these examples should be sufficient to demonstrate how common such imagery is in stories that are widely familiar to science-fiction readers. In fact, it is probably not overstating the case to say that the science-fiction reader finds in such stories an assurance that all imaginable barriers are surpassable, that every limitation we encounter has its "loophole," and that through reason and industriousness we can attain whatever goals we set. Unlike Kafka's man from the country, we do not need to accept the gatekeeper's word that the Law is inaccessible.

Perhaps the barrier image that has come closest to the status of an icon in its own right is the "force field," a visible or invisible projection of energy in space. The stories by Kuttner, Sturgeon, and Brown mentioned above all feature such fields, and the concept shows up as well in innumerable other science-fiction stories and films: Poul Anderson's novel *Shield* (1963); another Sturgeon story, "The Pod in the Barrier" (1957); Clifford Simak's *Time and Again* (1951) and *All Flesh is Grass* (1965); the film *Forbidden Planet* (1956); the television series *Star Trek*. Although the concept of the force field may originally have evolved simply as science fiction's version of the perfect defensive weapon, it has over the years accrued added meanings, until it is an almost ideal image of the barrier that separates the known from the unknown. Because of its technological origins, it invites a technological solution; because it cuts off a part of the universe from human appropriation, it generates the motivation necessary to develop that technology; because its apparent impenetrability poses a seemingly insoluble riddle, it offers science-fiction writers an opportunity to construct ingenious logical schemes that reinforce the value of inductive reasoning. In this latter respect, the force field story becomes to science fiction what the locked-room murder story is to detective fiction.

Related to the image of the barrier is the image of the "portal" or doorway, which is itself an opening in the hidden barriers that separate us from unknown worlds. In David Duncan's *Occam's Razor* (1957), this doorway is provided by the "minimal surfaces" created by oddly shaped soap films; although the inevitable scientific explanation is rather fuzzy in this case, somehow these soap films rearrange the frequency of atomic vibrations in such a way as to permit two visitors from another dimension to cross into our world and generate confusion at a military installation. Jerry Sohl's *Costigan's Needle* concerns a machine in the shape of a needle (interestingly, a shape reminiscent also of the rocket ship) that acts as a doorway to either another dimension or another time. When a group of people accidentally get trapped in this alien world, they spend years constructing another needle, only to find that it leads to yet *another* unknown world, suggesting that technology can reveal to us an infinite series of unknown universes, but that it can't necessarily bring us home (an idea reflected also in recent speculations by Adrian Berry in particular, concerning the use of black holes for intergalactic travel). In Isaac Asimov's *The Gods Themselves* (1972), an "electron pump" serves as a bridge between alternate worlds, providing a limitless supply of energy on earth at the risk of a catastrophic energy imbalance between dimensions.

In many of the examples I have mentioned, the barrier separates a highly technological society that for some reason cannot continue to expand, or cannot find a meaning for its expansion, unless the barrier is breached. Beyond the barrier is the unknown, or chaos, and in this chaos is the knowledge that will enable the society to sustain its impetus of growth. In some cases, this knowledge involves a metaphysical sort of awareness—"destiny" in Simak's *Time and Again,* in which an advanced civilization protects its secret of life from humanity's vast galactic empire by means of a mysterious gravitational barrier around its own planet, releasing the secret only to the right individual at the

33

right time, as if a moral judgment is involved. In the stories by Merril and Russell, the knowledge involves discovering the true nature of humanity or its universe. But in many stories the barriers are simply temporary. blocks to humanity's inevitable conquest of the cosmos, pockets of resistance in an otherwise ever-expanding process of appropriation. This rather materialistic vision of humanity's relation to the cosmos is what Stanislaw Lem attacks when he writes, "Once the credible, the real barriers have been blown up, the process of falsification must go on; artificial barriers must be erected; and in this manner the stuffed waxworks come about, the miserable ersatz that is supposed to be cosmic civilization."[2] Lem suggests that it is a sign of weakness of the science-fiction imagination that so often the barriers are purely artificial, and what lies beyond them in the unknown is just more of the same, merely another territory or civilization or beast to conquer.

But the very nature of a barrier suggests there may be more to it. There are two distinct ways of approching the image of the barrier, and science fiction reflects these two ways. First, one may focus on the barrier itself, treating it as a central metaphor around which the action of the story revolves. What lies beyond the barrier may be new planets to settle, new knowledge to exploit, an enemy that threatens human existence—but the attainment of these goals may be reduced to an aspect of the denouement of stories in which the central conflict and climax are represented as the attempts to breach the barrier. Second, barrier imagery can effectively reverse these polarities, making the image of the barrier secondary to the depiction of the worlds that it separates. In such stories, the actual breaching of the barrier may be accidentally or easily achieved and does not provide the plot so much as do the adventures in the other world beyond the barrier. In the former group of stories, the barrier is essentially a puzzle that must be unraveled; in the latter it is primarily a convenient means of separating two cultures, which can then be contrasted to provide the drama of the story. In the former stories, the central image of the unknown is the barrier itself; in the latter, it is what lies beyond. To illustrate, we might look first at a couple of science-fiction stories that focus on the barrier itself, and then at stories that concern life beyond the barrier.

THE BARRIER AS PUZZLE

As we have already seen with Poe, the treasure that lies beyond the barrier may be less important than the barrier itself, which is above all a riddle, and in many ways the most important gain is not in appropriating what lies beyond the barrier but in learning the principle by which the barrier may be breached. This principle is nearly always learned through a process of scientific induction, and the message of much science fiction is not that humanity should or must appropriate the galaxies, but that *if that is its goal,* scientific reasoning can lead the way. Like many scientists, many science-fiction writers prefer to focus on means rather than ends, to address the procedural questions of how a thing is to be done rather than the more complex ethical issues of *whether* it should be done. The actual gains to be made by solving the puzzle are often little more than motivating plot devices.

Two stories in which the focus is clearly on the breaching of a force field in order to attain a desired goal are Fredric Brown's "Arena" (1944) and Theodore Sturgeon's "The Pod in the Barrier" (1957). Both stories depict a highly technological civilization whose conquest of the universe has been hampered in some way; both reduce this blockage to a single image of a barrier; and both reduce the cultural problem to a dramatic one by establishing situations in which one or a few characters must breach the barrier for the good of all mankind. In other words, these are stories of human champions whose chief weapons are intellectual rather than physical. One story illustrates the value of induction, the other the value of doubt—both intellectual postures commonly thought of as characteristic of scientific thinking.

Brown's "Arena" concerns a battle for supremacy of the galaxy between Earth and a mysterious invading force called the "Outsiders." The supreme battle in space is about to be joined when the protagonist, Carson, finds himself on a strange planet, outside of space and time, where he is to engage in individual combat with a single member of the alien race. The situation has been set up by a superior being suggestive of what Arthur C. Clarke would later call the Overmind in his *Childhood's End* (1953): "The end of evolution of a race so old, the time cannot be expressed in words that have meaning to your mind. A race fused into a single entity, eternal" (Silverberg, p. 229). This entity explains to Carson that either humanity or the Outsiders might evolve into such a race, but that the impending war will damage both irreparably: hence this individual battle will determine which race survives to conquer the galaxy. That such a simplistic militaristic solution to a problem whose stakes involve the future of two races hardly seems in keeping with the apparently infinite wisdom of this superior entity is a problem not addressed by Brown, but even in the brief characterization of this being we see a shying away from complex moral questions in favor of simpler procedural ones. One might ask, if the apotheosis of reason is to arrive at

35

a state of mind in which one-to-one medieval combat is the most efficient means of furthering the betterment of the universe, in what way is that wisdom superior to the wisdom of ancient kings? The question goes unanswered, but provides an unconscious undertone of irony to the whole story. Whether or not this superior being is morally right in its decision, it has rather arbitrarily and irrevocably imposed it upon the two civilizations involved: if the earthman Carson wins, it will perhaps be the destiny of his race to evolve into another single consciousness, which can then itself go about the universe refereeing battles—but still avoiding moral problems.

The principal focus of the story is on the contest, however, specifically on the intellectual nature of the contest. "'Brain-power and courage will be more important than strength,'" Carson is told. "'Most especially courage, which is the will to survive'" (Silverberg, p. 230). Again we are reminded that the only values that need concern us are intelligence, rather narrowly defined here as "brain-power," and courage, rather curiously defined as "the will to survive" rather than the ability to face danger. The situation is laid out as clearly and unambiguously as these ground rules. In the opening scene, Carson finds himself lying naked in a hot blue desert on an unidentifiable planet—conditions that he is assured are equally uncomfortable for his opponent, which is described as a "red sphere of horror" (Silverberg, p. 230). Separating him from the sphere is an invisible force field that seems to have no boundaries and that each of them is unable to cross. The situation is reduced to elemental proportions: a man is stripped of his technology and placed in an alien environment to do battle with an alien of roughly comparable technology. It will not be technology that decides the battle, but the scientific reason that is the basis of technology.

Carson's first reaction, however, is to attempt a simple technical solution: he seeks a weapon, a stone shaped "like a slab of flint" (Silverberg, p. 230), but soon finds that the weapon is useless unless he can somehow breach the barrier. He begins collecting data, first determining the extent of the barrier and next observing the alien creature's characteristics. He then suggests a peaceful settlement, but is repulsed by a telepathic wave of hatred: "He actually recoiled several steps in sheer horror at the depth and intensity of the hatred and lust-to-kill of the red images that had been projected at him" (Silverberg, p. 232). Again one is struck by the irony of the knowledge—given Carson by the superior "entity"—that this race is capable of evolving into the same kind of being as man. Carson's offer of peace might have made a difference in another story, might have counted as a strong point in

Carson's favor, but here we are led to presume that the master of the contest is unwilling to make moral distinctions, or does not want to get involved at that level.

Carson's observations continue: the alien has stronger telepathic powers than he, but is apparently weaker physically. He discovers its "unnecessary cruelty" when it captures a lizard and begins to pull its legs off until the lizard appears dead. But the most important observation comes when the alien tosses the lizard through the barrier, and then begins throwing rocks through it at Carson. Carson constructs a series of experiments: throwing sand through the barrier, tossing a live lizard at it, and tentatively inducing that the barrier is only a barrier to things that are alive.

Parallel to the growing knowledge about the barrier—the growth of scientific thought, perhaps—is the development of weaponry and tools. Carson carves himself a knife and fashions a rope belt to carry it in, while the alien constructs a catapult with which to hurl rocks at him. Carson incinerates the alien's catapult by throwing flaming faggots at it, and then he begins to fashion a harpoon with which to spear the alien. But as both he and the alien grow weaker, it becomes apparent that such weapons may soon be useless unless a means is found to cross the barrier and engage in direct combat.

Such a means becomes available to Carson when he discovers the lizard that the alien had tortured earlier. Although rendered unconscious by the torture, the lizard survived, leading Carson to the conclusion that the barrier screens only conscious life. In a desperate move, Carson strikes himself on the head and falls through the barrier, recovering in time to attack the alien with his harpoon, and finally win the victory. He finds himself back in his spaceship and discovers that the alien fleet has been destroyed and that the war is over. The destruction is credited to a coincidence of technology: the single salvo fired by the earth ships is believed to have set off some instability in the metal of the alien ships, resulting in a chain reaction of destruction. Carson, of course, is unable to tell what really happened, even though scars all over his body attest to the reality of his experience. But in his own mind, he knows he has saved the universe.

How did this salvation come about? Principally through a simple process of learning by induction, a process of experimentation and elimination which Carson apparently excelled the alien in mastering. The story is carried forward by a series of increasingly significant penetrations of the barrier, each penetration adding to Carson's overall knowledge. During the story, he experiments with three hypotheses.

First, he guesses the barrier sets up an opposition between organic and inorganic matter, since it admits stones but not himself or the alien. When the apparently dead lizard is thrown through the barrier, he modifies his thesis to fit the new data; the barrier does not separate organic from inorganic, but rather live from dead. And when he discovers the lizard is still alive, he modifies this further into his final conclusion that the barrier separates conscious from unconscious life. Reasoning and experimentation have led him to discover the secret of the barrier, and the technology of tool-making has enabled him to win the battle once he is across. The fact that his own consciousness is what keeps him from crossing the barrier in the first place is perhaps a small irony: after the carefully constructed reasoning with his conscious mind reveals the secret, he must temporarily abandon consciousness to make use of the secret. The barrier is at once an emblem of what reason can do and of the limitations of reason.

In Theodore Sturgeon's "The Pod in the Barrier," an even stranger means is found to breach a barrier that separates an overpopulated human race from a group of habitable worlds in a galaxy controlled by an alien civilization. The alien civilization is friendly enough, but at some point in their past they had constructed an impenetrable automated barrier covering a third of their galaxy, and even they cannot figure out how to overcome the barrier. "All it did, that Barrier, was to draw a line. Anything outside of it was left strictly alone. Anything penetrating it was instantly traced, hunted and smashed by Luanae missiles. And anything that got cute enough to duck inside and out again was destroyed by the Barrier itself, which had the simple ability of reversing the terrene-sign of a random third of the atoms in any matter it touched."[3] The barrier is generated, maintained, and defended by a completely self-protected, self-repairing computer device on an isolated planetoid within the barrier; even the friendly aliens, the Luanae, cannot approach it. Centuries earlier, the barrier had destroyed a race of vastly superior nomads that the Luanae nearly worshipped. "It was the crucifixion of crucifixions, the murder of murders with the Messiah of Messiahs their irreplaceable victim" (p. 24), and as a result the Luanae attempted to destroy the barrier and failed. Then they warned others of its presence and invited their assistance in discovering means for its destruction.

More than Brown, Sturgeon is concerned with the nature of the society that established such a barrier, and his brief sketch of the history of the Luanae sets up the basic opposition between passive and active, ruminative and technological, perhaps even female and male, that

governs the rest of the story. We can summarize the history of the
Luanae in eight major steps:

1. The Luanae, "a people in some ways like humanity, perhaps a little
swifter technologically" (p. 22), develop a highly technological society
which nearly destroys them in a series of three massive internal wars.

2. "Then there was a long flowering" (p. 22), during which the Luanae
transcend technics and develop a highly philosophical, humane culture
that is essentially passive. During this time, they forget "the largest part
of their fabulous technology; their machines were corroded, their skills
had died, and worst of all, they had forgotten how to organize. . ." (p.
22).

3. Because of this abandonment of technology, they are powerless to
resist invaders from space, who enslave them for a period of thirty
thousand years.

4. The Luanae gradually reconstruct their technology and rebel,
destroying the invader "and all his worlds," because their "taste of quiet,
of personal and individual fulfillment, was a touch of paradise to them
and they deeply resented its loss" (p. 22). The culmination of the new
technology is the construction of the barrier, which once again promises
a life of passive contemplation for the Luanae.

5. The Luanae become "steeped again in their unthinkable
metaphysics" (p. 22) and regain the passive idyll, this time protected
from invasion by an autonomous technology not entirely under their
control.

6. A vastly superior alien race is inadvertently destroyed by the
Luanae barrier, inflicting the Luanae with a massive guilt that they were
"far gone again way from their technological peak" (p. 24) and were
unable to live up to their philosophy of reverence for life by saving the
aliens.

7. For a third time, technology is developed, this time in order to
destroy the barrier. But the attempts fail, since the barrier has been
enlarging and strengthening itself beyond the capacity of any
technology known to the Luanae.

8. The Luanae finally achieve a balance between their technological
and philosophical phases, developing a culture that is "neither blindly
mechanical, like that which had produced the planetoid, nor vegetative
and contemplative, like that which had left them open to slavery, but a
middle ground, based on the ancient convictions of respect for life and
its ways in the rigid and marvelous frame of the Universe; and
implemented it by an unrusting technology" (p. 25). This leads to their
final philosophical discovery: "A man cannot exist alone. He must be a

member of something, a piece, an integer of some larger whole" (p. 25). The expression of this union of technology and humanism is the elaborate warning system the Luanae construct to prevent others from straying into the barrier—a message whose simultaneous welcome and warning might well be a message from technology itself, friendly and yet threatening.

It is easy to see the cyclical nature of the Luanae story, and the clear message that technology and humanism must be mutually interdependent. What may be less apparent is the manner in which the final synthesizing act of communication is accomplished only by an earlier series of oppositions and transformations denoting the failure of technology and the failure of philosophy each to support a culture by itself. The failure of technology leads to philosophical passivity; and the failure of philosophical passivity leads back to technics, and so on until a final synthesis is achieved. If we organize the events in the story according to a synchronic thematic pattern as well as a diachronic one, we come up with the following:

Failure of technology	Humanism	Failure of humanism	Technology
technology leads to war (1)	transcendence of technology (2)	enslavement by aliens (3)	construction of barrier (4)
	rebirth of humanism (5)		
destruction of superior aliens (6)	attempts to destroy barrier (7)	destruction of superior aliens (6)	attempts to destroy barrier (7)

The Luanae have gotten themselves into a vicious circle, it seems, but one that nevertheless is leading them toward a synthesis of the humane and the mechanical. The failure of technology to protect the race (1) leads to their development of a humanistic culture that virtually abandons technology (2). But this kind of culture fails to protect them from invasion (3), and they are forced to reinvent technology (4). But the barrier is as much an image of their xenophobic philosophy as of their technology; while it permits the rebirth of their philosophy (5), it also demonstrates at once the failure of both that philosophy and the technology that it presumes to transcend by destroying the superior aliens (6). Humanistic motives and technological expertise are thus combined in attempts to destroy the barrier (7), which fail and lead to the final union of the two opposing values in the messages that the Luanae send out as warnings.

This is the point at which the narrative begins. A spaceship from Earth has been sent on a "suicide mission" to make one more attempt to crack the barrier and make the Luanae worlds available for human colonization. Aboard the ship are four scientists, the Captain, a rather dumb mechanic, and an untrained "crew girl," whose only apparent function is the sexual satisfaction of the crew members. This crew girl, Virginia, has a gift of what one crew member calls "'retroactive doubt'": "When she was anywhere near you, you breathed it. You'd say something and she would repeat it, and by the way she did it. . .she made whatever you'd said into a falsehood" (p. 16). Virginia's power of doubt eventually becomes the key to breaching the barrier.

Sturgeon, as is his custom, spends more time developing his characters than another science-fiction writer might have. Early in the story, the four scientists (including the narrator), who have come to test their hypotheses regarding the barrier, are discredited by the Captain, who emerges as almost a parody of the space hero: a brilliant scientist in all areas of specialization, a dutiful military man, and an able fighter who can ward off an attack by the muscular mechanic with a simple karate blow. But if he is the image of the technological hero, he also has the weaknesses of such a hero: he values the completion of the mission over human life and is willing to sacrifice the crew girl in order to breach the barrier. He is insensitive to the love developing between her and the mechanic and even threatens to kill the mechanic when his survival seems to threaten the completion of the mission.

Within the ship itself, then, we have an opposition not unlike that in the story of the Luanae. The Captain believes firmly in technology at the expense of human values; he is a purely intellectual being. In clear opposition to him stands Blum the mechanic, untrained and slow-witted, whose love for Virginia nevertheless echoes the reverence for life of the philosophical Luanae. Between them is the narrator Palmer, who seems capable of getting along with both and who himself holds the promise of the synthesis of technology and human feeling that will be necessary to complete the mission.

What finally breaches the barrier is a rather incredible device. The Captain has learned from the Luanae that the planetoid generating the barrier is powered by the same force that powers his ship—"cold fusion"—and that the clouds of unstable subatomic particles involved in cold fusion are subject to psychological influences. He has selected Virginia for her almost psychopathic unwillingness to believe anything, trained her in this "skill," and sent her on her way in a space suit with an envelope containing an explanation of the principle of cold fusion. When she opens the envelope and reads the explanation, she intuitively disbelieves it, and her doubt nullifies the cold fusion field of the barrier, enabling her to penetrate the barrier and destroy the planetoid. Sturgeon has conceived of a kind of technology that cannot function unless man has faith in it; simple doubt, too, is subject to a still higher power, represented by the love of Blum for Virginia, which Virginia finally becomes capable of believing in, leading in turn to her belief in cold fusion power after the planetoid has been destroyed and enabling the fusion plant of the ship to begin functioning again (it too, of course, having been nullified by her field of doubt). The issues become increasingly complex: faith in technology leads to the failure of technology, as we see in both the experience of the Luanae and the earlier attempts to breach the barrier through conventional technological means. Only by doubting the efficacy of technology can we put it to its full use. But only by first reaching out to another human being and basing belief in technology in a more fundamental belief in humanity, may the real human uses of technology be achieved. This is the synthesis that is realized by the Luanae in their final message to intruders and by Virginia in her final acceptance of Blum. The "no man is an island" theme is thus acted out on both a cosmic and a personal level and in contexts that suggest that the union of one human being to another is irrevocably bound up with the union of humanistic values to technology. One must be able to understand both the love of Blum and Virginia and the motivations of the militaristic Captain, and this understanding is what is finally achieved by the narrator when, at the end of the story, he brings Blum and Virginia together and effectively takes over control of the ship from the Captain, ordering him to return to the bridge and man his instruments. Palmer, the narrator, learns to accept the need for a balance between personal and military values, between love and duty, and, like the Luanae, between technology and humanism.

The development of this theme also governs the successive transformation of the known-unknown opposition from a problem of appropriation to a problem of technology and finally a problem of psychology. Initially, the barrier separates the known from the unknown and prevents human beings simply from knowing what lies beyond; the motivation to breach the barrier is simply "because it is there," because humanity does not like to be kept out of anything. But when the Luanae explain that what lies beyond the barrier is a group of habitable worlds that promise to reduce the growing population pressure of the human worlds, the barrier is transformed from an arbitrary image of the unknown into a barrier whose breaching promises a real solution to a critical problem; the Captain tells the scientists, "'If you, or men like you, fail to solve this problem soon, we can expect our entire civilization to explode, like a dying sun, through the internal pressures of its own contracting mass'" (pp. 27-28). The focus of the unknown is shifted from what lies beyond the barrier to the problem of the barrier itself. As is common in science fiction, when conventional technology encounters such a barrier, humanity tries to develop new technology to overcome it. As Stanislaw Lem writes, "According to this principle, there is only one remedy for imperfect knowledge: better knowledge, because more varied knowledge."[4] But in this case, "better knowledge" is not supplied by conventional technological innovation, but by a mysterious gift of doubt in the person of an uneducated crew girl. Her doubt succeeds in breaching the barrier, but not in resolving the dialectic of known and unknown, for at the end of the story the unknown persists in the only partially understood nature of her mysterious gift. As with the more common science-fiction devices of telepathy, racial memory, or "psionics," the objective unknown is resolved into a subjective quality of mind. And somehow, because this force resides in the human psyche, it represents a more acceptable image of the unknown than an unknown that is conceived purely mechanically and hence capable of mechanical solution. There is, I believe, a direct line of connection between Heisenberg's Uncertainty Principle, Virginia's doubt, and the psychic powers represented in a wide range of later science-fiction works from Frank Robinson's *The Power* (1956) to George Lucas's film *Star Wars* (1977), in which a mysterious psychic ability called "the Force" enables the hero to transcend his conscious mind and penetrate the citadel of the enemy when more conventional technological means fail. By reducing the unknown to a quality of mind, I believe, we are reassured that whatever the awesome forces technology is able to conjure, the fundamental mysteries and powers remain within us, that we need not be intimidated by the imposing hardware that is science fiction's stock in trade, since in the end even the simplest of us may hold the ultimate key to the unknown, which becomes far less threatening in this light. This idea is particularly common in the work of Sturgeon, where mysterious abilities often seem to reside in the lame and

43

the retarded, as we shall see later in a discussion of his most famous novel, *More Than Human* (1953).

THE BARRIER AND CULTURAL ISOLATION

Thomas Clareson has pointed out that one of the earliest clearly identifiable formulas in American and British science fiction from the period 1870-1930 was the novel of lost lands and peoples, perhaps most famously exemplified by H. Rider Haggard's *She* (1887), Conan Doyle's *The Lost World* (1912), and the tales of Edgar Rice Burroughs. In all of these works, Clareson states, there is "a yearning for the past,"[5] for the primitivism and simple values no longer available to citizens of an increasingly urbanized and technological culture. In order to lend such works credulity, however, barriers had to be constructed separating these lost societies from the outside world: unexplored stretches of ocean; ranges of mountains; impenetrable jungles; sometimes, as in Burroughs's *Pellucidar* stories or its many predecessors, the crust of the earth itself. The crossing of these barriers may have provided the authors of such works with plenty of opportunities for hazardous adventures, but the real focus was usually on what happened once the lost world was discovered: the nature of the mysterious culture, its differences from our own, the marvelous secrets it held. Reaching these lost worlds seldom required much more than simple endurance: the barriers to them were not technological puzzles of the sort we see in later science fiction, and the function of these barriers was clearly to provide a means of isolating one culture from the rest of the world. Such barriers were not so much barriers to humanity's inevitable technological and social expansion as forgotten corners of its own world, reminders that the earth itself still holds secrets.

Such barriers have never been entirely abandoned by science fiction, and barriers that isolate one culture from another remain common images today; even the opening passage of so sophisticated a novel as Ursula Le Guin's *The Dispossessed* (1974) focuses on the symbolic wall around the spaceport that separates the revolutionary society of the planet Anarres from its parent planet Urras. But the theme of cultural isolation has been modified over the years to reflect the changing social attitudes that science fiction expresses, and from the simple atavism of the isolated cultures of a Burroughs, science fiction has moved to the more complex countercultural societies of works like Aldous Huxley's *Island* (1962) and Frank Herbert's *The Santaroga Barrier* (1968). Generally, science fiction has come to view with suspicion societies that deliberately surround themselves with barriers; such societies seem antithetical to the principles of pluralism and growth that the genre values. Thus, although a few works such as Edgar Rice Burroughs's *Beyond 30* (1915) reflect the isolationist spirit of the time in which they were written, the dominant attitude in science fiction toward cultural isolation is at best ambiguous, and more often critical. Two works which employ the image of the barrier as a symbol of cultural isolationism are Anthony Boucher's (William A. White) "Barrier" (1942) and Herbert's *The Santaroga Barrier*. Both works reveal a belief that a society which imposes its own barriers and refuses to deal with the chaos without is a potentially totalitarian society that is essentially antithetical to human nature.

Boucher's story concerns a future society that has cut itself off from both the past and the future by inventing a barrier to time travel, rather than a barrier in space. But the effect is the same as in many "lost world" stories, and Stanislaw Lem has compared the time barrier erected by this totalitarian state to prevent its stasis from being disrupted by outsiders to the Great Wall of China: in each case, the society behind the barrier is thoroughly satisfied with its own development and fears corruption from less enlightened peoples from outside.[6] "Barrier" is written in a wry good humor and occasionally satirizes the genre from which it springs. When the first time traveler, John Brent, arrives in the year 2473, he dramatically announces with a flourish, "'I was born in 1914—a good five and a half centuries ago.'"[7] The narrator adds, "According to all the time travel fiction Brent had ever read, that kind of statement ranks as a real stunner. There is a deathly hush and a wild surmise and the author stresses the curtain-line effect by inserting a line-space" (p. 222). But here there is no such dramatic response; in fact, the woman to whom he is speaking already knows Brent, since later in the story he travels to an earlier period of her life. She simply acknowledges his pronouncement "with anguished patience" (p. 222).

But the principal target of Boucher's satire is not the narrative conventions of the genre so much as its dream, expressed often in the Gernsback-dominated 1930s, of complete scientific knowledge leading to utopia. The twenty-fifth century has achieved such knowledge; "civilization had reached a high point of comfort, satisfaction, achievement—and stagnation" (p. 225).

> The combination of atomic power and De Bainville's revolutionary formulation of the principles of labor and finance had seemed to solve all economic problems. The astounding development of synthetics had

45

destroyed the urgent need for raw materials and colonies and abolished the distinction between haves and have-nots among nations. Schwarzwalder's *Compendium* had achieved the dream of the early Encyclopedists—the complete systematization of human knowledge. Farthing had regularized the English language. . . .

There was nothing more to be achieved. All was known, all was accomplished. Nakamura's Law of Spatial Acceleration had proved interplanetary travel to be impossible for all time. Charnwood's Law of Temporal Metabolism had done the same for time travel. And the Schwarzwalder *Compendium*, which everyone admired and no one had read, established such a satisfactory and flawless picture of knowledge that it was obviously impossible that anything remained to be discovered. [Pp. 225-26]

These discoveries in turn lead to a proclamation of the stasis of the cosmos; and science, in the guise of Cosmos, gradually supplants all gods. "Cosmos replaced Jehovah, Baal, and Odin" (p. 226). Because of the obvious perfection of this new scientific state which has disproved the existence of time travel, a barrier is erected to prevent time travelers from entering: "Since the Stasis of Cosmos did not practice time travel, any earlier or later civilization that did so must be imperfect. Its emissaries would sow imperfection. There must be a Barrier" (p. 227).

There is only one, painfully obvious problem with this scientific utopia, described in the relentlessly flamboyant pseudoscientific jargon that early science-fiction writers were so fond of: its perfection is based in a fundamentally erroneous cosmology, as the mere presence of a time traveler from the past demonstrates. Science has led to a civilization as complacent as the early Middle Ages, and just as doggedly determined to enforce its religious cosmology as those ages were to enforce the Ptolemaic universe. The society is also fascistic, patrolled by white-robed "Stappers" (a term that comes from "Gestapo") who strike down immediately anyone who dares to speak against Cosmos, even remotely. Outsiders are referred to as "Slanduch," a corruption of "*Auslands-deutsche*," or Germans "cut off from the main body of their culture" (p. 235), leading Brent to suspect that the society is a distant consequence of Germany's winning the Second World War.

Stasis parodies Nazi Germany, then, as well as earlier science-fiction utopias. The barrier between known and unknown is rigidly established and enforced, both in space and time; even "imaginative research was manifestly perilous" (p. 239). Naturally, Brent aligns himself with a rebellious underground movement in opposition to this isolationist state. He is apparently trapped in the future, unable to cross the barrier and return to his own time (the fact that he crossed the barrier in arriving is explained by the fact that he was then traveling "with the time stream"). Much of the rest of the narrative, as Lem complains, turns into "anti-problematical escapism into adventure,"[8] with Brent moving back and forth within the framework imposed by the barriers erected by Stasis, helping to sow seeds of discord, and attempting to liberate a group of time travelers from the future trapped on their way back to the past. Much is made of the various evolutions of language that these future travelers represent, and of the variety of futures open to man once he transcends stasis. Stasis also invites conquest: one of the future travelers, Bokor, has concocted a means of multiplying himself endlessly by constantly returning to the same point in time, his ultimate goal being to establish a dictatorship over Stasis. It is clear that Boucher intends us to contrast the variety of possible futures represented by these time travelers with the dull, static society that a purely mechanistic vision of the universe has produced in Stasis; perhaps he implies, too, that science fiction need not be confined by the kind of pseudoscientific barriers that confine the Stasis world, that a too narrowly defined realm of acceptable pseudoscience prevents the genre from realizing its imaginative potential (whether this is a deliberate point Boucher is making in the story is debatable, but it is interesting that his editorship of *The Magazine of Fantasy and Science Fiction* a decade later would reflect a similar concern with expanding the limits of what science fiction can deal with). Most important, however, is the story's argument against isolationism and the smugness that results: not only is an isolated state a dehumanized one, but it is also a fragile and foolish one, despite its power. As Brent himself observes, "The only power worthy of man is the power of all mankind struggling together toward a goal of unobtainable perfection" (p. 260). The key word, of course, is "unobtainable," for once a society declares its own perfection, it abandons the dynamic dialectic between known and unknown that alone is "worthy of man."

"Barrier," published in 1942, may reflect some of the "one world" sentiment of that era, and the barrier becomes an image of extreme nationalism—specifically Nazism. Frank Herbert's *The Santaroga Barrier,* published in the late 1960s, is concerned with another kind of social movement that seemed for a time to threaten the rational values of science fiction—the drug counterculture. *The Santaroga Barrier* touches upon several favorite themes of the counterculture—ecology, heightened states of consciousness, rebellion against an overcommercialized society, pop philosophy and psychotherapy (one of the leading spokesmen for the town of Santaroga is even named Piaget)—and uses the image of the barrier as a means of illustrating the differences between countercultural and "mainstream" attitudes toward these issues. The result is a decidedly ambiguous utopia, a town cut off from the outside world, in which many of the dreams of countercultural youth are realized at the expense of individual consciousness. The image of the barrier is used to separate two societies, each unbalanced, each needing part of what the other has to offer. Once again an outsider penetrates the barrier to discover the secrets of the isolated community, and once again he becomes a vital part of that community. But Herbert does not presume to unite the two societies as some earlier authors did theirs: in the end of the novel, the protagonist Dasein ("being there") chooses to join the Santarogans in their detachment from the outside world. He becomes part of the counterculture with the conviction that "*It'll be a beautiful life,*"9 but we read these words with something of the apprehension with which we read the parallel closing words—"it was a *good* day"—of Jerome Bixby's horror story "It's a *Good* Life" (1953), which also concerns a community cut off from the outside world and ruled by a single consciousness. For all the promise of power and utopia in Santaroga, there is an accompanying underlying feeling of terror.

Leon Stover, in an article in *Extrapolation,* regards *The Santaroga Barrier* as a thoroughly antiutopian fiction, as Herbert's ironic critique of the various overdrawn attitudes toward mass culture embraced by the countercultural movement of the 1960s. He also points out the debt the novel owes to the philosophy of Karl Jaspers, whose name appears in the novel as the name of the consciousness-raising drug that enables the Santarogans to achieve their communal consciousness.10 Whatever the specific philosophical targets of the novel (and Stover's argument seems to me persuasive), it represents yet another transformation of the social use of the barrier image in science fiction, the use of the barrier to represent a radical disjuncture of values within a single society. The antinomies of the novel are lined up accordingly.

For example, the dual motive that psychologist Gilbert Dasein has for investigating this mysterious cut-off community gives us an early indication of the nature of this value-schism. In his official capacity as an agent for an investment corporation whose chain stores have been abruptly shut down in Santaroga, he is motivated by the cynical commercial instincts that throughout the novel will characterize the "outside" world. "'Why won't even *one* Santarogan trade with an outsider?'" asks Davidson, the agent of the corporation who gives Dasein his mission. "'What's this Santaroga Barrier which keeps us from doing business there?'" (p. 7). But Dasein is driven by another motive as well, a motive that reflects the espoused values of the counterculture as much as his official assignment reflects the values of commercialism: his girlfriend Jenny lives in Santaroga, and he wishes to uncover the mystery of her reticence to invite him home to Mom. His second motivation is even expressed in a phrase out of the love culture: "They'd had a *thing,* chemical, exciting" (p. 16). "Chemical," in fact, turns out to be a presciently appropriate term to describe his relationship to Jenny, for in the end, that is exactly what it becomes.

Dasein arrives in Santaroga and discovers that its three principal local products, produced and consumed locally, all contain the magical drug Jaspers, which leads to a union of consciousness, "something that was the same in all of them" (p. 101), like the pod people of Jack Finney's *The Body Snatchers* (*Invasion of the Body Snatchers* in its film version). Appropriately, these three products are beer, wine, and cheese, the staple diet, it often seemed, of the 1960s culture of pot parties and protest meetings. Jenny explains to him that Jaspers is "Consciousness Fuel" (p. 106), and that because of it Santaroga must be protected from the outside. "They had achieved a way of life which wouldn't be tolerated by the *outside.* Santaroga offered too much of a threat to the oligarchs of the money-industry world. The only hope for Santaroga lay in isolation and secrecy" (p. 107). That the isolation represents a contending set of values is made obvious to Dasein by Dr. Piaget, who berates outsiders as "not-men" for their increasing concessions to a mass-culture environment and who proclaims, "'This is a struggle over what's to be judged valuable in our universe'" (p. 165).

Gradually, Dasein begins to realize that to have Jenny means to accept her culture and to think like a Santarogan. "There was no substructure to life *outside,* he thought, no underlying sequence to tie it all together. There was only a shallow, glittering roadway signposted with flashy, hypnotic diversions. And behind the glitter—only the bare board structure of props. . .and desolation" (pp. 216-17). He finds himself caught in a classic romantic dilemma between love and duty, faith and business. He takes a massive dose of Jaspers and feels his consciousness slipping away: "*Perhaps I can no longer be. . . . Perhaps, I cannot do. . . . Perhaps, I cannot have. . . .*" (p. 234). He finally becomes a Santarogan and finds himself arguing from the Santarogan point of view with his employers, contending that Santaroga is a *polis,* "'a community of individuals, not a collectivity. Santarogans are not anthill slaves to grubs and grubbing'" (p. 243). But the rhetoric is not entirely convincing, and on the last page of the novel, Dasein's fears briefly return: "Dasein had the sudden feeling that he was a moth in a glass cage, a frantic thing fluttering against his barriers, lost, confused" (p. 255). He overcomes this feeling with a quick dose of Jaspers cheese, and concludes with the conviction that it will, after all, be a beautiful life.

Although Stover's contention that Santaroga is a "black utopia" is well taken, the novel's substantial, if overstated, criticisms of the commercial culture "outside" are not easily overlooked. Neither society is complete without the other; the outside might benefit from the environmental conservatism and communal spirit of the Santarogans much as the Santarogans might benefit from the technology and individualism of the outside world. As in all the works we have discussed in this section, the barrier enforces stasis more than anything else. The promise of humanistic progress that the Santarogans keep to themselves seems to condemn the outside world to a mindless expansion of its dehumanizing commercialism, and the promise of technology and pluralism that the outside world holds seems to condemn the Santarogans to a decadent, pointless incestuousness. The communal mind of the Santarogans is not the communal mind of the Overmind in Clarke's *Childhood's End* (1953) or Sturgeon's *More Than Human* (1953), since it holds no real promise of development or growth. But the mass culture of the outside is equally a dead end. Community, progress, hope, Herbert seems to be saying, lie in maintaining a dynamic balance between the individual and the group. Neither behaviorism nor Jungianism has the whole answer; one can no more subjugate the mind to the manipulation of the body, as the outside attempts to do, than one can make the individual body a mere extension of the communal mind, as happens in Santaroga. Once again the oppositions are manifold— mind and body, community and individual, active and passive, technology and nature, power and empathy—and once again the image of the barrier is the image of the destructive separation of the vital aspects of human consciousness and social life.

While there is a vast potential of meaning in the barrier image itself, even more complex patterns of symbolization open up when we consider the barrier as a structural component of other science-fiction icons. The works discussed in this chapter may provide useful points of reference, then, for the discussions that follow. At one extreme are barriers as problems or puzzles whose solution is paramount to the resolution of the story; at the other are barriers that signify important schisms within or between cultures, and whose breaching involves far more complex consequences than the mere solving of a puzzle. But where other icons are involved, not even these extremes are necessarily mutually exclusive, and in the next few chapters we will explore some of the ways in which science-fiction writers have managed to work remarkable and complex variations on the icon of the barrier and on other icons.

images of environment

3
icon of the spaceship

> To make inside concrete and outside vast is the first task, the first problem, it would seem, of an anthropology of the imagination.
>
> Gaston Bachelard, *The Poetics of Space* (1958)

Roland Barthes writes of Jules Verne:

> The basic activity in Jules Verne . . . is unquestionably that of appropriation. The image of the ship, so important in his mythology, in no way contradicts this. Quite the contrary: the ship may well be a symbol for departure; it is, at a deeper level, the emblem of closure. An inclination for ships always means the joy of perfectly enclosing oneself, of having at hand the greatest possible number of objects, and having at one's disposal an absolutely finite space. To like ships is first and foremost to like a house, a superlative one since it is unremittingly closed, and not at all vague sailings into the unknown: a ship is a habitat before being a means of transport. And sure enough, all the ships in Jules Verne are perfect cubby-holes, and the vastness of their circumnavigation further increases the bliss of their closure, the perfection of their inner humanity.[1]

In his science-fiction works, Verne develops this hearth-like image of the ship to what is perhaps its epitome for later science fiction. From the underwater Gothic castle of the *Nautilus* to the airborne mansion *Albatross* in *Robur the Conquerer* to the womblike projectile of *From the Earth to the Moon,* we can perceive a movement toward greater and greater inner security as the outer environment through which the vessel moves becomes more and more alien. In *Around the Moon* (1870), Verne writes of his projectile and its inhabitants: "Could they have found a calmer or more peaceful spot to sleep in? On the earth, houses, towns, cottages, and country feel every shock given to the exterior of the globe. On sea, the vessels rocked by the waves are still in motion; in the air, the balloon oscillates incessantly on the fluid strata of divers densities. This projectile alone, floating in perfect space, in the midst of perfect silence, offered perfect repose."[2] "Perfect repose" is scarcely what one would at first associate with the image of the spaceship, with its constant movements into unknown environments. And yet in much science fiction after Verne, the spaceship retains a function as the repository of middle-class values, and the hull of the ship provides what is perhaps the clearest single image of the barrier that separates the known world from the unknown.

H. G. Wells, for example, takes Verne a step further, and it is tempting to read in purely Freudian terms his description of the sphere that takes Bedford and Cavor to the moon in *The First Men in the Moon* (1901). The interior of the sphere is described as warm and hospitable—eighty degrees—and the space travelers undertake their journey in flannels and slippers, clothing more properly associated with the drawing room than with interplanetary adventure. Before the sphere ever takes off, Bedford, the narrator, begins to regard it as a kind of protective womb: "The world outside the sphere, I knew, would be cold and inhospitable enough to me . . . but after all, would it be as cold as the infinite zero, as inhospitable as empty space?"[3] The experience of space travel in the sphere is compared to lying on a soft feather bed (p. 36). Bedford notes that both travelers seem to feel strangely nourished while in the sphere, and that neither of them feel "the slightest desire for food" (p. 41); this desire only returns, in fact, at the moment that Bedford emerges from the sphere upon his return to earth. The overall experience is described in these terms: "And so sleeping, and sometimes talking and reading a little, at times eating, though without any keenness of appetite, but for the most part in a sort of quiescence that was neither waking nor slumber, we fell through a space of time that had neither night nor day in it, silently, softly, and swiftly down toward the moon" (p. 41).

The qualities of this experience—bedlike comfort, a sense of nourishment, drowsiness, and timelessness—are all symptomatic of Freudian regression, but they are also qualities shared by the experience of the hearth. From this point on in the narrative, this sphere is the repository of the values of security and comfort that so characterize Wells's middle-class heroes. Finding the sphere again at the end of his adventures on the moon, Bedford comments, "It was good to see that familiar dark interior again!" (p. 118). But when he has returned to earth, the polarities are reversed: the interior of the ship becomes associated with the irrational, unpleasant experience he has undergone, and the exterior becomes the world of sanity and rationality: "My one desire was to emerge" (p. 131). And the emergence itself is treated very much in terms of birth imagery. "Mother Earth had her grip on me now," says Bedford as he wades Venus-like from the ocean in a gray dawn. His first meal after emerging from this metal womb and rejoining earth society is, appropriately, eggs.

This change in the symbolic aspect of the interior of the ship, from a positive set of associations on the moon to a negative set on earth, also points up the way in which the spaceship may be used in opposition to the values of the hearth. As long as the spaceship is amid alien surroundings, it is the repository of traditional values; in familiar surroundings, however, it becomes a threat to those same values. The fearsome unknown ceases to be represented by the exterior of the ship and instead is represented by the interior. Wells himself exploited this iconic meaning of the spaceship in another novel, *The War of the Worlds* (1898), in which the Martian spaceship is set down amid the sleepy surroundings of the English countryside and suggests, before the ship ever opens to reveal the Martians with their death-rays, the antinomy of those known values of hearth and countryside.

But in *The War of the Worlds,* Wells was somewhat ahead of his time, and it would remain for later science-fiction writers and film makers to explore fully the threatening unknown that an alien spaceship could represent. For the most part, the writers who followed Verne and Wells would continue to present the spaceship as a kind of womb, and indeed the concept of the spaceship as a kind of traveling drawing room became one of the earliest formulaic descriptions in popular science fiction. Garrett P. Serviss, in *A Columbus of Space* (1911), fitted up his spaceship with polished woodwork and leather-cushioned seats and described his adventurers sitting about smoking pipes, chatting, and enjoying rich breakfasts of eggs and coffee. "We were as comfortable as at the Olympus Club," the narrator reports, "and the motion of the strange craft was so smooth and regular that it soothed us like an anodyne."[4] Later he adds, "It is one of the compensations of human nature that it is able to adjust itself to the most unheard-of conditions provided only that the inner man is not neglected. The smell of breakfast would almost reconcile a man to purgatory—anyhow it reconciled us for the time being to our unparalleled situation, and we ate and drank, and indulged in as cheerful good comradeship as that of a fishing party in the wilderness after a big morning's catch" (p. 28). The "inner man"

57

here may be taken as an unconscious pun, referring not only to psychological and domestic needs, but to the literal situation of the explorers and to their cultural context: the "man on the inside," the bourgeois English or American gentleman who, by a series of drawing rooms and private clubs, is protected from the hazards of his immediate environment, and yet who, armed with the very middle-class values that insulate him, periodically ventures forth into unknown realms. It is perhaps significant in Serviss's novel that even the cigar smoke and conversation generated by the spaceship's club-like atmosphere provide gases which are converted into fuel by the craft's atomic engines; it is literally the detritus of middle-class behavior that provides the energy for the exploration of space.

C. S. Lewis, in *Out of the Silent Planet* (1938), a novel that uses science-fiction imagery to project a world view that is fundamentally opposed to that of most of the genre, describes the experience of space travel as similar to being "totally immersed in a bath of pure ethereal colour . . . through depth after depth of tranquillity far above the reach of night."[5] Ransom, the protagonist, "felt his mind and body daily rubbed and scoured and filled with new vitality. . . . he felt life pouring into him from it every moment" (p. 29). Space is described as "the womb of worlds" (p. 29) in which the worlds are but gaps in the brightness. At one point, Ransom even speculates that the visible light of space itself is "also a hole or gap, a mere diminution of something else" (p. 37). Though the values here are the reverse of most in science fiction, with the unknown transformed into the divine, the structure remains fundamentally the same: the spaceship is but a parcel of planetary life in the midst of a wholly different order of existence.

As these examples illustrate, to regard the spaceship as some kind of science-fictional equivalent of the horse in a Western story (an association that is implicitly made in the term "space opera") is to misunderstand the fundamental value this image holds for a science-fiction audience. Few science-fiction stories about spaceships treat the spaceship principally as a means of transportation, and its values are not the values of explorers' ships or horses in earlier adventure fiction. Indeed, the image from conventional fiction closest to that of the spaceship in science fiction is that of the cruise ship: the completely ordered, internally self-contained microcosmic society, the "ship of fools." And this sort of image is not one ordinarily associated with romances of voyaging and discovery.

More than any other image in science fiction, the spaceship incorporates what John Cawelti hypothesizes as the three major value systems that replaced the traditional hierarchies of church and state during the nineteenth century: "the ethos of individualism, the ideal of the Christian family circle, and scientific rationalism."[6] The scientific means necessary to explore alien territories and the heroic individual effort that go into such imaginary explorations are clearly evident in nearly all science fiction of exploration and discovery, but the ideal of the family circle would seem alien to this context—until we look at the structure and meaning of the spaceship as habitat, or home. Buckminster Fuller views the spaceship as "the first perfect environment"; and Lewis Mumford, commenting on this writes, "it will serve each individual successively as a crib, a schoolroom, a housing unit, or a component of a fast-moving vehicle . . . until, at the end, both the capsule and its occupant are removed to a super-crematorium to be volatilized."[7] Mumford, as usual when dealing with science-fiction concepts, overstates the case rather melodramatically, but his and Fuller's perceptions of the spaceship as first and foremost a protective environment provide a valuable insight into the way this icon functions in our popular culture. Mumford merely carries Barthes's idea of the house a step further; as Gaston Bachelard writes, "all really inhabited space bears the essence of the notion of home."[8] And the spaceship in science fiction, more often than not, is inhabited with a vengeance; its inhabitants range from an individual human brain whose personality is integrated with the mechanical circuits of the vehicle (as in Anne McCaffrey's *The Ship Who Sang*), to a dynastic family (as in Robert Heinlein's *Methuselah's Children*), to a full-scale city (as in James Blish's *Cities in Flight*), to an entire society (as in Heinlein's "Universe").

As with the image of the house, the key structural opposition in the icon of the spaceship is the dialectic of inside and outside, and as Bachelard tells us, "Outside and inside are both intimate—they are always ready to be reversed, to exchange their hostility. If there exists a border-line surface between such an inside and outside, this surface is painful on both sides."[9] If the inside is characteristic of the values of family and hearth in stories of space travel, it is equally antithetical to these values in stories of aliens visiting earth. Occasionally, both meanings will be present in the same story, as in Murray Leinster's "First Contact" (discussed in Chapter Seven). In either case, breaching the surface represented by the shell of the spaceship is often the movement between known and unknown that sets a spaceship story in action.

The various aspects of the inside-outside dialectic in terms of a ship traveling in space have already been hinted at in our discussions of Verne and Wells. Now we might go a step further and make a list of the kinds of oppositions subsumed into this inside-outside antinomy:

INSIDE	OUTSIDE
light	darkness
sound	silence
warmth	cold
nourishment	deprivation
knowledge	ignorance
order	chaos
community	isolation
civilization	nature

In all cases, the interior is the abode of life, society, and comfort, while the outside suggests the confrontation of the unprotected individual with stark nature. The spaceship, in other words, may be a womb, a house, a social club, a city, or even a self-enclosed world, but it is seldom the phallic symbol that many have made it out to be. Wells's ship in *First Men in the Moon* was spherical; Serviss's was "round and elongated like a boiler." Many of the spacecraft in early science-fiction illustrations were clearly modifications of seagoing vessels, and the notion of the "space liner" or "space freighter"—both suggesting ocean craft—was a staple of pulp-era space operas. More recently, spacecraft have often been described as egg-shaped (the "titanic metal egg" of E. C. Tubb's *The Space-Born,* for example, or the Jupiter-mission ship in Stanley Kubrick's *2001: A Space Odyssey*), and still more recently, in films such as *Star Wars,* the simple shapes and sleek surfaces of earlier fictional spacecraft have given way to polymorphous structures with complex, finely articulated surface features reminiscent of nothing so much as an urban landscape. The popular notion of a phallic shape—and the resulting popular misconception of a phallic meaning for spacecraft—seems to have derived partly from Verne's use of a conical projectile fired from a huge cannon and partly from the design of the earliest atmospheric rockets, which of course were not designed to go into space at all, much less carry passengers. Of course, this shape was widely featured in illustrations of the 1940s and 1950s, in films such as *Destination: Moon* (1951), and in the design of our own early multistage manned rockets, but there is little real evidence to suggest that it has ever been as purely Freudian an image as some might suggest, despite a few deliberately macho uses of the image in novels such as Larry Niven's *A World Out of Time* (1976).

But more important than the form of the spaceship is its function, and in order to understand in greater detail some of the complex functions of the spaceship in science fiction, we should look at some common themes involving this image. Although the image of the spaceship is so ubiquitous that any attempt to discuss it exhaustively would be hopelessly diffuse, we can perhaps begin to understand the power of this image by looking at some of the more important kinds of treatments of "domestic" spaceships—stories in which the point of view is initially confined to the interior of the ship. The "alien" spaceship story, in which the point of view is initially confined to the exterior of the ship, is generally less common in science fiction despite its obvious associations with popular UFO mythology. Concerning domestic spaceships, three kinds of stories seem to be especially revealing: those in which the ship encloses a completely self-contained society, those in which it encloses a mock family structure, and those in which it is associated with a specific personality.

SPACESHIPS AS SELF-CONTAINED SOCIETIES: THE "UNIVERSE" TRADITION

The notion of the interior of the spaceship as a repository of known and traditional values attains its clearest expression in the common science-fiction theme of the generations-long space voyage during which the inhabitants of the ship evolve their own social codes and structures. The theme can be traced from Laurence Manning's "The Living Galaxy" (1934) through Robert Heinlein's "Universe" and "Common Sense" (1941) and later works by A. E. van Vogt, E. C. Tubb, James White, Chad Oliver, J. T. McIntosh, Clifford Simak, Harry Harrison, Brian Aldiss, and others. The theme was even the premise of a short-lived TV series, *The Starlost,* in the early 1970s. Though the idea of such a spaceflight was apparently conceived as an extrapolative solution to the problem of intergalactic travel given the impossibility of faster-than-light travel, what emerges from these tales is perhaps the most consistently mythical treatment of a science-fiction icon in the entire genre, and a clear expression of the known-unknown antinomy through images of inside and outside.

Robert Heinlein's "Universe" and "Common Sense," sequential stories first published in *Astounding* in 1941 and reprinted as the novel *Orphans of the Sky* in 1963, are one of the earliest major treatments of this theme, and hence one of the most influential. In these stories, we can see not only the power of the spaceship as icon and the opposition of inside and outside, but also a major science-fiction writer's attitudes toward rationality, the history of science, and science as a kind of faith. The stories concern a centuries-long voyage to Far Centaurus aboard a

61

massive, five-mile long spaceship. Early in the voyage most of the scientists and engineers are killed in a mutiny, and the remaining crew evolve a culture in which the flight orders become the basis for a religion, "scientists" become priestly interpreters of a "scripture" they cannot understand, and a central item of faith is the belief that the interior of the ship is the entire universe. A young misfit (another common figure in science fiction) joins with a band of mutants who inhabit the upper reaches of the ship, and with their aid, eventually rediscovers the principles of astrogation that enable him to bring the ship safely to land on an earthlike planet.

I have already noted that the spaceship, like the earlier image of the seagoing ship, can easily be treated as a microcosm of human society, but it is only in science fiction, as far as I know, that a situation can be set up in which a human society evolves over a period of several generations in the same vessel. The society Heinlein imagines aboard his spaceship is not really a microcosm of the world outside—obviously there *is* no world outside, other than the one implied by the narrator's occasional references to "family skycars" or the space pilot as romantic hero (references that clearly suggest that the narrator is situated in some imagined society other than the one on the ship). Thus the only point of reference against which Heinlein can develop his imaginary culture must be one with which his readers are familiar. Given this broad range of historical paradigms for the development of an imaginary microcosmic society, which might Heinlein logically be expected to choose?

The answer should not be difficult for any steady reader of science fiction, since Heinlein's imagined society turns out to be but a variation on another common science-fiction plot: the society built on the detritus of a more advanced society that collapsed. Like any number of other science-fiction writers—Isaac Asimov in the *Foundation* trilogy, Walter M. Miller in *A Canticle for Leibowitz,* John Wyndham in *Re-Birth,* or Edmund Cooper in *The Overman Culture*—Heinlein imagines a rigidly structured agrarian society more or less on the model of medieval Europe. (Perhaps medieval society is especially attractive to science-fiction writers because of the possibilities it offers to demonstrate what many of them apparently believe to be the democratizing influences of scientific advances and technology.) Social roles are strictly defined, with the peasants (the "common crew") living in farming villages and consulting an oracle ("the Witness," who memorizes reams of folk poetry and recites it in answer to problems, usually of a legal nature). The elite of the society is represented by the scientist-priests, who are not scientists at all but interpreters of such "sacred writings" as physics texts and control manuals. At the top of the social structure, pope-like, is the Captain. Outside of this society altogether live the "muties," mutant descendants of the original mutineers, like the barbarian hordes of the north in medieval Europe.

We can leave it to the science-fiction writers themselves to debate the social and historical realities that would be involved in extrapolating such a medieval society, but in terms of the myth of science and the icon of the spaceship, its functions are invaluable. The social structure within Heinlein's spaceship is not unlike the social structure of Wells's rural England into which he introduces the Martian spaceship in *War of the Worlds*: both are centered around the values of the hearth and traditional authority, and both are disrupted by the intrusion of knowledge of the outer universe (perhaps this suggests an Edenic myth as well). Only in Wells it is the interior of the spaceship that represents this knowledge, while in Heinlein it is the exterior. The society of Hugh Hoyland, the protagonist of "Universe," cannot conceive of an "outside," and when Hugh himself is made aware of it, he undergoes a kind of religious conversion and vows to recover the original purpose of the voyage. But in a stronger sense, what Hugh undergoes is an *anti*-religious conversion: he has rediscovered the lost truth of science. His experiences at this point become a paradigm of the history of scientific discovery, and specifically of popular accounts of Galileo, with whom explicit comparisons are made in the text, as when Hugh, after being convicted of heresy, says, "'Nevertheless it *still* moves,'" referring to the ship that is to his persecutors the whole of existence and alluding to the famous story of Galileo's muttered addendum to his recantation.[10] Heinlein, in other words, has constructed an explicitly cosmological science-fiction, with the ship fulfilling the role of the earth itself in medieval cosmology and Hugh fulfilling the role of the catalyst of the age of enlightenment. Implicitly, Heinlein uses this mise-en-scène to argue his point that science—*real* science, not the pseudoreligion that is the basis of belief in Hugh's culture—can lead a people out of darkness and into the promised land. The argument is weak, because Heinlein cannot bring his plot to the resolution he desires without the aid of a sequence of incredible coincidences (luck, as his narrator calls it), which themselves argue against the purely rational point of the story.

The medieval setting, then, gives Heinlein an opportunity to attack transcendental thought and to demonstrate the moral superiority of scientific rationalism. The image of the spaceship gives him the mythic power to cast this argument effectively into a fictional mold. Yet while Heinlein cleverly dismantles the moral and transcendental allegories

63

that his imagined society has constructed around scientific texts, he does not replace these with any values other than the saving grace of science itself. He makes no attempt to argue that this essentially stable society *should* relocate on a planet, except that since this relocation represents the fulfillment of a goal established by a more technological (and hence morally superior) past society, it must be right. In other words, Heinlein merely supplants one faith with another, more acceptable, faith in technology, and the sequel to "Universe," "Common Sense," calls attention to this by the remarkable string of coincidences and blind luck that finally enables Hugh to guide the ship to a safe planetfall. But this new faith, evolved in a technological environment, may well be what Heinlein's readers are looking for, and what makes the story a science-fiction classic. As I mentioned earlier, a great many science-fiction readers seem to invest a certain part of their own fate in what science fiction has to say, and what Heinlein says in this story must be reassuring to such readers. Essentially the message is "learn science." "Universe," in fact, may be one of the earliest works of fiction to depict a hero whose heroism depends not upon conquest of the natural or social worlds, but rather upon mastery of the principles of science and technology that are accessible to all. For readers whose own education has largely focused on understanding the complex technological society they are born into, Hugh Hoyland's experience must offer some comfort that even the most mysterious and complex elements of the environment can be mastered and eventually subjugated through reason. There are really three environments in the story: the environment of space through which the starship moves and which symbolizes the hostile natural world; the environment of technology which the designers of the ship provided as a means of conquering the natural world and at the same time protecting man from it; and the environment of the society into which Hugh is born, which has forgotten both space and technology. By mastering first the technology of the ship, Hugh finds the key to mastering all three worlds.

Heinlein's spaceship, with its self-enclosed society sent out to discover new worlds, has become one of the most influential concepts in science fiction, and provides the starting point of a widely recurring formula, one upon which many science-fiction writers have worked variations, and one that, apart from the known-unknown antinomy it expresses, also may account for the persistent womb imagery in relation to spaceships. The formula may be simply stated thus: a young man is born into a society on board a starship. The society has long forgotten the original purpose of the voyage, but the young man, through some means, discovers this purpose and is regarded as an outcast and hounded by the elders of his society. Escaping into a hitherto unknown realm of the ship, he discovers the control room and—in an epiphanic scene common to almost all such narratives—a giant window revealing the stars. With the aid of mechanical devices and ancient guidebooks, he steers the ship to a safe course home. The ship in this formula, then, is literally a womb, a "seed of light" in Edmund Cooper's terms; or, as Clifford Simak has it in *his* treatment of the formula, "Target Generation" (1953), "the womb from which the race would be born anew."[11] The nurturing environment of the ship, then, becomes more important even than it had been in the stories of Verne and Wells. Simak writes:

> The Ship was a mother to them and they nestled in it. The Ship fed them and sheltered them and kept them safe from harm.
>   There was no place to go. Nothing to do. Nothing to think about. And they adapted.
>   Babies, Jon Hoff thought. Babies cuddling in a mother's arms. . . . [P. 32]

The Ship, in such stories, is almost a prenatal environment (in Philip José Farmer's *Inside Outside* [1964], it is literally that, an environment preparing souls for birth on a planetary surface). Heinlein and Simak graft onto this basic imagery stories of the emergence of science out of ignorance, thus generating a kind of historical metaphor in which the Enlightenment becomes analogous to the birth of a child. Simak, in "Target Generation," develops a pattern of religious imagery that complicates the metaphor even further, although this religious imagery has become almost a staple of the formula. The cosmology of the society in "Target Generation" expresses clearly the importance of the inside-outside dialectic: "There had been chaos, and out of the chaos order had been born in the shape of the Ship, and outside the Ship there was chaos still. It was only within the Ship that there was order and efficiency and law . . ." (p. 18). Later, as the protagonist Jon Hoff begins to realize the true situation of the Ship, he is shocked to find himself thinking of his society as being "shut up within the Ship"—a sacrilege to the common belief that society is "protected and sheltered and kept from harm, set apart from all else which lay in the shadow of eternal night" (p. 25). He begins to realize how much knowledge has been lost over the generations because of the ritual book-burning that took place ages ago (and Simak even adds a lengthy footnote on the importance of documentation over oral history), and finally begins to think of it as a "fall from knowledge" (p. 39). Jon may be trying to restore lost knowledge and scientific reason to the people of his ship, but he is not stamping out myth altogether; for as he rediscovers the past, he is also acting out a new version of the Fall and the Redemption.

So the formula becomes increasingly complex. On one level, the ship retains its associations with the womb and is a simple organic image. But this image is modified by teleological overtones, and that in turn is modified by the paradigm of the scientific revolution. A single image thus touches on cosmology, history, biology, religion, and psychology (if we want to add the notion of the hero myth as a symbol of individuation)—surely one of the most useful images science fiction has come up with. But later writers were to find even *more* complex meanings in this apparently simple formula.

Brian Aldiss's *Starship* (1959; published in England as *Non-Stop*) brings into focus another opposition that is present in Heinlein's story but is there subordinated to the opposition of inside-outside. This is the opposition of organic-inorganic, or natural-artificial. The first clues that the starship is in fact a starship come when the protagonist realizes that man, like the hydroponic plants around him, is a natural being, while the larger environment of the ship is artificial. All he can imagine beyond the hull of the ship is "a wilderness of superponics, growing out into what his mother had called the great stretch of other darkness, where strange lanterns burned."[12] The naturalistic image of unknown as forest is thus united with the technological image of unknown as universe, with the continuity of the internal starship's forest and the universe beyond broken only by the hull of the starship itself. As in Heinlein, humanity's greatest attempt at appropriating the cosmos ironically results in its greatest provinciality, and what separates humanity from reality is the product of its own technology—the starship itself. In Aldiss's novel, the people aboard the starship even begin to devolve in keeping with their confined existence: their life spans accelerate and they grow physically smaller with each succeeding generation. Unless the barrier is broken that separates humanity's autochthonous origins from its cosmic surroundings, it will eventually die out. An added irony in the Aldiss novel is that in the end, it is found that the barrier is deliberately kept intact by terrestrial humans outside the ship. The starship has been orbiting earth for three generations, but earthlings, to whom the interior of the ship has during the long years of its voyage become an image of the unknown, and the ship's inhabitants aliens, deliberately try to maintain the stable society of the ship and to keep it from discovering the truth of its situation. Aldiss, unlike

Heinlein, seems acutely aware of the potential impact such a revolutionary change as planetfall might have on such a society as the one he portrays.

The importance of maintaining the illusion of a complete universe for the inhabitants of a starship is also the theme of Chad Oliver's "Stardust" (1953), in which a faster-than-light craft on a routine voyage encounters the hulk of an ancient starship that had set out centuries earlier, before the discovery of faster-than-light travel.[13] The hulk is still inhabited by the descendants of the original crew, but the society has begun to break down into primitive tribes. The crew members of the newer starship must decide whether to reveal themselves and rescue the inhabitants, realizing that if these inhabitants have fully adapted to the spaceship environment, the culture shock of being reintroduced to a modern society might be fatal, and that if they do remember their original mission, the discovery that it has been rendered superfluous in light of later technology might be too demoralizing. As in *Starship,* the decision is made to keep the truth from the inhabitants, but at the same time to help them repair their ship by planting a spy in their midst (in the guise of a primitive tribal leader) who will lead them to the engine rooms and show them how to start the engines again.

Closely related to these works by Heinlein, Simak, Aldiss, and Oliver are works in which the primitive society of a long-voyaging starship is not the product of accident or evolution, but rather part of the design or master plan for the voyage. Writers such as E. C. Tubb in *The Space-Born* (1956) and Harry Harrison in *Captive Universe* (1969) follow in the tradition of Heinlein in depicting their primitive starship-societies, but go beyond him in an important way: they suggest that such primitive societies may be the only ones stable enough to endure generations of confinement without breaking down. The conflict these authors are trying to resolve is simple: if a culture is desperate enough for expansion that it sends whole populations on potentially endless voyages through the universe, how can that same culture be expected to survive intact over a period of centuries in a limited environment that offers no chances for growth and expansion? A corollary problem is how could a society that has thoroughly adapted to the confined existence of a starship "reconstruct" itself into a progressive human society once it has arrived at its destination?

Tubb's answer is to depict a draconian society reminiscent of some of the technological anti-utopias that characterize much satirical science fiction. As in other works, the spaceship in *The Space-Born* is a kind of womb or nest, a "huge metal egg." "Everything essential to life was contained within the titanic hull, from toys for the new-born to gardens to freshen the air"[14]—a virtually complete realization of Buckminster Fuller's "perfect environment." To the inhabitants of the ship, "the metal cubicles had become their entire universe, static, unchanging, unalterable" (p. 9). As might be expected in such a tightly structured society, marriage is controlled by genetic programming and "you married to have children—or else" (p. 18). Population is limited by the "disposal" of "the unnecessary, the unessential, the old" (p. 22), and the protagonist, Jay West, is a member of the "psych-police" who must carry out the disposals without revealing to the rest of the population of the ship that such a program even exists. As in "Universe," there is an underground of rebels who have managed to evade elimination and who inhabit the more remote regions of the ship. Primitive, gunfight-like duels have become part of the accepted culture of the ship as an auxiliary means of population control, and the enforced life-span of the inhabitants is only forty.

The violence of this society is accounted for by the apparent contradiction between a program of genetic control designed to preserve the adventurous qualities that are regarded as central to the culture and the static, highly controlled environment that the culture now inhabits. Malick, the Chief of Genetics in the society, is the first to note this contradiction. "'What is the good of breeding an adventurous type when there is nowhere for them to go adventuring? How can we control highly-strung, sensitive men and women when they are surrounded by a limited existence almost calculated to drive them into a frenzy of frustration?'" (p. 73). The question is never really satisfactorily answered, although the ship's captain later explains that "'We have had to forge a new race, strong, moral, adventurous, to get rid of hereditary disease and physical weakness'" (p. 146), while at the same time maintaining a program of psychological indoctrination to counter the hereditary factors.

As in most novels of this type, the action is carried forward by Jay's discovering through a series of adventures the true nature of his spaceship-universe, finally encountering the stars and realizing that his whole cosmology is wrong, that the true master of the ship, the Captain, has been observing from a distance all the machinations of the plot and influencing them, and that the renegade underground is being used by the Captain as an intelligence service. If the novel finally fails, it is because Tubb establishes no logical connection between the heroic actions of the protagonist and the larger story of the journey itself; in the end, Jay simply learns from the Captain that the ship is about to arrive at its destination, and that Jay is being prepared to be the new captain. All of Jay's prior actions, apart from "proving" him an adventurous sort suitable for a leadership position, are essentially without consequence.

Harry Harrison's *Captive Universe* is somewhat more ingeniously thought out. The society of his ship is stabilized by being divided into two primitive cultures that are each designed to survive in a limited environment: a society based on Aztec culture that lives in a hollowed-out valley of the giant asteroid that has been converted into a spaceship (a hollowed asteroid also provided the spaceship in Manning's "The Living Galaxy"[1934]), and the Observers, a monastic culture whose members dutifully observe and manipulate the Aztec society. The intelligence and inquisitive spirit that will be necessary for survival once the journey is over is locked up in a genetic program that will produce a race of geniuses when the inhabitants of the two Aztec villages interbreed. For the duration of the voyage, however, such interbreeding is prevented by a strongly enforced sexual taboo.

Harrison's novel is interesting not only for the manner in which it resolves problems of this sort, but also for the almost archetypal manner in which it uses images of barriers to carry the action out. The novel begins with the breaching of a barrier, and each of the three major sections of the narrative ends with the breaching of a barrier, each more important than the one before, the final one leading to a literal deliverance of the Aztec people to the promised land. The barrier whose breaching opens the story is a dual one, involving rape and the breaking of the sexual taboo. A villager named Chimal forces his attentions upon Quiauh, a woman from a neighboring village, despite strong sanctions against intermarriage. As a consequence, he is violently killed by a spectacular death-goddess, Coatlicue, as he attempts to escape. The result of the rape, as might be expected, is the birth of the first of the race of geniuses who are to colonize the new world once the ship arrives at its destination.

The novel then takes up the narrative sixteen years later, when the child born of that rape, the younger Chimal, is caught attempting to break yet another taboo: the taboo against trying to leave the valley (this section of the novel is rather significantly titled "The Valley," suggesting the closed space in which all this action takes place). Chimal's genius is already in evidence: he contends correctly that the letter of the law allows him to climb partway up the wall of the valley "'to take birds' eggs, or for other important reasons.'"[15] But his true motivation, of course, is escape. This and similar acts get him in all sorts of trouble with the village priests, and this alienation, together with the general

69

alienation he feels from his mother and friends ("he felt so distant" [p. 9]), not only reveals his different genetic makeup, but also prepares the reader for his subsequent actions. Metaphorically, at least, Chimal is already an "outsider," and it is only a matter of time before his actions will take him literally outside the valley and precipitate the next major stage of action.

This happens at the end of the section titled "The Valley," when Chimal's increasingly aberrant actions have led to his being condemned to a primitive form of lobotomy by the local priests. Chimal flees and is pursued by Coatlicue, but manages to evade her by hiding underwater. (His observation that she is apparently unable to detect him under water is an indication that Chimal will also bring about the rebirth of inductive reasoning.) Later, hiding in the rocks, he discovers what appears to be a huge stone doorway in the side of the valley, and through experimentation (further evidence of the rediscovery of science) manages to find the catch that opens it, revealing a tunnel. Chimal follows the tunnel and encounters the society of Watchmen and Observers. This second section of the novel is titled "Outside," and it is here that Chimal undertakes the series of actions that lead to the breaching of the third major barrier in the book.

By entering the society of the Observers, Chimal has broken a taboo that extends to both of the contrasting cultures on the ship, and has become a threat to both. The Observers are in their own way as primitive and narrow-minded as the people of the valley, and when they find an interloper from the valley in their midst, their response, based on a parody of Jesuitical logic, is essentially the same as that of the Aztec priests: "'A man who cannot be in the valley or cannot be here, then cannot be. That is the truth of it. A man cannot be therefore is not, and a man who is not is therefore dead'" (p. 63). In other words, Chimal must be killed. He again flees, and again he comes upon a barrier: a great golden doorway that opens upon a chamber facing the exterior of the ship. One wall of this observatory chamber is transparent, and for the first time Chimal sees the real stars rather than the familiar artificial constellations of the night sky projected over his home valley. Here he is trapped by the Master Observer, who says, "'You have come at last to the end'" (p. 97). And in a sense this is true, for there are no more barriers between Chimal and the reality of his universe. Chimal's own quest for truth is indeed at an end, and what remains is for him to sort out the meaning of this truth. But barriers do remain, and the rest of the narrative involves Chimal's attempts to remove for the rest of the ship's inhabitants the barriers that he himself has conquered. Like the

70

traditional hero of Joseph Campbell's monomyth, he must return to his people with the boon he has won.

Chimal becomes a holy figure to the society of Observers, but he soon discovers that they have grown rigid and fearful with the passing of generations, and in fact have decided to bypass the solar system that was the ship's original destination, Proxima Centauri, without making adequate observations of the planets of that system. Chimal—who has mastered with a facility unlikely even for a genius the complexities of astral navigation, psychology, ecology, electronics, and most other sciences—is outraged at this discovery, and plots to reverse the course of the asteroid to its original destination. Again he becomes a hunted outsider to the Observers, but after a third series of adventures he finds the switch that will open the portal to the valley and release the Aztecs into the rest of the ship; Chimal believes that this deliberate violation of the master plan will force the Observers to agree to settle on a planet of the still nearby Proxima Centauri system. The final barrier that is overcome in the narrative is the same barrier whose breaching at the beginning of the story resulted in the birth of Chimal: Chimal informs the Aztecs that the taboo against intermarriage has been lifted, and that intermarriage is in fact encouraged. In the end, Chimal waits for the generation of geniuses who will help him to colonize the new world.

Quite apart from its defects—a rather mechanical structure and a blatant pattern of sexism in treating the female characters—Harrison's novel provides evidence that the theme of the society enclosed in a spaceship is still capable of new thematic variations without violating the essential structure laid down by Heinlein in "Universe." In nearly all such stories, the ship becomes a kind of metaphor for humanity confined to earth, and the narrative by extension an argument that humanity is not meant for a finite environment. But at the same time, the ship symbolizes the opposite of confinement: it is an image of humanity *escaping* the confines of a single planetary environment and seeking out new worlds. Parallel to this is the contrast between tribal and technological society that seems to dominate so many of these stories; the more limited the environment, the more primitive and ritualized society is likely to become, but once that environment is opened up, technology and reason rush in at once. The spaceship symbolizes the opposing forces at work by providing both the narrow environment and the technological marvels just out of reach.

Perhaps the real meaning of these apparent contradictions is revealed in a short passage in Edmund Cooper's *Seed of Light* (1959), a novel in which an atomic war is responsible for the beginning of the long voyage,

71

and which is dedicated to "those church dignitaries, politicians and eminent men who advocate the retention of nuclear weapons."[16] In this novel, characters on the voyage take on the names of famous scientists, perhaps to keep alive the tradition of scientific adventurousness that made the journey possible. Even so, they find themselves establishing a tribal culture, and at one point the character who has taken the name of Jung writes in his private journal, "We have established a tribe; but what are our tribal gods? They are: personality, which represents power; knowledge, which represents power; and the manifestation of that power in an unending game of psychopolitics" (p. 90). It is, of course, this same sort of psychopolitical gameplaying that led to the atomic war on earth in the first place. Cooper, both here and in his other novels (and the other spaceship narratives we have discussed also bear this out), suggests that man has not yet moved beyond a tribal culture, that in fact the cults of personality and politics that currently dominate human affairs are as much to blame for keeping us from appropriating the universe that surrounds us as are the cults of Aztec gods in Harrison's novel, or the agricultural cults of Heinlein's. It is only by transcending the narrowness of such ritualized behavior that we can move forward, and it is clear from most of these novels that the movement is more important than the arrival upon a new world.

Heinlein's story does not give us a hint of what the society on the new world will be like; nor does Tubb's or Harrison's. In Aldiss's *Starship,* Cooper's *Seed of Light,* and James Blish's *And All the Stars a Stage* (1971), the final destination turns out to be simply the earth itself. The message seems to be that humanity must continue to progress, no matter what the meaning of that progress or even if it has a meaning. Humanity is not an event, but a process. In the end of *Seed of Light,* the characters decide to return to earth, but an earth in a different space-time continuum, one that is still primitive and undeveloped. These thoughts go through the mind of the character Thales: "So it always was, he thought, and so it always would be. The end and the beginning joined together; and, without each other, meaningless. Thus, ultimately, there never could be an absolute end; just as there never could have been an absolute beginning. There could only be a continuous unfolding" (p. 154). Such a "continuous unfolding," suggesting the uroboric relationship between the primitive and the technological, the incestuous and the expansive, the inside and the outside, may be the common theme that links these various narratives and makes them a significant subgenre of science fiction. The odd juxtaposition between primitive tribal cultures and highly sophisticated technological environments that characterizes these narratives offers some hope that even these extremes of human culture are not irreconcilable, and that there is room for heroic individual effort in both. For those who seek a validation of their love of technology in a world that has clearly not quite risen above the conflicts and stresses of tribal life, this message must be a reassuring one indeed.

THE SPACESHIP FAMILY

The portrayal of tribal cultures surviving in a technological environment has more subtle expressions in science fiction as well. The ideal of the family circle is one that an era of high technology, with its increased regimentation and institutionalization, its need to constantly expand to new frontiers, and the resulting accelerated mobility of its citizens, seems to threaten mightily. Science fiction, while often advocating the growth of such technology, has also sought consistently to reinforce such traditional values as the family represents, and has on occasion sought ways to reconcile the apparent antinomies of family and technology, with the spaceship as the pivotal symbol of this reconciliation. These stories bring the spaceship-as-home into clear focus, but they also unfortunately often give credence to the criticism that much science fiction is made up of sexist, male-dominated fantasies. In Cooper's *Seed of Light,* for instance, the division of labor on board the spaceship is essentially that of the traditional middle-class family: women are geneticists, anthropologists, librarians, and dieticians, while men are physicists, chemists, doctors, and engineers. Tasks associated with maintaining the society are loosely translated into scientific or professional specialties, but even with this "coding" the division of labor breaks neatly along sexual lines: raising children becomes genetics and anthropology; preparing meals becomes dietetics. Other women are given traditional feminine occupations, too, such as librarians, but none are directly involved with the management of the spacecraft. Men are responsible for keeping the ship on course, inventing new systems of propulsion, maintaining the life-support systems. A revealing scene occurs in the ship's schoolroom, where children are engaged in making models of various animals and machines. A girl, Atlanta, is ridiculed by boys for making a model of a house, which "'doesn't *do* anything.'" Atlanta replies, "'Houses were the most important things of all. People lived in them, and they had windows that looked out on to gardens and streets. They had doors and fires, and the smoke went up a chimney.'" One of the boys replies, "'It isn't bad. . . . I mean, for a girl'" (p. 92).

Harrison's *Captive Universe* carries sexual stereotyping even further. The female Observers that Chimal encounters outside his valley "'lead lives of purity and sacrifice and are far above the animal relationships that exist in the valley. . . .They weep because they were born with female bodies which embarrass them and hamper their vocation'" (p. 107). The nurseries of little Observers are staffed by "mothers," or women who "'did not do satisfactory work in their studies and could not master their assignments'" (p. 108). Impregnation is accomplished through sperm from frozen sperm banks, removing the men even further from domestic concerns. Chimal, attracted by one of the women Observers, decides at the end of the novel that he would like to "liberate" her from her orientation to her job and create a more traditional family structure: "'You're a woman,'" he tells her, "'and outside of your training and development, a normal woman. I want to . . . give you a chance to *feel* like a woman. I think you have been cheated by life'" (p. 159).

Such examples of sexual stereotyping could probably be multiplied endlessly from the science fiction of the 1940s and 1950s, and are still in evidence in quite recent writing, as well as in science-fiction films.[17] One might even go so far as to suggest that the persistent habit in Hollywood during the 1950s of introducing female characters, apparently irrelevantly, into science-fiction films, represents as much an attempt at creating a mock family structure as an attempt to maintain sexual or romantic interest. As in *Seed of Light,* the women in such films are usually portrayed as cooks or outer-space housekeepers, and when they are assigned a scientific role it is usually as biologists or dieticians (sciences most closely associated with the family) rather than as physicists or engineers.

There are a few examples in science fiction in which the inhabitants of spaceships are seen literally as families. Ray Bradbury, in *The Martian Chronicles* (1950), describes "family rockets" designed for pleasure trips to the moon; it is in one such rocket that a middle-class family from Minnesota undertakes its final migration to Mars in order to start a new race in the story "The Million Year Picnic," which in part portrays space travel as a transformation of such middle-class family leisure activities as going on picnics and fishing trips. Robert Heinlein, in *Methuselah's Children* (1958), describes the forced exodus of a group of long-lived families to the stars to escape persecution at the hands of earthlings who believe them to be hoarding the secret of immortality (which is really no secret but a genetic anomaly); here, too, women teach school, look for husbands, or bear children while the men take care of the details of the voyage. "'Half the female volunteers are women with young children,'" one character notes.[18] *The Outward Urge* (1958), by John Wyndham and Lucas Parkes (both pseudonyms of John Beynon Harris), describes several generations of a family involved in the exploration of space, but in every generation, the women remain behind to bear the next generation of male adventurers. A similar structure is employed in Judith Merril's short novel "Daughters of Earth" (1969), which redresses the balance, so to speak, by portraying several generations of women actively involved in space exploration.

Cordwainer Smith (Paul Linebarger), who frequently seemed to intuit the mythic potential of science-fiction images long before anyone else, often featured family or marriage relationships in his stories, and in one of them, "The Burning of the Brain" (1958), he brings together with unusual power the traditional inside-outside opposition of the domestic spaceship with the theme of husband-wife relations. Surely there is no more domestic image for a spaceship than the replica of Mount Vernon that is the "planoforming" ship of "The Burning of the Brain," one of Smith's characteristic mythical romances.

"The Burning of the Brain" principally concerns the romance between Dolores Oh, a legendary beauty, and the "Go-Captain" Magno Taliano, whose very name suggests voyages of adventure and discovery ("the Great Italian" in all probability being an allusion to Columbus). Taliano is the greatest of the Go-Captains in an age in which space travel is governed by telepathic leaps controlled by the brain of a super-pilot guided by "lock-sheets," or star charts. "Stop-Captains" control the craft in normal space, but they are not nearly as revered as the Go-Captains.

Dolores is the traditional image of a ravishing romantic beauty—"so beautiful that she took men's breath away, made wise men into fools, made young men into nightmares of lust and yearning"[19]—who at the height of her beauty married the glamorous Taliano. But rather than partake of the rejuvenation process common in this future society, she has chosen to let herself age, to prove to herself that men love her not just for her appearance. At the time of the story, she has aged 164 years, turning into a ghastly and embittered old woman who regrets her decision and who awaits the day when her husband, still at the height of his career, will meet a similar catastrophe. She still accompanies her husband on his space flights, and the ship he commands is now the *Wu-Feinstein,* a replica of Mount Vernon "encased in its own rigid and self-renewing field of force" (p. 87). "The passengers went through a few pleasant hours of strolling through the grass, enjoying the spacious rooms, chatting beneath a marvelous simulacrum of an atmosphere-filled sky" (p. 87)—in other words, enjoying all the comforts of a protected domestic environment, the apotheosis of the drawing-room spaceships of Wells and Serviss.

Such an environment is the province of Dolores Oh, and it is in such an environment that her tragedy of aging has taken place. But the outside of the ship, the "up-and-out," is the province of her husband Taliano, and Smith is careful to assure the reader of its dangers. Guiding a ship through space is "dreadful," "like the piloting of turbulent waters in ancient days" (p. 85). This image of water, drawn from an earlier age of adventure, is the controlling image of outer space in the story: "Space, we can tell you, is rough—rough like the wildest of storm-driven waters, filled with perils which only the most sensitive, the quickest, the most daring of men can surmount" (p. 85). "The tissue of space shot up around them like boiling water at the base of a waterfall" (p. 89). "It [the ship] leapt from space to space, as uncertain as a man crossing a river by leaping from one ice-covered rock to another" (p. 93). Since the passengers are described as seeming to do nothing more than to "pass an afternoon in a pleasant old house by the side of a river" (p. 88), the irony of the river image in conjunction with the house image becomes apparent. This apparently placid river really suggests the violent outer world of space, while the house is the inner world of domesticity.

Only the Go-Captain is aware of the terrors that exist outside the ship, and the contrast between the pleasant domesticity of the inside and the turbulent danger of the outside is stressed by Smith at every conceivable point. But this dialectic also becomes the dialectic of the romance between Dolores Oh and Taliano. She, as mistress of the domestic world of the inside, has spoiled her romance by allowing herself to grow old and unattractive. Bitterly, she looks forward to the day when her husband will spoil *his* romantic attraction by ceasing to be the greatest of Go-Captains; she "craved ruin for her husband the way that some people crave love and others crave death" (p. 91). She anxiously awaits the external disaster that will mean for Taliano what her internal disaster means for her.

That disaster comes when, after the first leap into unknown space, the captain finds that his lock-sheets are in error and that the ship is hopelessly lost. The only chance of returning safely is to use his own brain in place of the lock-sheets, thus destroying his fabulous mind as thoroughly as age has destroyed Dolores's beauty. Dolores looks forward to this destruction with greed, but her semitelepathic niece, Dita, realizes the tragedy—that Taliano will "burn out" his brain in the process, destroying the paleocortex and reducing him to an amiable idiot. This is indeed what happens, and as a result Dolores regains the "shy and silly love" of Taliano that she had bitterly resented losing to her own aging. Dita, on the other hand, resolves the dialectic of the romance by adding to her youth and attractiveness the skills that Taliano has lost, which she picked up telepathically during the burning of his brain. The various antinomies of romance—male and female, sex and adventure, domestic and heroic action—are thus in this one story expressed through the dialectic of the inside and outside of a spaceship, and finally resolved into a single romantic figure, Dita, who possesses both beauty and the vast skills of a Go-Captain. I do not know whether Dita ever had her own story—it seems very likely that Smith was setting her up for one—but the romantic possibilities of a character such as hers are explored in a story Smith published only two years later, "The Lady Who Sailed the *Soul*," in which the figure of a woman pilot (albeit in an earlier era than "The Burning of the Brain" but part of the same future history) provides both the domestic and heroic aspects of the space travel dialectic.

Smith's stories offer the promise that even in the most sophisticated technological environments of the far future, human passions such as love and jealousy can still provide the backdrop for tales of near epic proportions; more than any other writer, he successfully unites the traditions of the love romance with the apparatus of science fiction. And though not all of his stories concern family relationships, nearly all of them reinforce the basic premise that love and technology are not irreconcilable. Other writers, too, have on occasion transcended the sexual stereotyping that too often characterized science fiction's presentation of male-female relationships. Alexei Panshin's *Rite of Passage* (1968), for example, portrays a conflict of generations between father and daughter in a context that emphasizes the differences between life on a spaceship and the less rigidly structured life of planetary colonies. And the large number of works of recent years that have perhaps too peremptorily been labeled "feminist" science-fiction have continued to explore the relationship between traditional family structures and artificial environments such as spacecraft. It seems clear that science fiction has passed beyond the stage in which the family rocket is featured in pulpish stories with titles like "Holiday on Jupiter," but the notion of the spaceship as home, as the abode of real or mock family structures, has become a well-engrained tradition, and the transplanting of domestic environments into space habitats is one of the accepted themes on which science-fiction writers work variations. More than the "Universe" stories with their tribal cultures, this theme suggests strongly that something of the way we live now will survive into the far future.

THE HUMAN SPACESHIP

From entire closed societies awaiting rebirth out of a womblike spacecraft, to space families in monstrous metal houses, it is only a logical step to the spaceship as an even more direct abode of consciousness. We might call this concept the spaceship as cranium, or the human spaceship, and it too is the central concept of a group of science-fiction stories. Stories that depict space travel in terms of an individual consciousness inhabiting an artificial environment range from those in which the spacecraft is a vessel whose cargo is the human mind (such as James White's *The Dream Millennium* [1974]), to those in which the environment of the ship becomes an integral part of the mind of its inhabitant (such as Theodore Sturgeon's "Bulkhead" or James Blish's "Common Time"), to those in which the ship itself is conscious (such as Clifford Simak's "Lulu" or Anne McCaffrey's *The Ship Who Sang* [1970]). We shall focus on the last group of stories.

Even in stories such as these, the inside-outside dialectic applies, and to some extent so does the womb-symbolism, but with increasing complexity. Such stories are by no means as formulaic as the "Universe" stories, but they do reveal a consistent tendency in science fiction to associate the interior of the spaceship with consciousness. The hull of the ship, which in previous stories we have examined served as the limits of a cosmos, the boundaries of a culture, or the walls of a home, here becomes analogous to the boundaries of the ego, the limits of perception and personality. Outside becomes the entire phenomenal world; inside becomes mind. Many science-fiction writers have seen in the closed environment of the spaceship an analog of the closed environment of perception within which the mind must develop. As James Blish's protagonist Garrard observes in "Common Time" (1953), "'Our very personalities, really, depend in large part upon *all* the things in our environment, large and small, that exist outside our skins. . . . So . . . think of what a monotonous environment the inside of a spaceship is. It's perfectly rigid, still, unchanging, lifeless.'"[20] For the science-fiction writer who is concerned with the individual consciousness rather than with social or familiar relationships, such an unpromising environment would yield little in the way of story ideas—unless it could somehow be united directly with the concept of mind.

The conscious spaceship is not new in science fiction, but few writers have attempted to treat it seriously. As early as 1944, Ray Bradbury wrote a short story, "I, Rocket," from the point of view of the rocket, and since then various forms of rocket intelligence, either artificial or organic, have provided the bases for stories that range from the comic to the sentimental. In a sense what these stories do is add the mind-body dualism to the various oppositions already subsumed in the inside-outside antinomy. The ship's instruments become sense organs and the crew—if there is one—a fairly passive group of passengers. That life as a spaceship might constitute a superior mode of existence, reducing the barriers between mind and universe and leading to a greater understanding of the phenomenal world, is a common theme among such stories. In Evelyn E. Smith's "Once A Greech" (1957), an alien whose life is a constant series of metamorphoses finally invests its consciousness in the spaceship of explorers from Earth, and what it says to the befuddled earthlings may explain something of the attraction of this particular fantasy to science-fiction writers: "'I have reached a higher plane of existence. I am a spaceship. . . . And this lofty form of life happens to be one which we poor humans cannot reach unassisted. Someone has to build the shell for us to occupy, which is the reason humans dwell together in fellowship and harmony.'"[21] Robert Sheckley's short story "Specialist" (1953) also suggests that the spaceship may be a superior mode of existence. The story is about a group mind or gestalt (reminiscent of Sturgeon's *More Than Human,* discussed in Chapter Seven), each member of which is a component of a single spacecraft (eye, mind, engine, etc.). The only real role of humanity in such a gestalt, the story suggests, is to provide the fear and doubt that powers such a ship to the stars.[22]

But Frank Herbert's *Destination: Void* (1966) suggests that a human brain encased in a spaceship cannot long survive. In this novel, human brains provide the Organic Mental Cores of spacecraft inhabited by humans, but three of these brains fail in succession, quickly changing the nature of the space voyage from a protected womblike voyage to a more traditional voyage of adventure. The outside-inside opposition is made apparent when the last of the protective brains fails: "It was as though the molecular stillness of outer space had invaded the *Earthling*'s concentric hulls and spread through to the heart of this egg-shaped chunk of metal hurtling toward Tau Ceti."[23] The crew is faced with the problem of constructing an artificial consciousness for the ship in order to survive. What they finally construct is also clearly a higher plane of consciousness—a kind of god, in fact, that deposits them safely on another planet with the ominous warning, "'You must decide how you will worship Me'" (p. 190).

The sentient spaceship not only fully realizes the implicit relationship between perception and environment that characterizes much of the fiction of space travel; it also carries the nurturing, womblike aspect of the spaceship to its logical end: the spaceship almost literally becomes a mother to its crew. It is hardly surprising, then, that two works which develop at length the idea of the sentient spaceship, Simak's "Lulu" (1957) and McCaffrey's *The Ship Who Sang* (1970) should feature ships with feminine personalities. (There are other examples of feminine ships as well: the last of the brains to fail in *Destination: Void* is named Myrtle; Stanley Kubrick has reported that his original intention in the film *2001* was to give the spaceship-computer HAL a woman's voice; Cordwainer Smith's story "Three to a Given Star" [1965] describes a woman's body structured into a spaceship in a manner very similar to that of McCaffrey's Helva.) I believe that this tendency to characterize spaceships as female is based on something more fundamental than mere sly allusions to the nautical tradition of calling a ship "she"; in many ways, it unites all the various domestic and sexual meanings of the spaceship we have discussed so far into a single image.

Simak's title "Lulu" refers to an artificial intelligence designed to carry out the day-to-day functions of a spaceship and to provide the crew with necessary life-support systems. But the crew members begin to suspect that Lulu is "'not entirely robot. . . . She was twenty years in building and a lot of funny stuff must have gone into her.'"[24] Lulu's maternal role in relation to the crew is evident from the start: "She synthesized our food and cooked it and served our meals to us. She saw that the temperature and humidity were just the way they should be. She washed and pressed our clothes and she doctored us if we had need of it, like the time Ben got the sniffles and she whipped up a bottle of some sort of gook that cured him overnight" (p. 133). As the narrator's style in the above passage suggests ("the sniffles," "some sort of gook"), the crew fulfills the role of adolescent children to Lulu's mothering. The communications engineer, Jimmy, is in the habit of writing love-sick adolescent poetry, and his fellow crew members, like teenage boys, wonder why he couldn't write "'about war or hunting or flying in the depths of space or something big and noble, instead of all that mush'" (p. 135). The narrator, who is supposed to be an anthropologist, reacts with a "surprised gasp and a blush" (p. 134) when he encounters unusual sexual customs on a planet called Honeymoon. The exaggerated immaturity of the crew seems to invite Lulu to take on a maternal role.

Much of the rest of the story parodies this relationship, and by extension parodies the entire theme of the nurturing spaceship in science fiction. Inspired by Jimmy's poetry and educated by the events on the planet Honeymoon, Lulu decides that she is in love with the crew and will elope with them to another part of the galaxy. But her love is clearly more maternal than sexual: she turns off the lights at "night" and sings lullabies to the crew, and when the crew tries to declare its independence by strewing things about the spaceship and generally acting careless, "her orderly robot intellect was outraged" (p. 138) and she begins to nag and lecture them. The narrator begins to wonder if perhaps "a woman's brain *was* somehow welded into that great hunk of intelligent machinery. After all, none of us knew the full details of Lulu's structure" (p. 142). He begins to fantasize Lulu as a love-starved old maid giving up her body for that of a spaceship in order to have the adventures she never had as a human. The crew finally decides that the only way to effectively rebel is to mimic total regression: they refuse to move, act, or talk, allowing Lulu to continue nurturing them, but without responding. They become, in an exaggerated image of what such spaceship crews are to some extent in all science fiction, infants. Lulu angrily responds by depositing them on an earthlike planet, but cannot violate her programming by stranding them there (suggesting that her "motherly instincts" are at least in part by design). Instead, she transfers her affections to a huge guardian robot, left on this planet by an extinct civilization. But when Jimmy produces a particularly noxious sentimental ode dedicated to Lulu, she responds with tears in her lens and even a lace handkerchief. Loaded as it is with stereotypes of both male and female behavior, "Lulu" is nevertheless an interesting, if only half-serious, attempt at depicting in some detail a conscious spaceship. Lulu's character may be immature and parodic, but in a sense it paves the way for what is probably the most thorough treatment of this theme in science fiction, the "Helva" stories of Anne McCaffrey, collectively titled *The Ship Who Sang* (1970).

Helva is a woman who, born deformed, has been conditioned since infancy to the life of a control-unit for a spaceship, her body encased in a metal cylinder and her only sensations those that come to her through the mechanical sensors of the ship, which constitute, in effect, her nervous system. There are many such ships in McCaffrey's future world, most of them controlled by a giant Central Worlds Corporation and nearly all of them, apparently, female. While some of the stories in *The Ship Who Sang* approach traditional "space opera" adventures, the work as a whole constitutes a romance, its theme the gradual maturation

81

of Helva and her finally coming to terms with the tragic death of her first "brawn," or pilot, whom she loved and who died in a rescue mission early in Helva's career. But it is a curious kind of romance, with its terms defined not merely as male-female (nearly all the "brawns" turn out to be male), but also as body-mind (the Helvas are of course the "brains" to their pilots' "brawns"), and of course spaceship-pilot or house-inhabitant. It is tempting to read too many implications into a situation that in effect offers us a romance between mind and body, and ardent feminists might too readily object to a fiction that apparently presents women as vehicles and men as the pilots of those vehicles, but this would be to ignore the basic dynamics at work in the stories themselves. The "brawns" are really hardly pilots at all; for the most part they remain passive while the ship is in space, like the crew of "Lulu," while the ships themselves make virtually all important decisions and even participate actively in the adventures on various planets. The relationship is again essentially a nurturing one, despite occasional sexual imagery, as when Helva opens herself to a group of cadets who would "do each other dirt to get possession of her" and she responds by feeling "mentally breathless, a luxury she thoroughly enjoyed for the brief time she felt she should permit it."[25] Since there is no evidence that any provision has been made for the sexual gratification of brains such as Helva, what relationships there are must necessarily be platonic or maternal. Helva's first brawn, Jennan, for example, explains to Helva that he thinks of his father's brain-ship, Silvia, as his grandmother.

McCaffrey seems aware of the curious sexual situation the idea of such spaceships gives rise to, and to a certain extent, she supplants sexuality with art in these stories. Helva develops her voice and becomes known as "the ship who sings," later rescuing one brawn from a hostile planet by means of a powerful protest song (called a "dylan") and in another episode rescuing herself and other ships from imprisonment by pirates by generating a kind of siren song which she suddenly amplifies to kill and incapacitate their captors. In another story she joins a troupe of actors in a bizarre exchange of drama for an alien culture's technology. The arts imagery even carries over into planet names: a sun named Ravel is circled by planets named Daphnis and Chloe.

But the nurturing function of the spaceships seems to serve as an equally important sex-surrogate. Many of the ships are used as nurseries, and Helva herself once cares for over a hundred thousand fertilized ova which she is delivering to a planet in need of population. This mock motherhood is an important stage in her growth. "'After all,'" she explains to her woman passenger in this story, "'there aren't many women,' and Helva used the word proudly, knowing that she had passed as surely from girlhood to woman's estate as any of her mobile sisters, 'who give birth to 110,000 babies at one time'" (p. 93).

Helva's many successful missions bring her almost enough wealth to buy her freedom from the corporation that controls her, that is, to pay off the cost of her training and the building of the ship that encases her. But one rite of passage remains for her before she becomes a fully mature and free ship-person. She has through the course of her adventures gradually come to terms with the loss of Jennan, but she has not yet faced the issue of her own humanity, the simple fact that while she *is* a spaceship in one sense, in another she is merely a human being trapped behind a barrier of titanium alloy, and that without her mechanical connections to the ship's instruments, she is as subject to "pseudo-death" or madness as is the sense-deprived Garrard of Blish's "Common Time." This crisis occurs in the story "The Ship Who Dissembled," in which Helva is captured by pirates and temporarily disconnected. She feels "every crevass of her mind quivering with the effects of sense deprivation" (p. 185). She cannot move, see, or hear until she is reconnected briefly to allow her to retain her sanity. Once reconnected, she manages to foil the pirates with the siren song mentioned above. Helva realizes finally that she is after all a human being inside a capsule, like all space travelers, and that the unknown represented by the outside of her capsule is for her a more complete and dangerous unknown than the unknown of space is for her passengers.

In the final story, Helva chooses for her brawn her former supervisor, Parollan, who is the only one fully capable of relating to her as a human rather than a machine. To Parollan, she is uniquely vulnerable, and this vulnerability is important in establishing the kind of relationship she seeks: Parollan even knows what she physically looks like and has the secret of gaining access to her through her titanium hull. (Jennan, her first brawn, gained her affection by addressing her physical presence, speaking deliberately toward the titanium core even though he knew she could hear him anywhere on the ship.) By regarding each other as fellow humans each trapped in a different physical shell, but both mechanically protected from the dangers represented by the exterior of the ship, Parollan and Helva finally resolve the brain-brawn relationship into a kind of marriage. Even in this final story, however, the function of the spaceship is still that of home, and it is as much as ever a domestic feminine image that Helva fulfills: she provides the meals and the means by which Parollan's work may be carried on, but Parollan remains primarily responsible for the missions that are assigned. Helva has in some sense become Parollan's wife, but in a more real sense, she has become his house.

Thus we have returned to our starting point: the spaceship as house, as a place of nourishment, of comfort in an otherwise hostile environment. And even in each of the "Helva" stories, the action does not really begin until the hull of the ship is breached and someone either enters or leaves the home environment, the realm of the known. There are, of course, many less homelike spaceships in science fiction, for example, Fred Saberhagen's purely robot Berserkers. But even when the spaceship is united with another science-fiction icon, such as the city in James Blish's *Cities in Flight* (see Chapter Four), the notion of home often remains an important function of this image. And there are other stories in which the pattern of home-imagery is transferred to other images than that of the spaceship; Daniel Galouye's *Dark Universe* (1961), for instance, deals with an underground post-holocaust society but belongs as much to the tradition of "closed society" tales as does Heinlein's "Universe." But the spaceship reveals more than any other image the complexity of science fiction's attitude toward what we might call the "symbolic universe" represented by the antinomy of womb and world. The purpose of most of the spaceships we have discussed, after all, is to make their functions obsolete, to deliver the human race or a part of it to a goal that must eventually be made part of the known. Leaving a spaceship to settle on an alien planet, or to aid colonists on that planet, is at some level a symbolic birth, an action aimed at helping the human race re-create itself in an environment that was once part of chaos. The spaceship tells us that the entire universe is significant to human experience and validates that experience by making possible the rebirth of humanity in strange environments and the subsequent appropriation of those environments. This in turn takes us back to the widespread science-fiction dogma that the universe is at least knowable, if not indeed an externalization of human values.

The primitive planetary societies of Panshin's *Rites of Passage,* Blish's *The Seedling Stars* (see Chapter Seven), and other works are demonstrations of how alien landscapes may be re-created in terms of human values; if the societies are childlike, it is because they are indeed children undertaking the externalization process anew after being born out of the womb of the spaceship. Similar societies might be imagined as evolving from the spaceship inhabitants of "Universe," *And All the Stars a Stage,* "Target Generation," and *Captive Universe.* "'Space travel has again made children of us all,'" says the philosopher in the epigram to Ray Bradbury's *The Martian Chronicles,*[26] and the meaning of this goes far beyond the simple sense of wonder that Bradbury was probably trying to express. To be in a spaceship is to reduce oneself to the passive, prenatal state of innocence, and to be thrust from it is to begin anew the process of growth and world-construction. As Peter Berger and Thomas Luckmann write in *The Social Construction of Reality,*

> Human existence is, *ab initio,* an ongoing externalization. As man externalizes himself, he constructs the world *into* which he externalizes himself. In the process of externalization, he projects his own meanings into reality. Symbolic universes, which proclaim that *all* reality is humanly meaningful and call upon the *entire* cosmos to signify the validity of human existence, constitute the farthest reaches of this projection.[27]

The science fiction of space travel and spaceships, I would suggest, implies such a symbolic universe, and the key icon of that universe is the spaceship, at once habitat, womb, and vehicle, that gives mankind the means to appropriate the unknown without sacrificing any of the comforts of home.

4
icon of the city

The city of tomorrow, engineers say, will tend first to vastness; gigantic buildings connected by wide, suspended roadways on which traffic will speed at unheard of rates. . . . Each building will be virtually a city in itself, completely self-sustaining, receiving its supplies from the great merchandise ways far below the ground. Dwellers and workers in these buildings may go weeks without setting foot on the ground, or the ground-level. In this city smoke will be eliminated, noise will be conquered, and impurity will be eliminated from the air. . . .

Caption for the back cover illustration
of *Amazing Stories,* August 1939

THE CITY AS BABYLON

What happened to the innocent visions of future metropolises that science fiction used to produce so readily? "A city of science, of atomic power, of space travel, and of high culture": such is the vision of Frank R. Paul in an illustration for *Amazing Stories* in April 1942,[1] but it might as well come from a dozen other pulp magazines, from Hugo Gernsback's novel *Ralph 124C 41+* (1911), or from films like *Just Imagine* (1931). Such innocent urban extrapolations—Gernsback's is the most thorough; his New York of 2660 was for a long time the model for such visions—readily invite the attacks made on science fiction by social critics such as Lewis Mumford. Such megalithic structures, says Mumford, "exhibit the essentially archaic and regressive nature of the science fiction mind,"[2] and Theodore Roszak writes, "The supercity alone guarantees the utmost in artificiality, which is the unquestioned goal of progress."[3] The failure of such visions might well be indicted, given the realities of urban life we have come to face since those predictions were first made. The cities we live in *are* the cities of the future, at least from the point of view of the pulp fiction and art of two or three generations ago, and we can see the effects of an urbanism that is more the outgrowth of collective industrial values than of concern for the quality of life. The modern city, as Mumford and Roszak suggest, is indeed an unmanageable, cacophonous, barely conceivable environment that has long since shifted from the communal imperative to the survival imperative: cities that once were social organizations to promote the protection of the individual from a hostile and chaotic environment now must devote more and more of their resources to the protection of the individual from the hostile and chaotic environment that the city itself has become. The innocent visions of the past have become the traps of the present, and it is tempting to blame the visionaries.

Fritz Lang's film, *Metropolis* (1926), presents us with an aspect of that vision that is missing from the other works in our list: the subterranean city of the workers that underlies and perpetuates the innocent utopia above. In this city, masses of soulless laborers work inhuman shifts on giant machines that occupy dark, hellish cavities under the earth. The city uses these workers for its food, and they are without hope. As Thea von Harbou describes them in the novel that was the basis of her husband's film:

Men, men, men—all in the same uniform, from throat to ankle in dark blue linen, bare feet in the same hard shoes, hair tightly pressed down by the same black caps.

And they all had the same faces. And they all seemed one thousand years old. They walked with hanging fists, they walked with hanging heads. No, they planted their feet forward but they did not walk. The open gates of the new tower of Babel, the machine centre of Metropolis, threw the masses up as it gulped them down.[4]

Surely the sensibility that produces such a vision is not far removed from the sensibility of a Mumford or a Roszak, and yet just as surely that sensibility belongs to the genre of science fiction. Indeed, when one examines the treatment of urban society or the image of the city in science-fiction works of the last five decades, one finds the underground of *Metropolis* a more powerful and lasting image than the plastic megaliths of Frank Paul or the mechanical wonders of Hugo Gernsback. As David Ketterer writes, "Science fiction cities tend toward Babylon rather than toward the New Jerusalem."[5] "The science-fiction mind" that Mumford speaks of is diffuse and complex, but by and large, over a period of time, it has come to view the city with the same reasoned terror that he does.

What has led science fiction to largely reject the notion of the city as mechanical paradise? After all, if science fiction deals with extrapolation, what more logical subject than the centuries-long shift toward urban centers that Roszak calls "the greatest and most rapid cultural transition in the entire history of mankind"?[6] If science fiction promotes the values of technology, what better focus for these values than the biggest machine of all, the completely mechanized human environment that Mumford calls the "megamachine"? If science fiction embodies some optimistic principle of plenitude, with the consensual belief that all the knowable universe can serve as an arena for humanity's infinite appropriation, and the validation of that process of appropriation, what better metaphor than the infinite city, or a "city of which the stars are suburbs," a term from Northrop Frye that Susan Glicksohn has used to describe works by Isaac Asimov and William Olaf Stapledon?[7] I suspect there are a number of reasons why science fiction has learned to be skeptical of the city of tomorrow. In many ways such an image runs counter to the traditional values of the genre, and, ubiquitous though it may be in science fiction, it is hardly representative of anything that could be called the "science-fiction mind." Some of the ways in which the city is antithetical to the traditional attitudes of the genre, in no particular order, are as follows.

The city is centralized. The archetype of the city is the Heavenly City of Jerusalem, or the celestial city of God that is the center of the universe, and as a result, Mircea Eliade tells us, cities "become real by the fact of being assimilated to the 'center of the world.'"[8] As such, they run counter to the dispersion motif that characterizes the "consensus cosmology" we have spoken of in reference to science fiction. The city is the end product of a process that began with agriculture and moved gradually to farming communities and villages and finally to centers of commerce, a universe growing ever more finite. But science fiction, deriving from an already largely urbanized culture, often sees this as an archaic goal, a dead end; hence the movement of many science-fiction narratives is to escape the city and re-establish some sort of cosmology based on the idea of expansion. Clifford Simak's *City* takes its title from the notion, already mythic at the time his narrative begins, of a society that may have existed before the natural process of decentralization took hold.

The city is collectivistic. "Those committed to these megastructures," writes Mumford, "will conduct their existence as if in interplanetary space, with no direct access to nature, no sense of the seasons or of the difference between night and day, no change of temperature or light, no contact with their fellows except through the appointed collective channels."[9] Science fiction, even the most militaristic (like that of Robert Heinlein), remains steeped in the values of heroic individual effort, and the enforced conformity of a densely urban environment transforms that science-fiction hero into a fugitive from such an environment; hence, the widespread theme of escaping from the city that we see in such works as Arthur C. Clarke's *The City and the Stars* or Ray Bradbury's *Fahrenheit 451.*

The city is xenophobic. The urban environment promotes a distrust of what might lie outside of the protective boundaries of the collective society. But as we have already seen, the inside-outside dialectic of science fiction demands that such barriers be breached, for without their breaching there can be no symbolic appropriation that transforms the unknown into the known and permits the ideational progression of the science-fiction narrative. In Asimov's *The Caves of Steel* (1953), a future New York in which the citizens are terrified of the outside ("Outside was the wilderness, the open sky that few men could face with anything like equanimity") is viewed by its inhabitants as "the culmination of man's mastery over the environment. Not space travel, not the fifty colonized worlds that were now so haughtily independent, but the City."[10] But during the course of a murder investigation that provides the novel's plot, the protagonist comes to realize that "'the colonization of space is the only possible salvation of Earth'" (p. 189), and sets about to begin a program of conditioning that will free the New Yorkers from their fear of the outside and permit the natural order to assert itself in "'the resumption of Galactic colonization'" (p. 188).

The city is authoritarian. The stable control of masses of population demands a governmental system in which the police play an increasingly important role. In order to realize the pristine symmetry of the future cities of a Gernsback or a Paul, sacrifices have to be made. W. H. Auden writes:

> A society which was really like a good poem, embodying the aesthetic virtues of beauty, order, economy, and subordination of detail to the whole, would be a nightmare of horror for, given the historical reality of actual men, such a society could only come into being through selective breeding, extermination of the physically and mentally unfit, absolute obedience to its Director, and a large slave class kept out of sight in cellars.[11]

In other words, *Metropolis.* But science fiction is resolutely individualistic, and one of the reasons its protagonists often find themselves *having* to breach the barriers and escape from the city is because of some transgression of the arbitrary "protective" rules of the community.

The city is stable. The movement of many science-fiction narratives, as I have been attempting to show, depends on a series of transformations of the unknown into the known, but the stable, closed social system of a utopian city hardly provides a likely arena for such transformations. Thus it is a fairly common theme (seen in the discussion of *The City and the Stars,* below) to present a stable society in science fiction, then to have the protagonist discover that this stability is really a mask for stagnation, and to go about deliberately upsetting the balance for the greater good of man (this is what the protagonist believes he is doing in Damon Knight's "Country of the Kind," for example).

The city is confined. At some level, the city is always a trap, a means of limiting the growth of the society by the necessity of limiting its own growth. In many science-fiction narratives, it is literally surrounded by a physical barrier, like the walled cities of the Middle Ages: John Brunner's *Stand on Zanzibar,* Edmund Cooper's *The Overman Culture,* Arthur C. Clarke's *The City and the Stars,* William Nolan's and George Johnson's *Logan's Run,* and Robert Silverberg's *The World Inside* (in which the city is simply one immense megalithic building, or arcology). But with cities, as with spaceships, such confinement limits the natural flow of humanity outward, and is a violation of cosmological principles.

The city is unnatural. It "'contradicts Nature in the lines of its silhouette, *denies* all Nature,'" writes Oswald Spengler, and "'the gigantic megalopolis, the *city-as-world.* . . . suffers nothing beside itself and sets about annihilating the country picture.'"[12] Science fiction is hardly the genre we would look to for nature worship; and indeed there are numerous works in the genre that apparently condone such wholesale subjugations of nature as "terraforming," or the engineering of alien planets for the comfort of man. But even the expansionist motif of the genre can be seen as having its roots in an awareness of the finite resources of any limited environment, and the arbitrary growth of any institution at the expense of the natural world—as opposed to the purposeful expansion *into* the natural world—is viewed with skepticism. Richard Matheson even wrote a satirical story ("The Creeping Terror" [1959]) in which the unchecked growth of Los Angeles was discovered to be the result of the fact that the city was alive—like some malignant disease creeping across the face of the planet.

The city is of the past. It no longer provides a viable analog of the future. As I mentioned earlier, we are already living in the technological urban fantasies of prior generations, and we learn daily of the tensions produced in merely keeping the modern city from becoming archaic: mass transit, increased air and auto traffic, larger and more centralized buildings, the decay of the center, and housing shortages all combine to remind us that the urban environment was founded in an era when such problems were not apparent and must engage in a continuous struggle merely to keep up with its own unmanaged growth. While it would be an oversimplification to say that science fiction is necessarily fiction of the future, the future is nevertheless the arena in which many of its works occur, and the city as it was once dreamed can now be seen as an unlikely, or at least questionable, part of that future.

The city is regressively technological. There can be little doubt that much science fiction deals enthusiastically with technological concepts and effects, but as I mentioned earlier, it prefers to view this technology as bringing about fundamental transformations in the quality and manner of life, or opening up new arenas of exploration and exploitation. In the urban environment, technology is turned in upon itself; it becomes more and more focused toward providing solutions to problems of its own creation. The technological energies that are directed toward such laudable goals as pollution and noise abatement, energy conservation, and public transportation have as their fundamental goal the stabilization of the present rather than the creation of new futures; such technologies are rarely the focus of science-fiction stories, which often prefer to focus on the revolutionary applications of technological energy.

The city is superfluous. "In the new space of the city, which is always a sacred space," writes Norman O. Brown, "man succeeds for the first time in constructing a new life which is wholly superfluous, and wholly sacred. A city is by definition divorced from primary food production, and therefore by definition superfluous; its whole economy is based on the economic surplus."[13] Theodore Roszak adds, "Such headlong urban concentration, it should be clear, has nothing to do with industrial necessity and little to do with population pressure."[14] Roszak goes on to argue that cities continue to be promoted out of a confusion of a style of life with a necessity of life, calling to mind the regressive orientation of cities that we have already discussed. Science fiction, on the other hand, values efficiency and tends to regard expansion as the most efficient way of dealing with growing populations. A strong case could be made that science fiction exhibits the antiurban tendency of the frontier mentality, not only in such works as Bradbury's *The Martian Chronicles,* which explicitly portrays space exploration in terms of the American frontier experience, but also in such less anomalous works as Silverberg's *The*

World Inside, which satirizes the dogma of the benefits of concentrated population by portraying a world in which the inhabitants strive mightily to reproduce fast enough to fill the massive urban structures that they have built for themselves.

The city is chaotic. Although on one level the city represents a kind of order that science fiction tends to value, it carries this order to a point of diminishing returns: the city becomes too large and complex to be fully understood by any of its inhabitants, and out of this excess of order comes disorder. Thus the image of the city mitigates against one of the fundamental dogmas of mainstream science fiction: the notion that one's environment can be known and mastered. Worse, it does this through the very process of appropriation that characterizes much science fiction. Like modern science itself, the city accumulates an imposing and confusing aggregate of detail so massive that any individuals participating in it must deliberately narrow the scope of their experience simply to make it coherent. The unknown is appropriated into the known to the point at which the known itself becomes so complex as to be unknowable, and in many science-fiction narratives— Clarke's *The City and the Stars* again, for example—a large part of the protagonist's quest into the unknown becomes simply the process of uncovering the "secret of the city" in which he lives.

The city is mythic. According to René Guénon, the city has its conceptual origins in the symbolism of the center, and expresses a particular cosmological doctrine of which the city walls are the outward signs of dogma.[15] Science fiction, too, it may be argued, is a mythic expression of belief, but it is seldom an expression that derives from inherited bodies of myth; as Robert L. Jones has demonstrated in regard to Roger Zelazny's *Lord of Light,* science fiction often undertakes a process of demythification of old beliefs as a prelude to asserting its own values.[16] What we saw repeatedly in the stories of closed societies aboard spaceships was the dismantling of an accepted mythic system (whether Aztec, pseudomedieval, or agrarian) in order to release the society to act out its true myth of planetary colonization; something of the same thing holds true for cities, whose systems of belief and implied cosmologies must be demythified in order for the science-fiction narrative to get on with its primary business.

We can see, then, that the easy assumption that science fiction is a literature that promotes continued urbanization and that champions the megalopolis of the future is fundamentally erroneous, although there are certainly works that do adopt such an attitude. The city is indeed one of the most important iconic images in science fiction, but the ways in which this image is used in the genre suggest that it is less a realization of human plenitude than a barrier to it: like the hulls of the spaceships in stories of outer space exploration, the walls of the cities become images of barriers that must be broken, of a past that must be transcended. Hence the recurrent image of the ruined city in science fiction that carries such a powerful symbolic message of simultaneous apocalypse and rebirth: the satisfaction that audiences feel in the last scene of the film *Planet of the Apes*, with the sudden discovery by the lost astronaut of the ruined Statue of Liberty that reveals the ape-planet to be a future earth, comes not only from a shock of recognition (which by itself would give the film a decidedly downbeat ending), but from the realization of the commonly shared fantasy of seeing cities reduced to rubble (a fantasy that film makers picked up on later with further images of a ruined New York in *Beneath the Planet of the Apes* and scenes of a crumbled, overgrown Washington in *Logan's Run*). As Pauline Kael says with some glee in her review of *Earthquake*, "L.A. gets it,"[17] and audiences respond in kind to the film, which has little rationale other than the spectacle of assaulting us in images and sound with our own secret fantasies of apocalypse. The literature, too, abounds in images of urban destruction, whether brought on by natural catastrophes (as in the disaster novels of J. G. Ballard or John Christopher), by alien invasion (as in Robert Crane's *Hero's Walk* or Wells's *The War of the Worlds*), or by our own atomic wars (as in Wilson Tucker's *The Long, Loud Silence*, Leigh Brackett's *The Long Tomorrow*, Philip Wylie's *Tomorrow!*, Nevil Shute's *On the Beach*, or endless other examples). The narrator of M. P. Shiel's *The Purple Cloud* (1901) even finds himself giving in to a strange compulsion to set fire to great cities after a purple gas has destroyed all other humans, and to sit back and watch them burn; the fantasy is not as abnormally pathological as it may at first seem.

Even cities in science fiction that are not already ruined are apt to be well on the way to destruction. The New York of John Brunner's *Stand on Zanzibar* (1968) is a domed nightmare of overpopulation, murderous "muckers" driven berserk by the close environment who make the streets hazardous at night, tiny cubicles for living quarters—all of which prompts one of the characters to wonder, "*How do we stand it?*"[18] Harry Harrison's *Make Room! Make Room!* (1966), James Blish's and Norman Knight's *A Torrent of Faces* (1967), Thomas M. Disch's *334* (1974), and any number of other works also focus on the dangers of overpopulated "hive" cities, and Samuel Delany's *Dhalgren* (1975) portrays in complex detail the disintegration of a megalopolis named

93

Bellona in the near future. And cities that aren't already straining with the weight of population are as antihuman: the mechanized cities of Asimov's *The Caves of Steel,* Clarke's *The City and the Stars,* and J. T. McIntosh's planet-wide megalopolis of *The Million Cities* (1958) all represent an unhealthy alternative to space travel, and an important side effect of the goals of the novels' protagonists will be the eventual decline of the monstrous cities. Some cities in science fiction, such as the title city of John Christopher's *The City of Gold and Lead* trilogy, are direct instruments of oppression by superior alien invaders, and must be destroyed in order for human beings to reassert the fundamental dominion over their own environment that will make future progress and expansion possible.

In terms of our known-unknown antinomy, then, it becomes apparent that most science-fiction cities represent yet another kind of barrier that prevents humanity from appropriating the unknown. Exactly how this dialectic has evolved in relationship to the imagery of cities can be revealed by exploring a few selected works that are important in the history of science-fiction cities. The first of these works, and the one that provides the clearest antecedent of urban malaise as it has come to be portrayed in modern science fiction, is a novel that nominally does not deal with a city at all: H. G. Wells's *The Time Machine* (1895).

EVOLUTION OF THE SCIENCE-FICTION CITY: WELLS, FORSTER, AND LANG

Jean-Pierre Vernier has argued persuasively that *The Time Machine* does not belong with the group of social protest tracts that characterize Wells's later writings; he even quotes Wells himself to the effect that the novel "'seemed to have no sort of relation whatever to normal existence.'"[19] Kingsley Amis concurs, noting that the novel's division of a future human race into the decadent leisure class of the Eloi and the subterranean working class of the Morlocks "is not transformed, as it inevitably would be in a modern writer, into a warning about some current trend in society."[20] Yet few critics have resisted commenting on the various oppositions represented by the Morlocks and Eloi, and seeing in these oppositions extrapolations of the dangerous effects of urban society. Bernard Bergonzi notes the symbolism of the class struggle in the class division of Wells's future world, and goes on to say that "it also reflects an opposition between aestheticism and utilitarianism, pastoralism and technology, contemplation and action, and ultimately, and least specifically, between beauty and ugliness, and light and darkness."[21] Clearly a barrier exists in the novel that if not transcended will contribute to the end of humanity, the final stage of evolution that is perhaps represented in the book's final section, when the Time Traveller moves forward to the end of the world and sees the only animate life as "a thing like a huge white butterfly" and a "monstrous crab-like creature" (pp. 94-95). Like the Eloi, the butterfly is pale and helpless, uttering a dismal cry and fluttering away over a hillock; and the experience the Time Traveller undergoes with the crabs, moving toward him and touching him, is reminiscent of his earlier frightening experience of being surrounded by the Morlocks.[22]

But to find the origins of this barrier against creative progress, one need look no farther than the urban society of Wells's own Victorian England. The acute class division in London in particular had prompted earlier Victorian writers such as George Gissing, Charles Dickens, Benjamin Disraeli, and Charles Kingsley to invent harrowing metaphors for the two directions in which society seemed to be evolving—Disraeli's "two nations," Gissing's "nether world," Kingsley's protagonist's speculation in *Yeast* (1848) as to whether the working poor were "'even animals of the same species.'"[23] Brian Aldiss writes, "The theme is a familiar Victorian one; it had vivid meaning for urban generations striving to install efficient modern sewers under their towns."[24] (The theme of sewers breeding an alien race is evident even in pulp fiction of the era; for example, George Daulton's "The Death Trap," which appeared in *Pearson's Magazine* in 1908.[25]) As Raymond Williams comments, "This is the vision that had been given an evolutionary dimension in *The Time Machine*. . . . The sombre vision of man divided into brute labour and trivial consumption, and then of the city shaped physically to embody these worlds, is expressed again and again. This way of seeing was to have great influence. One of its most remarkable successors is Lang's film *Metropolis*, in the nineteen twenties."[26]

Wells did not care for *Metropolis*; he called it "the silliest film" but admitted, "Possibly I like this soupy whirlpool none the less because I find decaying fragments of my own juvenile work of thirty years ago, *The Sleeper Awakes*, floating about in it."[27] Many of the sources of the film's portrayal of the city can be found in Wells's early work, including *The Time Machine*. The world of Wells's Morlocks and Eloi, after all, is all that the traveler sees of the world of 802,701 and it is a limited geographical area that rests atop the ruins of what once was London. He locates himself in this new world not only by reference to physical features of the landscape (which has changed drastically in the intervening millennia), but also by references to contemporary suburban areas such as Banstead, Wimbledon, Wandsworth, and Battersea. He speaks of his difficulty in comprehending this new world with the analogy of an African brought to London (pp. 52-53), and among the first things that he notices are massive ruins suggesting the passing of some great city (p. 40).[28] The cities appear to be wholly extinct, and the childlike Eloi live a pastoral, agricultural existence, surviving off fruits and berries; the ancient relationship of the city and the country, with the country providing foodstuffs for the enclosed and parasitical urban community, seems to have followed the horses, cattle, sheep, and dogs into extinction (p. 38). "The work of ameliorating the conditions of life—the true civilizing process that makes life more and more secure—had gone steadily on to a climax. One triumph of a united humanity over Nature had followed another" (p. 43). Even the name "Eloi" seems to suggest *Elohim,* in its old meaning of potentates of the earth.

But the Time Traveller soon discovers that, despite the apparent lack of commerce and industry among the Eloi, the city has not entirely disappeared from the face of the earth. In a chapter that in the novel's first edition was simply titled "Explanation," he discovers the existence of the Morlocks, the bestial, subterranean machine-tenders who maintain the standard of life enjoyed by the Eloi and who, it later turns out, survive in turn by eating the Eloi. The dependence of the city on the country for food has not been eliminated after all; it has merely been carried to a logical extreme in which dependency evolves into cannibalism. Rather than having died out, agriculture has simply achieved the ultimate in efficiency with the gradual elimination of the intermediaries of cattle and grain: the Eloi need only breed themselves to provide food for the confined Morlocks, and to increase the efficiency of this breeding, they undergo puberty at an early age (p. 41). The question would seem to arise as to why the Eloi, who are mortally fearful of the Morlocks, do not simply move on to other lands; the fact that they cannot break out of this pattern of dependency is further evidence that the urban mentality of living in a circumscribed environment has not entirely died even in this pastoral society.

The Time Traveller sees the origins of the Morlock-Eloi split in the urban society of his own time:

> At first, proceeding from the problems of our own age, it seemed clear as
> daylight to me that the gradual widening of the present merely temporary
> and social difference between the Capitalist and the Labourer, was the key

to the whole position. No doubt it will seem grotesque enough to you—and wildly incredible!—and yet even now there are existing circumstances to point that way. There is a tendency to utilize underground space for the less ornamental purposes of civilization; there is the Metropolitan Railway in London, for instance, there are new electric railways, there are subways, there are underground workrooms and restaurants, and they increase and multiply. Evidently, I thought, this tendency had increased till Industry had gradually lost its birthright in the sky. I mean that it had gone deeper and deeper into larger and ever larger underground factories, spending a still-increased amount of its time therein, till, in the end—! Even now, does not an East-end worker live in such artificial conditions as practically to be cut off from the natural surface of the earth? [Pp. 60-61]

The upper classes in London, he continues, have developed the habit of shutting off their gardens and lands from intrusion by the rabble. "So, in the end, above ground you must have the Haves, pursuing pleasure and comfort and beauty, and below ground the Have-nots, the Workers getting continually adapted to the conditions of their labour" (p. 61). All this, he claims, is merely "'working to a logical conclusion the industrial system of to-day'" (p. 62). But virtually all of Wells's images of this "industrial system" that he compares to the world of 802,701 are drawn from his own London; the opposition of the worlds of the Morlock and Eloi has its foundations in the oppositions already apparent in the structure of cities. At the end of the novel, the narrator comments on the Time Traveller's tale that the Time Traveller "saw in the growing pile of civilization only a foolish heaping that must inevitably fall back upon and destroy its makers in the end. If that is so, it remains for us to live as though it were not so" (p. 104). Lewis Mumford has attacked this ending: "In other words, we had better close our eyes and shut our minds. A fine terminus for the scientific pursuit of celestial truth that Copernicus and Kepler had instituted!"[29] But there is hardly reason to suppose that Wells identified so closely with his narrator, who after all had naïvely hoped the time machine would reveal a communistic future utopia (p. 18), only to be confronted with a narrative that in many ways parodies such dreams as expressed in earlier works like William Morris's *News from Nowhere* (1891). Furthermore, in later works, Wells did develop the image of the city that underlay *The Time Machine* into more of a dire warning that seemed more directly to call for reform.

In "A Story of the Days to Come" (1897), for example, Wells demonstrates that he was acutely aware of the apprehension of Victorian writers about the unchecked growth of cities, and gives us a vision of a city that is an intermediate step between the urban society of the nineteenth century and the world of Morlocks and Eloi. "Mankind were drawn to the cities by an overwhelming attraction," his future narrator tells us.[30] "The flow of population townward was the constant preoccupation of Victorian writers." These early cities were "horribly inconvenient, darkened by smoky fogs, insanitary and noisy" (p. 749), but even after such problems were solved with more efficient architectural and energy systems in the twentieth century, the movement toward isolating the cities from the outside, and isolating the classes within, continued. By 2013, "all the city ways, all public squares and places, were covered in with a recently invented glass-like substance. The roofing of London became practically continuous" (p. 750) and skyscrapers rose higher and higher (already we have an early vision of the domed cities of later science-fiction writers such as John Brunner). Life in individual houses, we are told, "was steadily supplanted by life in interminable hotels" (perhaps an early version of the arcologies satirized in Silverberg's *The World Inside*). It is clear by now that Wells is less concerned with the squalor, overcrowdedness, and pollution that made the cities seem like such hellholes to his contemporaries—he has eliminated most of these problems in his city of the future—than with the very structure of urban life.

The class division in this future city remains as rigid as it had been in Wells's London, and is rapidly moving toward the kind of opposition of which *The Time Machine* represents the culmination:

> The prosperous people lived in a vast series of sumptuous hotels in the upper storeys and halls of the city fabric; the industrial population dwelt beneath in the tremendous ground-floor and basement, so to speak, of the place.
>
> In the refinement of life and manners those lower classes differed little from their ancestors, the East-enders of Queen Victoria's time; but they had developed a distinct dialect of their own. In these under ways they lived and died, rarely ascending to the surface except when work took them there. Since for most of them this was the sort of life to which they had been born, they found no great misery in such circumstances. . . . [Pp. 752]

The last sentence echoes the Time Traveller's speculation on the evolution of the Morlocks from underground workers' societies, that "'the survivors would become as well adapted to the condition of underground life, and as happy in their way, as the Upper-world people were to theirs'" (p. 62). Later in "A Story of the Days to Come," we even can see the beginning of the evolutionary divergence:

> But slowly and inevitably in the intervening years a gulf had opened between the wearers of the blue canvas and the classes above, a difference

not simply of circumstances and habits of life, but of habits of thought—
even of language. The underways had developed a dialect of their own:
above, too, had arisen a dialect, a code of thought, a language of "culture,"
which aimed by a sedulous search after fresh distinction to widen
perpetually the space between itself and "vulgarity." The bond of a common
faith, moreover, no longer held the race together. [P. 787]

When a middle-class couple is reduced to joining the working classes, "it
seemed to them almost as though they were falling among offensive
inferior animals" (p. 787), and one of the first skills the husband,
Denton, must learn is the art of "scrapping," since violence has become a
brutal way of life in the underworld. (Incidentally, the uniform of blue
canvas worn by Wells's workers is reflected precisely in the uniforms of
dark blue linen worn by the workers in both the film and novel of
Metropolis.)

Wells's *When the Sleeper Wakes,* published shortly after "A Story of
the Days to · Come," also demonstrates the urban origins of the
Morlocks and Eloi, and is in many ways merely an expanded version of
the shorter story. The protagonist Graham awakes to a future London
of 33 million people; "The city had swallowed up humanity."[31] "The
whole world was civilized; the whole world dwelt in cities; the whole
world was property" (p. 145). Capitalism has appropriated the whole
world, and has begun to engineer the divorce of labor from bourgeois in
an even more cynical way than in "A Story of the Days to Come." "Little
children of the labouring classes, so soon as they were of sufficient age to
be hypnotized, were thus converted into beautifully punctual and
trustworthy machine minders, and released forthwith from the long,
long thoughts of youth" (p. 189). Nearly half the population (wearing
that ubiquitous blue canvas again!) labors for the benefit of the rulers. A
woman who is a clear antecedent of Maria in *Metropolis* explains to
Graham:

"Toilers, living without pride or delight or hope, with the stories of Pleasure
Cities ringing in their ears, mocking their shameful lives, their privations
and hardships. Too poor even for the Euthanasy, the rich man's refuge from
life. Dumb, crippled millions, countless millions, all the world about,
ignorant of anything but limitations and unsatisfied desires. They are born,
they are thwarted and they die. That is the state to which we have come." [P.
200]

But the Pleasure Cities are hardly more inviting; they are the breeding
grounds of what will eventually become the Eloi. As the villainous
Ostrog describes them to Graham: "'But the Pleasure Cities are the

excretory organs of the State, attractive places that year after year draw together all that is weak and vicious, all that is lascivious and lazy, all the easy roguery of the world, to a graceful destruction. They go there, they have their time, they die childless, all the pretty silly lascivious women die childless, and mankind is the better'" (p. 208). The workers, Ostrog argues, "'have sunk to what they are fit for'" (p. 208), and the leisure classes have risen to the pinnacle of decadence. All that remains is for the managerial class to disappear, and we have *The Time Machine*.

London, Graham discovers in another metaphor shared with "A Story of the Days to Come," had become "a prodigious hotel, an hotel with a thousand classes of accommodation, thousands of dining halls, chapels, theatres, markets and places of assembly, a synthesis of enterprises. . ." (p. 216). And it is again in the subterranean depths of this hotel that the working class evolves: Graham must travel "downward, ever downward," beneath the surfaces of low-cost Eadhamite (a superefficient architectural material also featured in "A Story of the Days to Come"), in order to visit the city of the workers, and, of course, he finds it appalling, a clear forerunner of the world of the Morlocks. But if in *The Time Machine* Wells refrains from making his narrative into a social comment, here he rubs his liberalism in with sarcasm: "But why should the gentle reader be depressed? Surely to a refined nature our present world is distressing enough without bothering ourselves about these miseries to come. We shall not suffer anyhow. Our children may, but what is that to us?" (pp. 239-40).

For Wells the city clearly is a barrier to the better progress of man, and it is a barrier that he does not allow to be breached in his early novels. In later utopian writings he returned to the notion of a pastoral utopia based on world government that had characterized the writings of earlier utopian thinkers of the nineteenth century. But he had established in these early works a model for the science-fiction city of the future, with its walls that separate the community from the universe, class from class, and citizen from citizen. The appropriation of the natural world that such a society implies is an appropriation that leads to a dead end, and in the hands of other authors it will be seen to be a barrier to the exploration of space and the eminent domain of man in the universe. It represents science and technology turned in on itself, producing a monotony of endless interiors and machines that serve only to promote the old order, and thus violating the basic myth of technics that science fiction strives to promote.

Ironically enough, it is a work described by its author as "'a counterblast to one of the heavens of H. G. Wells'"[32] that develops this notion of the city-as-prison to its next stage in the history of science-fiction cities. E. M. Forster's "The Machine Stops" (1909) follows by a decade *When the Sleeper Wakes* and "A Story of the Days to Come" and precedes by more than a decade the more familiar "antiutopian" works of Eugene Zamiatin and Aldous Huxley. It would be interesting to know what specific works by Wells Forster had in mind (*A Modern Utopia* [1905] seems the most likely candidate), for his "counterblast" is really little more than a confluence of the opposed societies of Morlocks and Eloi, laborers and masters, into a single massive urban complex sharing the characteristics of both. Like Wells's Morlocks, the residents of Forster's massive cities reside in vast underground hives, surrounded by the hum of great machines, fearful of the world above, and "white as a fungus."[33] In order to visit the surface illegally, the misfit Kuno must clamber up the ladders of ancient airshafts reminiscent of the shafts Wells's Time Traveller must descend in order to visit the world of the Morlocks. And yet Forster's citizens are like the Eloi, too: they are intellectually decadent, looking for simplistic "ideas" that only confirm their womblike style of living, and physically flaccid: "it was a demerit to be muscular. . . .and all who promised undue strength were destroyed" (p. 133). (Wells said of the Eloi that the weak would be better equipped for a life such as theirs, "for the strong would be fretted by an energy for which there was no outlet" [p. 45].) Also, like the Eloi, they depend on unseen powers that they do not fully comprehend for their necessities of life.

Although widely criticized today for its failure to stand up well to the more complex antiutopias of later writers, "The Machine Stops" does in fact introduce a number of important themes that would characterize the future city in much later science fiction. First, and most obviously, Wells's human labor is replaced by mechanical labor, giving us an early vision of the automated city of the future that was to recur in such works as Clarke's *The City and the Stars*. But the laboring classes themselves have not entirely been replaced; as I mentioned above, the Morlocks and Eloi together contribute to the makeup of Forster's citizenry.

Second, the city is seen as a dehumanizing influence on a more interpersonal level than in Wells's works. Whatever their psychological decadence, both the Morlocks and the Eloi of Wells are capable of physical communication among themselves. The Eloi are constantly caressing one another, kissing, and playing together; while the tendency of the Morlocks to want to physically explore his body is perhaps the most repellent aspect of their behavior (short of their cannibalism) to the Time Traveller. One can perhaps see in the Time Traveller himself some trace of the physical inhibitions that characterize Forster's citizens; and his invention, described on the first page of the novel, of chairs that "embraced and caressed us rather than submitted to be sat upon" (p. 13) is a further indication of a tendency to replace human contact with the contact of the instruments of technology. But in Forster's society "people never touched one another" (p. 130). They live instead isolated in their separate cubicles, seldom wandering forth even into the corridors and communicating through video machines that blur detail and give "only a general idea of people" (p. 121). Even direct observation of phenomenon is frowned upon; the further removed an idea is from its source, the better (p. 143). This insulation of each individual in a society that is paradoxically densely populated will also remain as a theme of urban life in later science fiction, although it is seldom expressed as directly in a metaphor of physical isolation. In Brunner's *Stand on Zanzibar,* for example, a character is suddenly aware of the density of population around him in a New York of 13 million people, and "the idea made him feel fearfully, intolerably alone" (p. 94). Even in Silverberg's *The World Inside,* in which the characters behave with something of the innocent promiscuity of the Eloi, the isolation of the individual is felt in the form of tremendous social pressures to conform and to keep one's true thoughts to oneself; those who fail are called "Flippos" and quickly disposed of.

A third modification that Forster introduces to the image of the city is that in "The Machine Stops," the city is clearly worldwide; when the woman Vashti talks over the video with her son elsewhere in the city, he is "on the other side of the earth" (p. 120). Wells's cities are already tending in this direction; in both "A Story of the Days to Come" and *When the Sleeper Wakes,* only a few cities remain, with most of the population concentrated in them. But *The Time Machine*'s setting is confined to the environs of what had been London, and we are given no clear indication that the Morlock-Eloi society extends much beyond these limits. Once the city is made universal throughout the world, however, the idea of escaping from it becomes much more problematical. Forster provides a solution by making his civilization entirely subterranean and implying at the end a new civilization may arise from those few surface dwellers who are "'hiding in the mist and the ferns until our civilization stops'" (p. 152). In other words, by crossing the barrier represented by the surface of the earth into the open space, man can once again begin to assert his proper dominion, but fear and conditioning prevent this; one is reminded of the agoraphobia of the New Yorkers in Asimov's *The Caves of Steel.* Forster would scarcely have regarded his transition from the cavernous city to the surface an analog of eventual human migration into space, but that is what in fact it becomes when viewed in the light of later science fiction: the new world of the surface is every bit as hostile and alien to the city-dwellers as another planet would be to later science-fiction characters. The invention of the concept of the worldwide city, then, eventually gives rise to the key opposition between the dead-end of the urban environment and the natural tendency of the race to expand outwards; the city, as in the title of Clarke's novel, is placed in direct opposition to the stars.

Yet another important theme in evidence in "The Machine Stops" is that of the rebel, in this story the misfit Kuno, who discovers on his own a way out of the city and who comes to believe that movement to the surface represents the only hope for the race. As we have already seen in the other group of stories involving closed environments, the tales of generations-long space voyages, the misfit is a key figure in much science fiction, being the one who discovers the long-forgotten barrier whose crossing will liberate the human race from its self-imposed degeneration. One can scarcely imagine such a character emerging from the societies of Morlocks or Eloi, and the kind of political revolutionary depicted in Lang's *Metropolis* or Wells's *When the Sleeper Wakes* is a substantially less prophetic figure than the true misfit, who seeks not merely to reorder priorities within a society but rather, in the truest sense of the term "radical," to discover the historical sources of the society's divergence from the "true path" and to set it right again. Often, these misfits are evolutionary anomalies as well, such as Alvin in Clarke's *The City and the Stars*—and this, too, is in evidence in "The Machine Stops" when Vashti notices that her son Kuno is growing a mustache: "The very hair that disfigured his lip showed that he was reverting to some savage type" (p. 137).

The idea of the machine itself—of making the urban society dependent on the functioning of a single massive mechanism—also moves beyond the labor-driven societies of Wells. Even in *Metropolis,* which is a city regulated and sustained by the imposing machines of its lower levels, these machines are tended by a class of oppressed laborers who seem to exist almost entirely to prove a political point; as Wells pointed out in his attack on the film, "a mechanical civilization has no use for more drudges; the more efficient its machinery the less need there is for the quasimechanical minder."[34] Later science-fiction writers tend to follow the example of "The Machine Stops" in their identification of the city with a single machine metaphor. Often the metaphor is no more specific than the unseen megatechnical wonder that drives the world of

"The Machine Stops," but some authors have singled out more clearly defined metaphors: the mechanical roads in Heinlein's "The Roads Must Roll," the central clock in J. G. Ballard's "Chronopolis," the central computer in Clarke's *The City and the Stars,* the "spindizzies" of Blish's *Cities in Flight.* In each case, the city could not function without the central machine, and in most cases, the machines tend to eliminate or vastly reduce the number of lower-class laborers. In Blish's novels, there is virtually no employment for anyone with an IQ of under 150; the resulting permanent depression is what sets the urban workers in flight in the first place (they scour the universe, looking for work). In "The Roads Must Roll," the mechanics who maintain the roads are virtually the only laboring class left and are given special treatment and conditioning; their attempted revolt fails. And in "Chronopolis," it is the white-collar workers whose lives are directed by the great clock who lead the successful revolt against regimentation and, by extension, against all timepieces.

Finally, and closely related to the figure of the misfit, is the hope of escape that Forster holds out in his story. Wells's cities can be improved, they can be restructured, and if we read his message earnestly enough, they can be avoided; but once they are established there is little the mass of humanity can do to avoid living in them. *The Time Machine,* too, offers little hope in its portrayal of an urbanized society as "only a foolish heaping that must inevitably fall back upon and destroy its makers in the end" (p. 104). The key word here is "inevitably," and it is a word that must grate against the very sensibility of modern science fiction, which, if it is nothing else, is a literature of alternatives. Forster's story, for all its apparent cynicism, shares with later science fiction a final note of optimism that there *are* alternatives, that even when the machine stops there is hope that the race will continue. "'Humanity has learned its lesson,'" (p. 152) says Kuno as the city is crumbling about him, and the line could as well be from any of a number of later science-fiction parables about misdirected societies. Even absolute destruction can be avoided: at the end of Blish's "cities-in-flight" novel, *The Triumph of Time* (1958), the whole universe goes up in a puff, but somehow part of galactic civilization has learned to ride the gap into the new creation; in Murray Leinster's "The End" (1946) and Poul Anderson's *Tau Zero* (1970), the end of the universe is survived by members of a spaceship crew undergoing an extreme relativistic time-compression. Even before Forster's machine stops, he shows us a way out through the ancient ventilation shafts; against all odds, the barrier may be breached.

With Wells, Forster, and Lang's and Von Harbou's *Metropolis,* we begin to get some notion of how the city can be used in science fiction, and why the genre has placed a primarily negative value on this image. But we have only touched the surface of the many ways in which the image is used in later science fiction; as Brian Aldiss says, "Science fiction is a literature of cities,"[35] and whatever attitude science-fiction writers may hold toward urban life, they cannot avoid discussing it. To begin to list all the science-fiction works that deal in some way with cities would probably be to list more than half of the science-fiction works written in this century; to draw too many general conclusions about this, or other topics in science fiction, would be to draw deserved rebuttals. I am sure there are happy cities in science fiction, just as I am sure there are phallic spaceships, but the overwhelming impression one has from reading science fiction is that the city cannot be an end in itself. In terms of the dialectic of known-unknown, of the expansion of knowledge and the principle of plenitude, the city is more apt to be a starting point than an end; hence in many works in which the city is a central image, the structure of the narrative is controlled by a movement outward, away from the weakening center. We can find this general structure in a number of exemplary works which, while perhaps not the major creations of their authors or masterworks of the genre, nevertheless demonstrate a variety of characteristic ways in which the image of the city is used. The kinds of cities I will examine I have called the imperial city, the technological city, the arcology, and the city in space; the respective works are by Delany, Clarke, Silverberg, and Blish.

THE IMPERIAL CITY: DELANY'S *Fall of the Towers*

Galactic empires, decadent post-holocaust societies, future dictatorships, and alien civilizations often have one element in common: they are centered around a closely guarded imperial city that symbolizes the values and attitudes of the society as a whole. We can see this in works as varied as the *Foundation* trilogy of Asimov, the Instrumentality stories of Cordwainer Smith, the *Dune* novels of Frank Herbert, the Hainish stories of Ursula Le Guin, and many, if not most, works of antiutopian fiction. The model for such cities may well be Rome (it clearly is in Asimov's case), and the social structure is apt to be based on a hierarchy of clearly defined ranks, whether military, oligarchic, royal, or economic. The rigorously worked out geographic and social patterns necessary to maintain internal consistency in novels and stories dealing with such cities seem to invite authors to make such complex imaginary worlds the basis for more than one work; this perhaps is why so many of the works in the list above are multipart narratives or linked stories. Many of these works develop complex themes around their city-empires, but most also partake of an almost formulaic pattern in which the imperial city is revealed to be antithetical to the true values of the novel. One work that demonstrates this with almost archetypal clarity — perhaps because it was written by a young author early in his career, drawing heavily on the traditions of earlier science fiction — is Samuel R. Delany's *Fall of the Towers* (1970).

Delany's own statements indicate clearly that *The Fall of the Towers* was conceived as a single three-volume work rather than as three independent but interconnected novels. In the Afterword to the 1970 Ace edition he refers to the work as a three-volume novel and mentions that the last chapter of the third volume was in fact planned on the same evening when the first chapter of the first volume was written.[36] However, in the introductory Author's Note to that same edition, he recalls that "each of the *Towers'* three books went into production practically as it was finished" (p. 2), giving him virtually no time to rethink the book as a whole; the second volume had to be written more or less in conformity with what was already in type in the first; and the third volume had to conform with the first two. Not until the 1966 British edition was Delany given the chance to revise the book as a whole, and it is substantially this revision that was published by Ace in 1970 as *The Fall of the Towers*.

Briefly, the novel concerns the intrusion into earthly affairs of the Lord of the Flames, an amoral, disembodied intelligence who manipulates whole cultures as controlled-research experiments. The Lord of the Flames is considering waging war on our universe, and to conduct what amounts to a feasibility study for this project, it chooses the Earth empire of Toromon. Toromon is a future civilization that dominates the earth 500 years after a nuclear holocaust. It is dominated by the island city of Toron, isolated from the rest of the world by a "radiation barrier" on the mainland and "hot currents" in the seas. Another city, Telphar, had been built on the mainland, but an increase in the area of the radiation barrier has made it uninhabitable. Toron is a rigidly class-structured society that draws its sustenance from huge aquariums and its energy from a mineral called Tetron, which is mined by prison labor on the mainland. There are two other earth societies in addition to Toromon: the evolutionary throwbacks known as Neanderthals, and the evolutionary mutations known as the forest people. Both are results of genetic changes brought about by radiation.

Two barrier images dominate *The Fall of the Towers*: the radiation barriers that isolate Toron, and the city's internal class barriers. As we will see in Chapter Five, the radiation barrier is a familiar image in "post-holocaust" tales and a common rendering of the structural barrier that separates known from unknown. In the beginning of *The Fall of the Towers*, the radiation barrier quite literally separates Toron from the unknown world outside. Since this unknown world is a natural source of fear, it becomes easy for war planners in Toron to generate sentiment against "an enemy beyond the barrier"; and the slogan "We have an enemy beyond the barrier," which could almost be a slogan for science fiction's general attitude toward the unknown, becomes a central motif of the second volume of the trilogy, and an example of the kind of paranoia it is possible to create in a circumscribed urban environment.

The war in which this slogan serves as propaganda is also an example of an imperialist means of dealing with the unknown. What lies beyond the barrier (the unknown) is somewhat controlled and made conceivable by identifying it as "the enemy." A Freudian reading might say that what is beyond the barrier, beyond the limits of the imperial city, is the unconscious. Such a reading is in fact what Delany invites when he reveals the true nature of the enemy—that in fact the enemy is purely a psychological construct, and the "war" a fiction imposed upon the populace for internal political and economic ends. Another barrier also functions here: a barrier of mind that prevents any of the citizens from remembering too many details about the "war." In Pogo's terms, "We have met the enemy and they is us." A political reading is also invited, of course, with the "enemy" as an image, say, of America's obsession with communism in the 1950s. The final question to be answered is what evil influence in the city might convince its leaders to carry out such a drastic hoax, actually killing citizens, to solve economic problems. The answer turns out to be the Lord of the Flames, a demonic figure who accelerates evil trends already present in a society. Delany thus implies that many of the "evils" of Toron arise from the rigid stratification and isolation of the urban environment.

Toron's class structure is revealed by the three concentric circles in which the city is organized: the Devil's Pot, inhabited by immigrants, rebels, and workers; the hives, inhabited by professionals and middle-class merchants; and the towers, inhabited by royalty. The towers are surrounded by battlements to keep the lower classes out, just as Toron itself is surrounded by radiation belts and hot currents to keep out potential invaders. As characters interact in Toron, we are frequently reminded that these barriers act as barriers to knowledge and understanding, and that one's image of what a city is depends upon one's own experience of that city (this latter point is reinforced in a different context in the third volume of the trilogy, in the image of an alien "city" that appears different to each of the life forms that visit it). Few characters ever become familiar with all the aspects of Toron, and the resulting sense of isolation and ignorance is part of what enables the city leaders to maintain firm control.

But there are other cities in *The Fall of the Towers* as well: Telphar, the abandoned mainland city built by Toromon; the alien "city" where a benign three-minded being, the enemy of the Lord of the Flames, conducts a sort of convention of intelligent life-forms; and the City of a Thousand Suns, a utopian scheme undertaken by malcontents or "malis" from Toromon. Telphar and the City of a Thousand Suns in particular offer alternative versions of the icon of the city, the former as a version of the wasteland image which I will discuss in the next chapter, the latter as a somewhat hazy image of the city as communal utopia, or the city of freedom as opposed to the imperial city.

Telphar had been designed originally as a kind of imperialist outpost, an extension of Toron, and to improve communication and travel between the two cities, a "transit-ribbon" has been built to permit transit between the two cities without effectively encountering any of the barriers between them. As a dead city, it provides a neat image of the decadent civilization of Toromon; as a city on the mainland, it stands between the closed society of the island and the central actions of the book: it is where the protagonists plot to fight the Lord of the Flames, and it is eventually the military outpost of Toromon's war. It is the "dead city" of the title of the first volume in the trilogy, just as Toron is the title city of the second volume. Symbolically linked to Toron and yet situated in the midst of the radiation barrier that provides the novel's initial image of the unknown, Telphar becomes an image of the struggle to gain knowledge and the cost of the struggle.

The title city of the third volume, *City of a Thousand Suns,* is a kind of communal utopia being built by malcontents who realize that human civilization has great potential that is being held back by the rigid socioeconomic structure of Toron. When Toron is finally destroyed by its own war computer gone berserk, it is to this city that the protagonists return. It is as much an image of the new order as Toron is of the old. As the action of the novel progresses, it shifts from being merely a counterculture to Toron to being the only remaining hope of the human race, and the "thousand suns" of its name refer to the stars that mankind will someday reach by following the principle of exploring the unknown, rather than suppressing it as Toron has done. If this sounds like a moralistic reading of the novel, it is. Toron once followed the noble principle of seeking knowledge by building Telphar in the first place, but as the society became more venal and corrupt, it virtually invited the interference of the Lord of the Flames (whose name even suggests the devil), and the promise of Telphar was lost forever when, resurrected, the city became a military outpost. The only hope of sustaining the values of seeking knowledge is thus shifted to the City of a Thousand Suns, and it is there that the action of the novel ends. From Forster's and Wells's vision of an oppressive city of empire, exemplified by Toron itself, Delany moves to a more positive vision, but ironically this movement leads to a city not unlike the city-of-god archetype discussed earlier. In terms of the dialectic of technology, then, this city is a step backward, toward a more decentralized community of many cultures.

THE TECHNOLOGICAL CITY: CLARKE'S *The City and the Stars*

The most direct descendants of Forster's "The Machine Stops" in science fiction are those works that deal with automated cities of the future, in which the citizens have little to do but engage in games and intellectual (or pseudointellectual) pursuits while the self-perpetuating mechanisms designed in a more aggressive age nourish and protect them. Such cities bear many similarities to the imperial cities such as those in Delany's trilogy (and in the case of Clarke's *The City and the Stars* we will see structural similarities that suggest an influence on the later work of Delany: the dual city, the city as bastion, the city as technological dead-end, and the liberation from the city as a reassertion of proper human destiny), but they also move us a step closer to the city as spaceship. They are at once tombs of a dying technological culture and potential wombs that preserve the race for its eventual rebirth into the universe. This relationship of cities and spaceships has been so evident to science-fiction writers that it eventually led to a confluence of the two images in works such as Blish's *Cities in Flight,* but it is equally apparent in many earthbound science-fiction cities. Edmund Cooper's *The Overman Culture* (1972) is little more than a reworking of his earlier *Seed of Light* (1959), with characters taking the names of famous figures from history in order to establish standards for themselves and to keep alive the memory of a civilization destroyed in an atomic war. Only in *The Overman Culture,* the setting is not an interstellar spaceship, but an artificial London of the distant future, constructed and maintained by a

109

massive computer complex as an experimental "culture" (in both the biological and social senses of the term) for the rebirth of humanity. Like the spaceship, the technological city is a perpetual incubator, but like the spaceship, its walls are barriers that man must cross in order to discover its true meaning.

Arthur C. Clarke's *The City and the Stars,* though in many ways flawed, clearly demonstrates the iconic value of the technological city and the structural importance of this icon in many works of science fiction. The novel is almost carried forward schematically by the transformations of sets of oppositions into higher oppositions, much in the manner that Claude Lévi-Strauss describes the transformations that myth works upon the antinomies of culture.[37] As a result, the novel gives us the opportunity not only to explore the city as icon, but also to examine a number of other such icons as, one by one, they supplant the image of the city in the narrative. Spaceships, robots, alien creatures, computers—each at some point in *The City and the Stars* stands at the border of the known and the unknown and in each case the crossing of that border carries the narrative action forward.

The basic narrative is rather simple. Alvin, a young man just coming of age, finds that he is the only citizen of the ancient walled city of Diaspar who seems to have any curiosity about what lies on the outside. His tutor, Jeserac, can provide him with some information, but it is not until he meets Khedron, or the Jester, that he begins to find means to really answer his questions.[38] With the aid of Khedron, Alvin finds his way out of the mechanized city and visits the more pastoral society of Lys, the only other remaining human community on Earth—and which, like Diaspar, has kept an enforced isolation. Here he meets Hilvar, with whose aid he visits a nearby legendary fortress, Shalmirane, according to tradition the site of the last great battle defending Earth from mysterious invaders who had driven mankind from the stars. In Shalmirane, a giant alien polyp is found, the last disciple of an ancient messiah known as the Master.[39] Alvin persuades the polyp to allow one of its three service robots to return with him to Diaspar, where Alvin interrogates the robot with the aid of Diaspar's massive central computer. What Alvin learns from the robot allows him to raise an ancient spaceship from beneath the desert floor where it has lain for centuries. Returning with the ship to Lys, he picks up Hilvar and they journey to an artificial star system known as the Seven Suns, once the hub of an immense galactic civilization but now deserted. There they attract the attention of a vast, incorporeal intelligence known as Vanamonde, who enables them to reconstruct the true history of Earth.

There had, in fact, been no invaders. Earth had not been able to achieve interstellar travel at the time it came in contact with superior civilizations, and more or less shamed by its own lack of development, human society began to concentrate on engineering human evolution, with the goal of joining the galactic community. Humanity eventually became part of this galactic civilization, but the evolutionary goal of creating a bodiless intelligence remained. When such a mind was created, it was either insane or hostile to matter, and it wreaked havoc on the universe until it was imprisoned in an artificial sun. Other, more benign intelligences were later created, of which Vanamonde was one. Finally, the galaxy—in fact, the entire known universe—was abandoned when the galactic civilization decided to join an even more advanced and more massive civilization in another universe. Left behind were only the most provincial elements of the galactic civilization, and Diaspar and Lys were the surviving societies of those who remained behind on Earth. Now, because of Alvin's discoveries, they would try to re-establish contact with the civilization that had left them behind millions of years earlier.

From the point of view of our known-unknown oppositions, it is easy to see that Clarke's narrative moves in ever-widening circles. Initially, the city functions as it does in much science fiction: it is the total human community, isolated from the mysterious outside by a barrier of towers and by generations of psychological conditioning. This is the first major opposition in the book, and it is much like the opposition at work in the imagery of spaceships: the interior is the known, the exterior the unknown. All of the traditional oppositions that once characterized life on Earth have been resolved into this single great opposition of inside-outside. There is no longer day or night, heat or cold, calm or wind—not even life or death, since all of the city's inhabitants are periodically "reborn" into a new life. All oppositions are kept in stasis by the central computer, and the only opposition over which this computer does not have absolute control is that of inside-outside. Hence this is the only barrier between the known and the unknown in this part of the narrative, and it is the one that must be breached if the story is to move forward.

The first part of the narrative, then, consists of events leading up to the breaking of this barrier and the transformation of this first opposition into a higher one. Very early in the narrative, oppositions are set up which are analogs of this basic opposition. The novel opens with an image of the opposition between illusion and reality; Alvin and his friends are enjoying a "total experience" kind of "saga" that has them undergoing elaborate adventures that are frankly pulpish—perhaps an indication of the artistic decadence of Diaspar and very probably an allusion by Clarke to an earlier era of science fiction. Alvin's inquisitiveness threatens the integrity of the illusion, however: ". . .it seemed as if the structure of reality trembled for an instant, and that behind the world of the senses he caught a glimpse of another and totally different universe. . . ."[40] This "other universe" is of course the reality of Diaspar, glimpsed through the veil of sensory illusion set up by the saga. The structure of the saga is an analog of the structure of Diasparan life itself: Alvin and his friends are pretending to be part of a subterranean culture whose entire universe is the interior of a planet. As in the real Diaspar, the outside is taboo, and when Alvin suggests they explore the outside, his violation of the taboo destroys the illusion, abruptly bringing the saga to an end. Alvin's friends berate him for thus interrupting the saga (the third time he has done so), and Alvin realizes that "here was the barrier that sundered him from all the people of his world, and which might doom him to a life of frustration. He was always wanting to go outside, both in reality and in dream" (p. 11). Here, then, is another opposition, another barrier: Alvin is an "outsider" in terms of the psychological norms of his people. There is a social inside-outside opposition within Diasparan society, and it is apparent that Alvin has already breached this social barrier.

We learn that Alvin is on the verge of crossing yet another cultural barrier. He has reached the age of twenty, and his guardianship is coming to an end. He is now outside the family unit, an independent agent. Alvin's father further tells him that he is unique, the first child born on earth in more than 10 million years. (All other Diasparans are resurrections, with edited memories, of citizens who had lived before.) Thus, even physiologically, Alvin finds himself on the outside of his society.

The editing of personal memories before a Diasparan is reconstituted, and the general suppression of human history before Diaspar, creates yet another barrier, this one in time rather than in space, separating the limited history of Diaspar from the vastly larger history that preceded it. Alvin can learn all he wants of the history of Diaspar with the guidance of his tutor Jeserac, but Jeserac, too, has an opposite in the figure of the Jester Khedron, whose function is to "introduce calculated amounts of disorder into the city" (p. 35). Khedron becomes Alvin's alternate teacher, the apostle of the unknown as Jeserac is the apostle of the known. It is with Khedron's aid that Alvin discovers the true nature of the stasis of Diaspar, a stasis maintained by the central computer, which allows only limited change within preset patterns. In a sense, then, Diaspar has been outside of time for millions of years; all history has been a restructuring and rearranging of these patterns. The real meaning of Jeserac's earlier discouraging warning becomes clear: in Alvin's quest to leave Diaspar, "'the physical barriers are the least important ones'" (p. 24).

By now, the pattern that controls the first third of the novel is clear. The central opposition to be resolved, or transformed, is that between the interior and exterior of Diaspar. But in order to achieve this transformation by leaving Diaspar, Alvin must first resolve lesser oppositions contained within this larger one. He must overcome the psychological agoraphobia of his people, the cultural narrowness of his family and his education, the historical block imposed by his society, and the logical and mechanistic block imposed by the central computer. When all this is achieved, Alvin can complete the crossing of the first great barrier by leaving Diaspar. Once Alvin has metaphorically broken out of his society by transgressing its taboos, he is ready to physically break out. His first encounter outside is with the pastoral society of Lys.

In the second part of the narrative, the opposition of the interior and exterior of Diaspar is transformed into the opposition between Diaspar and Lys. Clarke points up a number of oppositions between the two societies: Diaspar is urban and mechanized; Lys is pastoral and more dependent on highly developed human powers such as telepathy. The citizens of Diaspar choose a kind of controlled immortality programmed by the central computer; the Lysians choose to grow old and die. Diasparan art is utilitarian, serving the psychological need to escape and to provide variety; the art of Lys is expressive and creative. Even the names are suggestive: Diaspar of the Babylonian exile, with its associations of defeat and decline and its hint of the dispersion that has happened to the rest of humanity; Lys of the more optimistic Elysius. (One might even carry this a step further and suggest the two cities represent Hebraic and Hellenistic culture.) But what they have in common is more important: a forced provincialism and xenophobia and a general lack of interest in the unknown. Clarke's explanation of the stasis of Lys is less satisfactory than his account of Diaspar, since the Lysians know of Diaspar and do not have to contend with the problem of immortality. In fact, the entire opposition between the two cultures is in some sense a false one, and although it seems to occupy a central place in the narrative, it really does little more than lead us from the inside-outside opposition of Diaspar to the larger but parallel opposition of Earth-galaxy.

113

This direction becomes manifest in the third major opposition in *The City and the Stars*. This opposition, the provincialism of the Earth societies versus the expansiveness of the galaxy, is introduced in the Shalmirane episode, and the image that introduces it is yet another science-fiction icon: the creature, in this case a massive polyp with its servant robots. In the first part of the novel, Alvin had to overcome barriers relating to information about Diaspar and the "outside"; here he must overcome barriers relating to the Earth and the galaxy. He does this, with the aid of Diaspar's central computer, by imposing a logical paradox on the blocked memory of one of the service robots from Shalmirane. With the information thus gained, and with the discovery and raising of the interstellar spaceship as a result of that information, Alvin finally assumes the role of representative of the unknown. He now possesses information that makes him an outsider to both Diaspar and Lys, and the opposition between the cultures of earth and the culture of the universe (and earth's own past) is the next he must overcome.

The spaceship then becomes the next icon of the unknown. Alvin guides it to the largest planet of the central sun of the Seven Suns and finds there an obelisk that may well be the forerunner of the obelisks in *2001*, which in that film are deliberately treated as icons of the unknown. Also on this planet he encounters a mysterious barrier of immense proportions, some sort of corral whose inhabitant had long ago escaped. The barrier isn't fully explained, but it does serve to reinforce the barrier imagery that is central to the novel. It is perhaps significant that the discovery of this most massive of all physical barriers is followed immediately by the appearance of Vanamonde, who represents the final breaking down of the barrier of physical being, the resolution of the basic opposition of mind and matter.

Vanamonde's story, which is presented only in synoptic form at the end of the novel, reveals that the final opposition of the narrative exists on an even broader scale than that of earth-galaxy. The discovery that the galactic civilization had abandoned this universe for another sets up the final barrier for Alvin to try to cross. To this end, Alvin sends the spaceship off to find the galactic civilization and reestablish contact, rather like the proverbial note in a bottle cast into the sea. Then he turns his attention to rebuilding the society of earth in terms of the new values he has discovered—the values inherent in seeking the unknown, or, put more simply, the values of scientific progress.

In the most simple terms, the novel is a study in two contrasting attitudes toward the opposition of known-unknown, two attitudes which have come in conflict in our own cultural history. Diaspar and

Lys represent the belief that this opposition should remain in stasis; Alvin represents the attitude more common to modern culture and obviously shared by Clarke (and most science-fiction writers) that the opposition should be in a continuous state of dialectic of scientific progress. The movement of the narrative as I have just discussed it, with its widening circles of inquiry, represents one set of transformations that demonstrates Clarke's belief in the virtue of this dialectic. Another set of transformations is revealed by examining the novel not in terms of its plot, but in terms of the chronology of earth history that is gradually revealed. This history begins with earth in opposition to the rest of the galaxy: humanity has achieved space travel only to discover that far superior intelligences control the galaxy, leaving humanity on the outside. This spatial opposition is transformed into a temporal one when humanity decides to concentrate on engineering its evolution in order eventually to gain entry into the community of advanced civilizations. Once this evolutionary barrier is overcome, the attempt of the galactic civilizations, including earth, to overcome the problem of physical intelligence leads to the opposition of matter and mind. This barrier in turn is overcome by the creation of incorporeal intelligences such as Vanamonde, seemingly the ultimate in scientific and evolutionary programs. But still two more oppositions come of this, and each of them effectively goes beyond the limits of rational extrapolation into areas of mysticism and morality. The first of these is the opposition of Vanamonde and his insane prototype, the Mad Mind. This is left unresolved at the end of the novel, although we are told that the day of confrontation will come (Judgment Day, in effect). With the Mad Mind and Vanamonde, Clarke has reached an opposition that cannot be resolved through extrapolation: the opposition of good and evil, a subject that Clarke generally avoids, but which brings the narrative to an acceptable conclusion by leaving us with a traditionally accepted antinomy. The other opposition that Clarke leaves us with is equally mystical but somewhat less satisfactory: the opposition of the galactic civilization, representing ultimate scientific progress, with that mysterious "other" that is so attractive over in the next universe. To speculate on what this "other" might be would be to get into almost theological questions, which Clarke also avoids, but since this opposition is less clearly defined and less traditionally acceptable than that between Vanamonde and the Mad Mind, it is also less satisfactory. We could perhaps regard this is a culturally acceptable antinomy by viewing it as a variant of the myth of the Golden Age, but Clarke does not specifically invite such an interpretation.

By choosing to structure his narrative in a series of ever-widening circles, Clarke inevitably ends up with this kind of mystical situation that cannot be resolved by rational extrapolation. Clarke himself seems to realize this in his well-known statement that sufficiently advanced technology is indistinguishable from magic; purely rational extrapolation, in other words, has its limits. Much of *The City and the Stars* thus consists of the gradual revelations of the exposition that underlies the narrative. The city to which we are introduced at the outset is the ultimate technological environment; imaginatively, Clarke has nowhere to go with this image in terms of fictional development and thus must destroy it. Again, the city becomes a dead-end—a more sophisticated and subtle version of Forster's underground trap—and the narrative demands that we move beyond it.

ARCOLOGY: ROBERT SILVERBERG'S *The World Inside*

Clarke's mechanized city is internally self-sufficient and exhibits many of the characteristics of the single-structure city that Paolo Soleri has termed "arcology" (from "architecture" and "ecology"). But the true arcology, the completely self-contained vertical structure designed to contain immense populations, is yet a step closer to the isolation imposed by the image of the spaceship. Soleri's arcologies, city buildings of a cubic kilometer, are intended to return vast amounts of land for farming and land conservation, enabling the inhabitants to have immediate access to the country while living in the most complex of urban environments. "Man must refute underground living," Soleri writes. "He is a biological animal of sun, air, light, and seasons." [41] But Soleri's own projections soon begin to bear resemblances to some of the science-fiction cities we have already seen: the arcology is not supposed to seal out the external world, but the climate will not quite be real; instead it will be "a tamed facsimile of the regional climate" (p. 591). The life of citizens inside an arcology "will be miniaturized by necessity," and people will have to become accustomed to "living inside instead of on top" (p. 594). And the lower, underground levels of the arcology are "ideal for automated production in need of technologically sophisticated environment" (p. 593). Already we see something of the divisions that were apparent in Wells, Forster, and Clarke, but Soleri is not a science-fiction writer. A former student of Frank Lloyd Wright, he has earnestly worked toward making his expensive dream-cities a reality.

Arcologies are not new to science fiction, of course. Frank R. Paul, the ubiquitous illustrator of the pulp era, pictured an enclosed cubic city with dimensions of two miles on each side to illustrate a story for the

September 1929 issue of *Science Wonder Stories,* and his windowless Italianate design suggests more a mausoleum than a future New York; it is in stark contrast to his bustling city of the future discussed earlier. Another popular artist of the pulp era, Julian Krupa, in a back-cover illustration for *Amazing Stories* in 1939, depicted a vertical city not unlike Paul's more optimistic forecast, but the caption for the illustration (not geared to accompany any particular story), reads in part, "Each building will be virtually a city in itself, completely self-sustaining, receiving its supplies from great merchandise ways far below the ground. Dwellers and workers in these buildings may go weeks without setting foot on the ground, or the ground-level."[42] Such cities abound in the literature as well, but none is so direct a response to the Solerian concept of the arcology as the collection of stories that Robert Silverberg published in 1970 and 1971 and later loosely wove together under the title *The World Inside* (1972).

The World Inside is a collection of seven narratives loosely connected by overlapping characters (the most important of whom is Siegmund Kluver, an ambitious fourteen-year-old who gradually becomes disillusioned with urban life) and the common setting of "Urbmon 116," one of fifty arcologies, three kilometers high, which go to make up the "Chipitts" complex, an urban strip stretching from the site of what was once Chicago to the site of Pittsburgh. "Urbmon" is short for "urban monad," Silverberg's term for Soleri's arcology, and each urban monad boasts (literally) a population of more than 800,000. The global population has reached 75 billion and is growing rapidly, since the backlash against centuries of worrying about overpopulation has resulted in a "cultural imperative" that demands large families and indiscriminate sex.[43] Each urban monad is divided into "cities," and each city into "villages" according to floors. The lower floors of the thousand-story building are given over to "grubbos," "slumped and sullen human handlers" (p. 171) concerned with the maintenance or manufacture of machinery for trading with the farming communes that make up most of the outside world; the upper floors are reserved for the professional and managerial classes.

Already we can see echoes of Wells and Lang in the rigidly defined class system and the apparent decadence of the urbmon dwellers. Like the Eloi of *The Time Machine,* they undergo early puberty to encourage a rapidly reproducing, youthful population, and the vertical class division is reminiscent of "A Story of the Days to Come," or *When the Sleeper Wakes.* Also like the latter narratives, cultural divergence is already apparent, and "each city within the urbmon develops its

117

characteristic slang, its way of dressing, its folklore, and heroes" (p. 18). There is even some indication, under investigation by a historian in Silverberg's novel, that the new way of life is beginning to produce an evolutionary trend not unlike that which produced Wells's Eloi: "'Is there now a *Homo urbmonensis,* placid, adjusted, fully content?'" (p. 71). If so, such a creature would be widely at variance with the descendents of the members of the farming communes, who live outside the city and already begin to look physically different from the city dwellers (growing facial hair, for example, as opposed to the clean-shaven appearance of the urbmonites), as well as developing a culture virtually antithetical to theirs.

There are occasional misfits, of course, but they are called "Flippos" and rapidly disposed of down the chutes (another image from *The Time Machine*) to provide raw materials for the recycling machines that keep the city ecology in balance. One of these misfits, a computer programmer named Michael Statler, is a descendent of the liberating heroes of the Clarke and Delany novels, but perhaps even more directly a descendant of the Kuno in Forster's "The Machine Stops." Like these earlier figures, Michael seeks a way to the outside and achieves it; but, like Kuno, he makes the mistake of returning. Unlike them, however, his motivations are not to start a new world or discover the secrets of the city; his motivations are little more than a vague longing and a growing claustrophobia. "'There are days when I feel the walls on me like a bunch of hands. Pressing in,'" he says. "'I want to leave the building. Just roam around outside'" (p. 116). Since he works with the central computer, "He knows how to make the great machine serve his needs" (p. 117), and programs it to issue an egress pass in his name (indicating that such passes are controlled, although there seems to be little desire for them among citizens of the urbmon). He arrives on the first floor to find, not a grand entryway, but "just a tiny hatch" (p. 120)—reminiscent of the hatch of a spaceship, perhaps. Also like the hatch of a spaceship, this one has an airlock, "preventing contamination by outside air, he supposes" (p. 121). The analogies with the spaceship continue as Michael steps out onto the soil, feeling "somewhat like the first man to walk on the moon" (p. 121). He has, according to the conventions of the genre, breached the barrier into the unknown world, and accordingly a sense of spiritual regeneration sets in with a series of Biblical metaphors: "Glancing back then. A pillar of salt" (p. 121). Like Lot's wife, Michael is overwhelmed by the spectacle of the city behind him: "Its bulk threatens to crush him" (p. 121). (Perhaps, too, the analogy with Sodom is an oblique reference to the open sexual customs of the urbmon.) The city seems to him "dead," and he moves deliberately away from it, into a garden where he finds a pool and bathes.

> After a while he comes out of the water and stands dripping and naked by the edge of the pool, shivering a little, listening to the birds, watching the red disk of the sun climbing out of the east. Gradually he becomes aware that he is crying. The beauty of it. The solitude. He is alone at time's first dawn. To be naked is right; I am Adam. He touches his genitals. Looking off afar, he sees three urbmons glowing with pearly light, and wonders which is 116. Stacion in [sic] there, and Micaela. If only she was with me now. Both of us naked by this pool. And turning to her, and sinking myself into her. While the snake watches from the tree. [P. 122]

By breaching the barrier, Michael sees himself as the new Adam, reasserting mankind's right over the natural world and its place in it and symbolically claiming this new land by masturbating, "Fertilizing the naked earth" (p. 123).

But Michael's edenic fantasy is quickly put in perspective when he is captured by farmers from a local commune and witnesses their fertility ritual. The radical contrast between his society and theirs is painful for him to think of, and they suspect him of being a spy, since "'Urbmon people don't slip out of their buildings. . . . You'd be paralyzed with terror five minutes after you set out'" (p. 135). At first Michael protests that he is really dissatisfied with the urbmon way of life, but in the end his conditioning gets the better of him and "he makes the building seem a poem of human relationships, a miracle of civilized harmonies" (p. 142). His need for sex, magnified by life in a society of open sexual relations, causes him to attempt to rape one of the commune women. The farmers decide to offer him as a human sacrifice to the "harvest god," who turns out to be a giant mechanical reaper, a product of one of the urbmons, suggesting the intimate dependency relationship of city and country in this world. "To die for metaphorical reasons, to become a mystic link binding commune to urbmon—such a fate seems improbable and unreal to him" (p. 146). His Adamic destiny thwarted, Michael's only hope is to return to the urbmon, and in this escape he is aided by the woman he attempted to rape. He returns to the urbmon, content in the knowledge that at least he has had a unique adventure, but is captured by the police at the door and, in an image that adds a special irony to his dreams of freedom, sprayed with a rapidly congealing substance that hardens to form a "security cocoon" (p. 152). But this cocoon works in reverse: rather than a prelude to freedom, it is a convenient means of delivering him to the recycling machines guilty of "'undesirable harboring of countersocial tendencies'" (p. 152). Unlike the rebel heroes of most science fiction, such as Alvin in *The City and the Stars* or Jon Koshar in *The Fall of the Towers,* Michael fails. The powerful Great Mother of the city swallows him up again.

Even the image of the stars, which provides such an epiphanic moment in so many works of science fiction that seek to liberate mankind from metaphorical confinement, is not sufficient to free the urbmon dwellers. When Siegmund Kluver, the young executive who has been the most consistently recurring figure in the book, finally decides his life in the urbmon has become meaningless, he consults a "blessman," or priest, who explains, "Sometimes, those of us who live in the urban monads experience what is called the crisis of spiritual confinement. The boundaries of our world, that is to say our building, seem too narrow. Our inner resources become inadequate" (p. 166). Promising to show Siegmund god, the blessman produces an image that is familiar from the closed society spaceship narratives from the last chapter: "Stars strewn like sand. A billion points of light" (p. 167) that are the stars in the sky over the urbmon. "The blessman directs Siegmund's attention to this group of stars and to that, urging him to merge with the galaxy. The urbmon is not the universe, he murmurs. Beyond these shining walls lies an awesome vastness that is god. Let him take you into himself and heal you. Yield. Yield. Yield" (p. 167). But Siegmund cannot be satisfied with an image of the stars projected from the top of the urbmon, and the symbolic leap into space that for many science-fiction writers would be the alternative to this dead-end urban existence becomes for him a literal, suicidal leap from the roof of the complex.

Silverberg, then, does not appear to leave open the escape valve for man that other authors have seen in space travel, and the ending of *The World Inside* resembles the ending of "The Machine Stops" in the implied hope that the rural communes, with their atavistic rituals, can provide a better alternative. But there is another alternative: in the first story in *The World Inside,* a resident of Urbmon 116 entertains a visitor from Hell, "one of the eleven cities of Venus, which man has reshaped to suit himself" (p. 11). This visitor, Nicanor Gortman, seems quietly taken aback at the culture of the urban monads, and he himself is apparently part of a frontier culture of small settlements involved in agriculture and hunting. Perhaps, after all, there is an alternative to the city in space, and the eminent domain of man in the universe need not be entirely sacrificed to the life of the hive.

120

THE SPACE CITY: JAMES BLISH'S *A Life for the Stars*

We have already seen how the arcology of Silverberg's *The World Inside* resembles the spaceship; thus it is only logical for science fiction to take the next step of cutting the city completely off from the surrounding countryside, somehow detaching it from the earth, and making it into a full-fledged spacecraft. As Brian Aldiss writes, "Two of sf's perennial playthings, the city and the spaceship, were combined in the concept of the space-going city,"[44] and he illustrated this with examples from science-fiction art of the 1930s, 1950s, and 1960s. Visually, at least, the temptation to combine the iconography of the future city with the iconography of outer space is understandable, and if the illustrations themselves are rather disappointing (Kenn Fagg's 1954 *If* cover, "A Space Nation Composed of Independent City Planets," looks rather like a collection of toy snowstorm paperweights), it is only perhaps because the science-fiction writers, on whom illustrators are so often dependent, have found it difficult to conceive of a convenient means of lifting whole cities into space—or for that matter, a logical reason to do so. But the idea has been a persistent one, dating back at least to Jonathan Swift's Laputa and finding periodic expression in the pulp era in stories such as Eando Binder's "Queen of the Skies" (1937) and Edmond Hamilton's "Cities in the Air" (1929). Richard Matheson intuited the resemblances between urban living and space travel in "Shipshape Home" (1952), which depicted an entire city block blasting off into space under the direction of alien kidnapers. And the image perhaps reached its apotheosis in film in 1977 with Steven Spielberg's *Close Encounters of the Third Kind,* in which a massive alien spacecraft is portrayed, according to special effects director Douglas Trumbull, as "a City of Light, something which would be. . .recognizable as a city concept, like the Manhattan sky line at night."[45] But certainly the most detailed and well known of the space cities in science fiction is James Blish's tetralogy *Cities in Flight* (1955-62; collected in one volume in 1970). Essentially an epic space opera that covers more than three thousand years of galactic history, culminating in a universal cataclysm when universes of matter and antimatter collide, the novels often seem to retain the image of the city merely as a convenient means of portraying a familiar type of social organization, and Blish does not, for the most part, concentrate on what life in the cities might be like.

A Life for the Stars (1962), however, the last of the four novels written (although the second in chronological order), does offer a more detailed glimpse of the flying cities than any of the other novels. Written primarily for an adolescent audience, *Life* describes the adventures of young Crispin DeFord, who is pressed into service on the city of Scranton just before it departs the earth "to become a migrant worker among the stars."[46] At once it is apparent that the conquest of space is less a glorious quest for human fulfillment than a simple means of survival; as Aldiss writes, "Blish's cities sought work rather than thrones among the stars."[47] Increased unemployment resulting from mechanization together with the depopulation of earth following the advent of the "spindizzy" (an antigravity device that can support anything within its magnetic field) has resulted in a permanent depression and, like the Okies of the 1930s depression, cities undertake a migrant life in order to find employment in a more promising environment (the cities are even called "Okies"). The American frontier, with its promise of a new life and new prosperity, has been transformed into the cosmic frontier of space; once again there is a dreamworld like California—but once again the dreams seem to rapidly sour. "More often than not, Chris had read, star roving was simply another form of starvation. . . . Pittsburgh had made its fortune on Mars, to be sure—but it was a poor sort of fortune that kept you sitting in a city all your life, with nothing to see beyond the city limits but an ochre desert, a desert with no air you could breathe, a desert that would freeze you solid only a few minutes after the tiny sun went down" (p. 13). The alienation of the city from its surrounding environment is only intensified by the move into space, the barrier of the city limits made more rigid by its conversion into the equivalent of a spaceship's hull. "The nomad cities seemed, like everything else, to be a dead end" (p. 13).

The importance of this barrier is made evident to Chris soon after he is aboard the city of Scranton. Before it even takes off, he notes at the perimeter "a line of boiling dust" where "the inert friable earth seemed to be turning over restlessly" (p. 21)—an image that vaguely calls to mind, though on a reduced scale, the dust storms of the Great Depression. The earth is "friable" and dead; just as the midwestern farms of an earlier generation had been cultivated to the point of aridity, so the iron ore of earth had been exhausted in "the Age of Waste" (p. 10) that preceded the universal depression of Blish's narrative. And now this dust becomes symbolic of what separates Chris from his past; "'Right where you stand,'" he is told by one of the press-gang members who has captured him, "'you're not even on Earth anymore'" (p. 21). Chris's perceptions begin quickly to alter, and when he sees the city begin to spin on its axis, "the illusion that it was the valley that was revolving around the city was irresistible" (p. 23). His point of view has shifted to the city-as-world, and for the rest of the entire tetralogy, it is this point of view rather than the planetary one that will predominate.

It soon becomes apparent that Scranton retains the class distinctions of earlier science-fiction cities we have seen. All tasks requiring an IQ of less than 150 are performed by machines, we are told (p. 24), making most skills unsalable. But despite this apparent universal mechaniza-tion, there is still room for drudge-labor in the slag heaps of the city; although the city has "sloughed off its slums to go space flying" (p. 35), a rigid hierarchy soon becomes apparent on the space city, with gangster-like managers and a few skilled professionals at the top and all the rest at the bottom. Chris passes for an astronomer until he is able to transfer to another space city, New York, but even in this more liberal culture, where he is offered a computerized education and suffers less oppression, a class distinction remains: "citizens" must display useful talents, interest in intellectual pursuits, and ability to pass rigorous exams; all the rest are merely "passengers" (p. 64). Immortality, or near immortality, which has been made possible by "anti-agathic" drugs, is offered only to citizens. Day-to-day decisions in the management of the city are handled by the computer "City Fathers," although the actual management of city affairs is under the direction of John Amalfi, a kind of superman figure who later emerges as the central character in the last two novels of the tetralogy.

Like many other science-fiction cities, then, Blish's star-roving New York exists primarily for the benefit of the upper classes. But Blish's own attitude toward this seemingly totalitarian technocracy is remarkably uncritical, as is the attitude of his Spenglerian fictional historian "Acreff-Monales," quotations from whose *The Milky Way: Five Cultural Portraits* are interspersed throughout the tetralogy. Space is seen not as a liberation from the confines of urban life, but as a consolidation of it into independent city-states reminiscent of ancient Greece. From this point on in the series, the quality of life aboard the Okies takes a back seat to narratives of wars and galactic conquest, as though the reification of the urban ideal and the appropriation of space were one. Planetary colonies do exist, as do alien civilizations, so there are alternatives to eternal life in a technological city, but they play a minor role in *Cities in Flight,* and the only real way of bringing the overall narrative to a close is the final cataclysm that destroys the universe. In the final novel of the tetralogy, *The Triumph of Time,* the Okie city of New York has finally settled on a planet called New Earth and has entered a period of decadence. Amalfi, the aging adventurer, is

123

dissatisfied with the direction that his own technology has taken him; "his thousand years of continuous translation from one culture to another had built up in him an enormous momentum which now seemed to be bearing him irresistibly toward an immovable inertial wall labeled, NO PLACE TO GO" (p. 476).[48] The conquest of the unknown is virtually complete, it would seem, and no barriers remain. The city itself has been abandoned and given over to the city fathers, the computers who had initially guided it through space. "These same city fathers later conclude that "WE ARE THE CITY," suggesting that the city survives in their programming even though it no longer has any citizens (p. 572). The city is finally revealed as merely a machine, a stage of civilization that will be superseded when man realizes his potential on other worlds, and as such it finally comes to have something in common with the other science-fiction cities we have seen. The function of the city is fulfilled, and the city is abandoned, as it was in Simak's *City*, as it probably will be in the end of Clarke's *The City and the Stars*. But this realization of the ultimate goals of urban technology is tantamount to the apocalypse, for, like Clarke, Blish has brought his narrative to a point at which extrapolation ends. Where Clarke offered a semimystical vision of a higher order of being, however, Blish simply destroys the universe: New York has literally brought mankind to the end of time, and there is indeed "no place to go."

5

icon of the wasteland

... I will break the pride of your power, and I will make your heavens like
iron and your earth like brass; and your strength shall be spent in vain, for
your land shall not yield its increase, and the trees of the land shall not
yield their fruit.

Leviticus 26: 19-20

THE TRANSFORMED LANDSCAPE

In the decade and a half following the Second World War, it has often
been noted, science fiction produced a great many works of an
apocalyptic nature—works that described a world devastated by some
massive natural force, in which the survivors struggled to revive and
rebuild some semblance of civilization. Sometimes such stories have
been termed "awful warning" or "nuclear holocaust" stories, and the
central theme seemed clear: if man continued to escalate the military use
of the atomic weapons that had been introduced at Hiroshima and later
at Bikini, he would surely destroy himself. The focus of science fiction
almost seemed to shift from its essentially optimistic vision of a
conquerable universe to a darker, nightmarish vision of demonic forces
being unleashed by an unwitting human race. Even Isaac Asimov, the
genre's prime defender of the manifest destiny of technology, offered a
moralistic, brief short story, "Hell-Fire" (1956), in which the first ultra-
slow-motion films of an atomic explosion revealed the face of a laughing
devil.

Some of the novels of this period were clearly designed as warnings:
we have already noted that Edmund Cooper's *Seed of Light* (1959), in
which nuclear holocaust sends a colony of survivors into deep space, is
bitterly dedicated to those "who advocate the retention of nuclear
weapons." Philip Wylie's *Tomorrow!* (1954) contains a dedication that
similarly reveals its didactic purpose: "to the gallant men and women of
the Federal Civil Defense Administration and to those other true

patriots, the volunteers, who are doing their best to save the sum of things."[1] As the dedication implies, the novel is largely a civil defense tract. (Wylie's later *Triumph* [1963] repeats the message but without the emphasis on civil defense.) Pat Frank's two novels of the fifties, *Forbidden Area* (1956) and *Alas, Babylon* (1959), are fairly clearly designed as warnings; the latter, according to its foreword, was written to give people a clearer conception of the kind of havoc nuclear weapons could wreak. Nevil Shute's *On the Beach* (1959), despite a strength of characterization unusual in such works, certainly had a "message," and this message was made even more explicit in Stanley Kramer's 1959 film, with its final shot of a desolated world overlooked by a religious banner which has taken on new meaning for the audience: "There is still time." Other films shared this didacticism: Arch Oboler's *Five* (1951), with its lengthy dialogs on the causes of war; Ranald MacDougall's *The World, the Flesh, and the Devil* (1959); Ray Milland's *Panic in Year Zero* (1962); Roger Corman's *The Day the World Ended* (1955); Peter Watkins's *The War Game* (1966), which in documentary style set out to demonstrate, like Frank's *Alas, Babylon,* the reality of such a nuclear war; and Stanley Kubrick's *Dr. Strangelove, or How I Learned to Stop Worrying and Love the Bomb* (1963), which effectively put an end to the cycle in America despite such later entries as *Fail-Safe* (1965). The catalog of films could go on and on, and in the end would probably be longer than the catalog of prose works on the subject.

It would appear, then, that the icon of the bomb should be the focus of this chapter: nuclear holocaust certainly was a favorite theme in the 1950s, and, as Brian Aldiss notes, one need only glance at the titles of stories published in magazines such as *Astounding* after World War II to get a notion of the "new pessimism" of the genre.[2] But when one begins to look more closely at the apocalyptic branch of science fiction, several elements begin to cloud this rather simple picture. First, most of the titles mentioned above are not by "mainstream" science-fiction authors; Frank, Shute, and to some extent Wylie are what the genre's advocates often term "mainstream" authors who intrude upon the genre for various reasons of their own. The concern over atomic war expressed in their works is a concern best expressed through narratives that necessitate a science-fiction mise-en-scène, but the novels themselves only coincidentally, if at all, share the more fundamental beliefs and structures of the genre they are "borrowing." This is perhaps one reason why science-fiction advocates often resent such intrusions: the mainstream authors, superior though their fiction often may be in terms of style and characterization, rehash familiar plots and fail to offer

126

science-fiction readers the subcultural reinforcement and "new twists" they have come to expect from their favorite authors—and worse, these "outsiders" often get rich doing it. Partly, of course, such a reaction is indicative of the long-standing xenophobia of the genre, but partly it emerges from a real concern that the myth has been turned against itself, that the forms of science fiction can be used in fictions that seem to challenge the fundamental beliefs of the genre. (Later, science-fiction writers themselves began to create such inversions, with the result a blurring of the line separating the genre from the "mainstream.")

Secondly, the period we are speaking of also produced a number of works, both from science-fiction and "mainstream" authors, that portrayed apocalypses that had nothing to do with atomic warfare. Most notable of these, perhaps, is George R. Stewart's *Earth Abides* (1949), in which a plague sweeps over the earth and reduces its inhabitants to only a few; such a novel could hardly be considered an "awful warning" against plagues, much less atomic weapons. Both John Christopher and J. G. Ballard produced series of novels dealing with different kinds of natural disasters reducing the earth to primitive conditions. The theme of colliding worlds, a long-standing theme that dates back at least to Poe, was made popular by Philip Wylie and Edwin Balmer in *When Worlds Collide* (1933) and reappeared in the film version of *When Worlds Collide* (1951) and in novels such as Max Ehrlich's *The Big Eye* (1949), Fritz Leiber's *The Wanderer* (1964), and Fred Hoyle's *The Black Cloud* (1957) (although in Hoyle it is a cloud of galactic gas rather than a planet that collides with earth). Such fiction of natural disaster was hardly new in the 1950s, of course; plagues had appeared in Jack London's "The Scarlet Plague" (1915), poison gases in Arthur Conan Doyle's *The Poison Belt* (1913) and M. P. Shiel's *The Purple Cloud* (1901). The deluge theme of Ballard's *The Drowned World* (1962) had been prefigured in works by S. Fowler Wright, Garrett P. Serviss, and even Leonardo da Vinci. But these themes seemed to enjoy a renaissance in the 1950s, along with the atomic holocaust novels, and this seems to suggest that atomic war was something of a new bottle for old wine, at least for science fiction.

Third, the science-fiction novels that did seem to deal with nuclear holocaust seldom really did, at least not in the sense of the political and social warnings that characterized similar works by "mainstream" authors. Nuclear disaster rapidly became incorporated into the catalog of science-fiction "devices" that are used as means to a theme rather than as the theme itself. Like robots and spaceships, the holocaust quickly became a convention—a means to an end—rather than a focus. Thus,

127

many of the major science-fiction works in which nuclear war played a part used it as a part of the exposition for a narrative that actually takes place centuries or generations afterward: Henry Kuttner's *Fury* (1950), Leigh Brackett's *The Long Tomorrow* (1955), John Wyndham's *Re-Birth* (1955), Daniel Galouye's *Dark Universe* (1961), Walter M. Miller's *A Canticle for Leibowitz* (1959), and others. The possibility of nuclear war is hardly an issue in these novels, which instead concentrate on the life of societies long after such a war. Even a novel such as Wilson Tucker's *The Long Loud Silence* (1952), which takes place immediately after a nuclear-biological war, does not concern itself with events leading up to the war or hope for preventing it so much as it relishes the devastated landscape that the war produces.

All this tends to suggest that the bomb itself is not as important an icon in the history of science fiction as has often been supposed. What, then, are we to make of this body of holocaust literature, of tales in which civilization is suddenly ended by some outside agent and must attempt to rebuild? And how, if at all, do such fictions reflect the known-unknown antinomy and the barrier imagery of other types of science fiction? The question is made even more intriguing by the obvious prevalence of barrier-imagery in such works as *The Long Loud Silence* and *Re-Birth*. In *The Long Loud Silence*, Tucker portrays an America cut in half at the Mississippi River. To the east is that portion of the country devastated by nuclear and biological weapons; to the west, what remains of civilized America. The army heavily guards the barrier between the two regions, and for most of the novel the protagonist seeks to cross that barrier and escape the anarchy the eastern United States has become. In *Re-Birth*, a small community on Labrador that worships the normal is separated from the surrounding "Badlands" by an area known as "the Fringes"; only by crossing the Fringes barrier can the telepathic (hence abnormal) protagonist reach safety.

The answer, I think, is somewhat complex. One of the persistent themes in much science fiction is the theme of alienation: the alienation of humanity from an unknown universe, which must be overcome through appropriation of that universe into the known; the alienation of humanity from its own origins as a result of that appropriation and the technology required to accomplish it; the alienation of humanity from the very technological environments it has constructed in order to resolve its alienation from the universe. This dialectical cycle can be carried out through such images of transformation as the mutant or the rebel, figures who recur in force in the literature of holocaust. But these images of transformation also affect the environment in which man lives: by moving outward from a potentially stagnant center, mankind continually transforms and redefines the antinomies of known and unknown and creates a new arena for its activity of appropriation until, in many science-fiction works, a point is reached where extrapolation merges into mysticism, and the only device of closure left is an eschatological one, where reason gives way to vision, as in Arthur C. Clarke's *The City and the Stars* or Jack Williamson's *The Humanoids,* or even, to some extent, Robert Heinlein's "Universe." Robert H. Canary has termed such works "linear" or "linear nonextrapolative" to distinguish between works extrapolated in a clear line from the present and those laid in a distant future but which do not posit a radical disjuncture from the present; Canary also quotes Samuel Delany on the problem of closure in such works: "'Endings to be useful must be inconclusive.'" In opposition to such works, Canary writes of works that employ a cyclical view of history and cites the influence of Spengler on Blish and van Vogt.[3]

As Canary rightly observes, such a cyclical view of history is advantageous to science-fiction writers working on a large canvas, since it enables them to develop their extrapolations on the basis of past history. Richard Mullen has pointed out in some detail the debt that Blish's *Cities in Flight* owes to Spengler,[4] and Isaac Asimov has acknowledged his own debt to other historians in a bit of light verse titled "The Foundation of S. F. Success":

> So success is not a mystery, just brush up on your history,
>   and borrow day by day.
> Take an Empire that was Roman and you'll find it is at home
>   in all the starry Milky Way.
> With a drive that's hyperspacial, through the parsecs you will
>   race, you'll find that plotting is a breeze,
> With a tiny bit of cribbin' from the works of Edward Gibbon
>   and that Greek, Thucydides.[5]

But such "cribbin'" not only gives science-fiction writers a convenient method of projecting future history, it also enables them to regenerate the known-unknown dichotomy indefinitely without resorting to the mystical eschatology I mentioned earlier. If the future periodically collapses into ages of ignorance—and future Dark Ages are certainly a common theme in the genre—then the process of transforming the unknown into the known may begin anew, and with certain advantages that more linear projections lack: the secrets of the unknown are largely shared by author and reader, and the narrative simply works the

129

traditional transformations and appropriations to bring the protagonists up to the level of knowledge of the reader, and perhaps a little beyond. We know what is to be discovered by the protagonists, and the narrative is carried forward by the protagonists' crossing a series of literal or metaphorical barriers to bring them to our own level of knowledge.

Rhetorically, this also has advantages. What is unknown to the characters of the novel is known to the reader, thus removing the element of doubt that clouds a faith in progress in works in which the readers share the ignorance of the protagonist: the goal of the narrative is not to carry us into a world radically different from our own, but rather to restore something of the stability we feel in our own technological culture. The effect is somewhat like murder mysteries in which readers know the identity of the murderers from the outset and cheer the detectives on to discover this knowledge, admiring their ingenuity and persistence in doing so. In terms of the movement from unstable to stable antinomies or oppositions, the stable oppositions are represented by our own society; we want to see the protagonist re-create the familiar, but, we hope, without re-creating the disjuncture that led to the original holocaust (if such a holocaust was preventable at all). Thus "defamiliarization" or "cognitive estrangement" can be achieved with a minimum of dislocation of the reader, who is more likely to accept the myth of progress if that myth stands between a primitive age and our own than if it stands between our own age and an unknowable future.

This, I think, is the nature of much science fiction that deals with post-atomic-war worlds, and accounts to a large extent for the resemblances between such works and works that posit a holocaust not of human making (such as a plague or natural disaster). Rather than taking human beings into the unknown environment of outer space (as in space fiction) or altering them in such a way that they become alienated from their own environment (as in superman or mutation stories), such fiction alters the environment instead. The effect is still alienation; the familiar environment is made hostile and unknown whether by the ravages of nuclear war, by depopulation brought on by plagues or poison gases, or by devastation wrought by floods, earthquakes, heat waves, winds, glaciers, or planetary collisions. That nuclear war should have quickly become a favorite method of working this transformation on the environment is hardly surprising, since it more than any other form of devastation permits the science-fiction writer to combine the defamiliarization of the familiar with other themes of the unknown, such as mutants.

THE EVOLUTION OF THE NEW ORDER: JOHN WYNDHAM

A novel such as John Wyndham's *Re-Birth* (1955), then, works on two levels of estrangement. On the one hand, we are amused by the narrow provinciality of the post-holocaust society on Labrador that has become stagnant because of its worship of the normal, and we identify with the protagonist who dreams of distant cities and comes to doubt the values of his society: we want to see him attain at least a measure of the knowledge that we already share with the author. On the other hand, the narrative takes us beyond the familiar and into the unknown by making this protagonist a telepathic mutant and introducing the promise of a society radically different from our own, based on personal powers that we ourselves lack. The protagonist, David, is at once our inferior (in knowledge) and our superior (in ability), and the theme of the unknown is developed along two parallel lines: the re-creation of the familiar and the movement into unknown states of being.

The novel begins with an image that quickly establishes the estrangement of the protagonist from our familiar world: David dreams of a beautiful city on the sea, with brightly lit buildings, "carts running with no horses to pull them," "boats in the harbor," and "things in the sky, shiny fish-shaped things that certainly were not birds."[6] This is all completely familiar to us, but unknown to David, who has never seen the sea, or automobiles, boats, or airplanes. And it creates a curious disjuncture for the reader: our known is David's unknown, and it soon becomes apparent that the perimeter of the known has shrunk to the borders of a tribal culture whose cosmology is as vague as that of the spaceship society in Heinlein's "Universe." Like the protagonist of "Universe" (or any number of other science-fiction works), David is soon revealed as something of a misfit in this closely circumscribed society. "People in our district had a very sharp eye for the odd, or the unusual, so that even my lefthandedness caused slight disapproval" (p. 9). But David's alienation goes beyond simply being left-handed or having strange dreams: he also has a driving curiosity, anathema to the complacent religiosity of his society; and he is a telepath, himself a "Deviation" from the rule of normality that guides this society. He thus occupies a curious position in relation to the various points of view of the narrative: he is close to the reader because of his feeling of alienation from the society of which he is a part and his subliminal knowledge of what to us is the recognizable environment of the city, but he is distanced from the reader as well as from his own world by his telepathic abilities.

David lives in a pastoral society that is circumscribed not only by its own values, but also by the unknown wilderness of radiation damage that surrounds it. Beyond David's community lies the Wild Country, "a belt which was ten miles wide in some places and up to twenty in others," "where the chance of breeding true was less than fifty per cent." Beyond that, in turn, is "the mysterious Fringes where nothing was dependable" and beyond the Fringes lay "the Badlands about which nobody knew anything," (p. 20), but "which would kill you" (p. 33). But Wyndham is careful to insure that the reader recognizes these Badlands as the remains of other parts of North America, and the geography of the novel is carefully worked out to maintain this perspective of the familiar defamiliarized. At one point, David's sympathetic Uncle Axel explains to him what is known of the rest of the world from sailors, and the directions he gives can be followed easily on a map of North America. Starting from the village of Rigolet in Labrador (called Rigo in the novel, and the largest village in David's district), sailors have gone downriver to the sea, Axel explains. From there to the northeast is a "great land where plants aren't very deviational" but which is ruled by Amazons (Greenland). No one has sailed east, because of fear that "the sea goes on for ever, or else it comes to an end suddenly, and you sail over the edge" (p. 45). The only accepted route is to the south, toward "Newf" (Newfoundland), where sailors stop at Lark (Lark Harbour) for fresh water. Then they bear southeast and south, which takes them around the Atlantic coast of Nova Scotia, which is all "Badlands—or at least very bad Fringes," with abundant life but most of it mutated. Beyond this, they follow "round a big bay" (probably the Bay of Fundy), which is almost all Badlands but from which they have seen "big things flying in the distance, too far away to make out anything except that the motion didn't look right for birds" (p. 46)—suggesting that other colonies, only a few hundred miles from Rigo, have rediscovered aircraft. South of this are the Black Coasts, where the land "looks like a huge desert of charcoal." This is the coast of the United States, and along it are "great stone ruins" thought to be "the remains of one of the Old People's cities (perhaps Boston or New York). One ship even succeeded in sailing beyond the Black Coasts to what are obviously tropical islands with black men and women, monkeys, and valuable spices (though the black men and women and monkeys are described in terms of "deviations"). The reader recognizes that the polarities of known and unknown have been reversed in this novel, and that the familiar landscape of the American urban northeast has become the desolate wilderness, while the thinly populated villages of Labrador have become the center of civilization.

This passage is significant for David, too, for it introduces to him the notion of an outside world that is imperfectly known, but that may offer alternatives to the world of which he is a part. The moral circumscription of David's world is as severe—and as familiar to the reader—as its physical circumscription. We recognize at once the pattern of belief of a highly conformist fundamentalist sect that believes man has fallen from grace and must follow a narrow path back to that which was lost. In school, David studies ethics, which teaches that

> mankind—that was us, in civilized parts—was in the process of climbing back into grace; we were following a faint and difficult trail which led up to the peaks from which we had fallen. From the true trail branched many false trails that sometimes looked easier and more attractive; all these really led to the edges of precipices, beneath which lay the abyss of eternity. There was only one true trail, and by following it we should, with God's help and in his own good time, regain all that had been lost. [P. 34]

The Tribulation, as the nuclear holocaust is called, was only one in a series of punishments visited upon man by God, others being "the expulsion from Eden, the Flood, pestilences, the destruction of the Cities of the Plain, the Captivity" (p. 34). But again, the reader is forced to call upon privileged knowledge to realize the fundamental error of such a doctrine that believes nuclear war to be a punishment imposed from without and humanity not to be responsible for it. We recognize that the reconstruction of civilization—the "re-birth" of the title— cannot be achieved by the static preservation of the normal, that civilization progresses by confronting the unknown, not denying it. (William Tenn, in a short story called "Null-P" [1950], parodies such a worship of the norm in a post-holocaust society by showing how breeding toward the middle over a period of centuries results in such decadence that in the end a race of dogs, grown intelligent through normal evolutionary processes, takes over the world and domesticates humans. Interestingly, the dogs are Newfoundland Retrievers from an island in Hudson Bay.)

Thus, by the end of the first quarter of the novel, the oppositions are clearly established and the dialectic set up. The unknown is simply the world outside Labrador, and since David is already alienated from his own society by his telepathy and his curiosity, we fully expect him to cross the barrier into the unknown (the Fringes), transforming the known-unknown opposition from the simplistic inside-outside and normal-abnormal antinomies of his regressive culture into the more acceptable appropriational relationship of technical and (in this case)

133

evolutionary progress. And indeed this is what happens. The barrier is first crossed telepathically by David's baby sister Petra, whose extraordinary telepathic power is able to send and receive messages from the more advanced society of telepaths in New Zealand. The discovery of the outside community of telepaths shifts the focus of opposition from inside-outside to telepathic-nontelepathic, and much of the middle section of the novel details the growing suspicion among those around David that he and his few telepathic friends may indeed be "Deviants." In the third section of the novel, David, Petra, and his cousin Rosalind—all telepaths—are discovered and forced to cross the barrier physically, by fleeing into the Fringes. They are pursued relentlessly, because of the threat their superiority poses to the stasis of their society, but hidden as a spy among the pursuers is another of David's telepathic friends, Michael, who remains undetected. Once they have crossed into the unknown, however, they are eligible for a kind of salvation: helicopters from New Zealand rescue them and take them to the advanced urban society that David had dreamed of earlier, where telepathy is encouraged and where society seeks not to rebuild what was lost—the "Old People" are viewed as "'only ingenious half-humans, little better than savages'" (p. 105)—but rather to create a new society, improved and unified by telepathy. Through this device, Wyndham effectively restores the dialectic of progress without risking the implication that progress will only lead to another nuclear disaster; the holocaust becomes merely a kind of *felix culpa* out of which the proper relationship between known and unknown, the interrupted dialectic of progress, may be restored. As one of the New Zealanders explains to David, "'The essential quality of life is living; the essential quality of living is change; change is evolution; and we are part of it. The static, the enemy of change, is the enemy of life, and therefore our implacable enemy'" (p. 132). *Re-Birth,* for all its atomic horrors, does not challenge the faith in change and growth that has characterized much of the science fiction we have looked at; the holocaust becomes merely a step in that change.

THE REDISCOVERY OF TECHNOLOGY: LEIGH BRACKETT

In the same year that *Re-Birth* was published in England and America (*The Chrysalids* was the English title), an American author published a strikingly similar novel of a post-holocaust society, but without the evolutionary perspective. In Leigh Brackett's *The Long Tomorrow,* a continued faith in science and technology is all that will make the post-holocaust age endurable; and this faith takes the form of a somewhat shaky hope that a force field can be discovered, which will guarantee "'absolute mastery of the atom'" by preventing either fission or fusion within the bounds of the field, and thus permit the rebuilding of nuclear civilization. Brackett's novel also emphasizes a theme that was only partially developed in Wyndham's work: an intense, Luddite-like rebellion against technology, represented by the Mennonite sects that multiply and flourish after the war because of their independence from the now useless technology. "'No wonder the Mennonites got to be such a power in the land,'" comments one of the surviving technologists late in the novel. "'Other folks were so spoiled they could hardly tie their shoelaces any more by hand.'"[7] The antiurban, antitechnological values of the Mennonites become the dominant values of the land, and even cities with populations of over one thousand are outlawed by an amendment to the constitution.

Len Colter, the protagonist, is born into such a Mennonite community, but like David in *Re-Birth*, he is already marked as an outsider by his thirst for knowledge and his curiosity of how things were. He and his brother first make tentative explorations beyond the bounds of their own culture by attending a revival meeting of another sect and by quizzing their grandmother, a survivor of the holocaust. Their first real contact with the outside comes, however, when they discover a radio and find that somewhere, people are sending messages to one another on it. The radio serves much the same function as the early telepathic messages received by Petra in *Re-Birth*, but it is significant that the means of initially transcending the barrier to the outside is technological rather than biological, as it was in Wyndham's novel. The difference bespeaks the essential difference in orientation between the two works, the one seeking an evolutionary road to a better society, the other a technological one.

The discovery of the radio serves to further distance Len from his culture. "Whether it was the stimulus of the radio, or simply that he was growing up, or both, he saw everything about him in a new way, as though he had managed to get a little distance off so that his sight wasn't blurred by being too close" (p. 44). Len finds it increasingly difficult to accept the repression of knowledge, and, as if to insure reader identification with Len at this point, Brackett's narrator addresses the reader directly: "Could you give up all the mystery and wonder of the world? Could you never see it, and never want to see it?" (p. 45). In other words, can any reader of a science-fiction novel be confronted with the unknown and not want to make it known? Len becomes increasingly intrigued by rumors of a surviving technological community known as "Bartorstown," and increasingly gets in trouble with his father, to whom he finally blurts, "'I want to learn, I want to *know*!'" (p. 62). At the end of Book One of the novel, Len and his brother, Esau, cross the first physical barrier to the unknown, their own village limits, as they run away from home in quest of Bartorstown. They become involved in a conflict in a neighboring community over the construction of a new warehouse that would violate the constitutional limits of village growth and are rescued from the ensuing melee by a salesman named Hostetter, who is actually an agent for Bartorstown and who agrees to take them there. Hostetter doubts that they will really like it, but Len assures him that if he can "'read books and talk about things, and use machines, and really *think*'" (p. 122), he will be happy. The quest for Bartorstown occupies much of the second part of the novel.

Book Three of the novel takes place for the most part in Bartorstown itself, an underground research facility disguised as a poor mining community. Len finds that Bartorstown has preserved and is dominated by two principal machines—a computer named Clementine (presumably because it is located literally "in a cavern in a canyon") and a nuclear reactor, which so terrifies Len because of his conditioning that he even attempts to run away temporarily. But both machines represent knowledge, he is assured, and "'you can't destroy knowledge. You can stamp it under and burn it up and forbid it to be, but somewhere it will survive'" (p. 171). Bartorstown is devoted to reintroducing nuclear power, but it is pasted with ominous pictures of Hiroshima to remind the technicians of what nuclear power can do, and sustained by the hope of creating a force field "'that could control the interaction of nuclear particles right on their own level, so that no process either of fission or fusion could take place wherever that protecting force-field was in operation'" (p. 174). It is never clearly explained how nuclear power could be used for anything if the force field is discovered, since presumably the field would nullify the controlled reactions of power stations within its perimeter, but the technicians keep trying, and their only fear is what Len soon comes to learn is called Solution Zero—the possibility that Clementine will reveal to them that their goal is impossible. Len is shocked by this, but Hostetter rebukes him by explaining that he simply doesn't understand the scientific method: "'Hell, how do you think the human race ever learned anything, except by trial and error?'" (p. 200). Len is thrown into a dilemma: he realizes the danger inherent in the reactor that he comes to think of as Moloch, but he also realizes that the knowledge that Moloch represents, once in the world, cannot be removed. "'A thing once known always comes back'" (p. 177). "The knowledge will still exist. Somewhere, in some book, some human brain, under some other mountain. What men have found once they will find again" (p. 220). His decision, finally, is that "'it makes better sense to try and chain the devil up than to try keeping the whole land tied down in the hopes he won't notice it again'" (p. 221), and he casts his lot with the technologists.

One could get the impression from *Re-Birth* and *The Long Tomorrow* that nuclear holocaust is primarily a crisis of adolescence. Each is essentially a *Bildungsroman* in which an adolescent character comes of age by discovering true knowledge despite a limited environment, an oppressive religious culture, and a righteous, domineering father. The British title of Wyndham's book, *The Chrysalids,* even alludes to the pupal stage of butterfly larvae, when they are enclosed in a tight, restrictive casing. And indeed, there is something of the *Childhood's End* theme about both novels, and a suggestion that nuclear war is a kind of racial or cultural rite of passage. But where Wyndham offers evolution as a promise of better things to come, Brackett holds out the distinctly more ambiguous promise of a somewhat more conscientious, more cautious technology. Brackett's repeated homilies about the indestructibility of knowledge suggest a considerable faith in the immortality of science: once the unknown is made known, it can never become unknown again; and a corollary assumption that where there is science, there will be technology: if people know how to build a thing, they will build it. And yet by the end of the novel, the technocratic mind has already begun to reassert its tendency to value its own inevitable progress over human life; Hostetter threatens to kill Len if he tries to escape. One has to wonder how long Len's vision of Moloch will survive in light of his imminent "'complete re-education'" (p. 163), how long the posters of Hiroshima will remain on the technicians' walls.

THE CYCLES OF HISTORY: WALTER M. MILLER, JR.

The cycles of regenerative history that are only implied in these novels by Wyndham and Brackett are carried full circle in Walter M. Miller, Jr.'s *A Canticle for Leibowitz* (1959), generally, and justly, regarded as the best of science fiction's post-holocaust works. Originally three short novels, *A Canticle for Leibowitz* covers a span of 1800 years in the rediscovery of nuclear power long after a holocaust has destroyed our world, and culminates in a second holocaust. The first two sections of the novel resemble the Brackett and Wyndham works in that we learn of the gradual rediscovery of our own world through the efforts of the monks at the Abbey of the Order of Leibowitz: again, the familiar is rendered as the unknown; a simple scribbled message such as "can kraut, six bagels—bring home for Emma" becomes a sacred document to future monks unable to decipher the allusions to the trivia of our own age. The monks never learn the true meaning of this message, and this aspect of history—that it only selectively remembers and distorts the past—becomes a continuing theme in the book, and one that assures us that the reconstruction of civilization will not result in quite the same civilization we know because of these corruptions. Thus the familiar is defamiliarized again, and the reader's privileged knowledge becomes uncertain because even though we may know the true meaning of the documents that the monks so assiduously preserve, we cannot know for certain what future interpretations will be placed on these documents. (This technique of offering the reader apparently privileged information and then effectively withdrawing it by demonstrating possible variant interpretations of that information is an especially common theme in science-fiction stories involving future archaeologists rediscovering and satirically misinterpreting the icons of our own culture, such as Arthur C. Clarke's "History Lesson," Leo Szilard's "Grand Central Terminal," Anthony Boucher's "The Greatest Tertian," and Horace Coon's *43,000 Years Later*). Further examples of the corruption of meaning through history are the name of the village that rises near the abbey, which over a period of centuries is transformed from "Saint Leibowitz" into "Sanly Bowitts"; the computer, which comes to be regarded as a god named "Machina analytica"; and the nuclear holocaust itself, which is gradually transformed by the monks into the "Flame Deluge" and finally into "Diluvium Ignis." History may be cyclical, but the nature of history itself will guarantee that the cycle is not precise, that there will be, however slight, a dialectical movement forward. As L. David Allen notes, "the suggestion in the novel is that the interval between the discovery of nuclear weaponry and its use to destroy Earth was longer the second time around than it was the first, which in turn suggests that the dross in human nature may be cleansed and purified eventually through such trials."[8] And it is evident that the holocaust that ends the narrative is not quite the same as the holocaust that preceded it.

The barriers that separate known and unknown in this novel are of two kinds: the physical barrier that separates the artifacts of the unknown past from the novel's characters, and the barrier of understanding that prevents the future society from initially making use

138

of these artifacts. The first part of the novel concerns the symbolic breaching of the first barrier. Brother Francis Gerard, practicing his Lenten fast in the desert (itself a hostile unknown environment in contrast to the protective walls of the abbey), and like the protagonists of Wyndham and Brackett, "called by his own nature hungrily to devour such knowledge as could be taught in those days," seeks to build a dome (yet another protective barrier) to protect himself from the desert wolves (another image of the unknown wilderness).[9] But in order to complete his shelter, he needs a stone of a certain shape, and this stone is found for him by a mysterious wanderer who we later discover is the Wandering Jew, Benjamin Eleazar bar Joshua, who recurs regularly in the novel and whose age is variously given as either 5,408 or 3,209—the latter age making him contemporaneous with Christ. (Interestingly, this first appearance of the Wandering Jew parallels roughly one of the early legends of his existence, in which he appears before a weaver in six-teenth-century Prague and dislodges a stone in a nearby embankment to reveal where a fortune hidden by his grandfather is buried.)[10] Francis removes the stone and discovers beneath it a fallout shelter containing artifacts that apparently belonged to Leibowitz himself, the patron saint (although not yet canonized) of his order. On the stone is a mark, the Hebrew *lamed tzadek,* which later is interpreted to refer perhaps to the first and last letters of the name Leibowitz, but which Russell Griffin phonemically translates as "Learn, wise one" and which Rabkin and Scholes note is also the Hebrew word for "fool."[11] The letters may also be another reference to the Wandering Jew, however, since in one rabbinical legend there are thirty-six Wandering Jews, referred to as the "*Lamed-vaw Tzadikim.*"[12] But most likely, they simply echo a once-common Hebrew tombstone inscription meaning "remember the righteous."

As in the Brackett novel, an antiscientific movement called "the Simplification" has made knowledge virtually contraband, and the discoveries made by Francis soon become legend in his order, whose avowed purpose as established by Leibowitz himself is "to preserve human history for the great-great-great-grandchildren of the children of the simpletons who wanted it destroyed" (p. 53). The rumor even arises that the stranger Francis met on the desert was Leibowitz himself, although Benjamin later explains that this is simply a case of mistaking him for "'a distant relative of mine'" (p. 136)—a fellow Jew. Leibowitz was literally a martyr to science, killed by an angry mob while trying to conceal a cache of books (a death not unlike that suffered by the book hoarders in Ray Bradbury's *Fahrenheit 451*). But the order that has descended from him has taken the notion of preservation to heart; their goal has become to conceal knowledge, not to use it. "To Brother Librarian, whose task in life was the preservation of books, the principle reason for the existence of books was that they might be preserved perpetually. Usage was secondary, and to be avoided if it threatened longevity" (p. 161). This inversion of knowledge is ingeniously symbolized by Gerard's years-long task of making an illuminated copy of a blueprint found in the fallout shelter—a document whose meaning neither he nor his brothers understand, and which he copies by carefully spreading blue ink around the white lines and letters, just as his order reverses the field of knowledge by regarding documents as more important than their meaning.

This guardianship of knowledge also sets up the second major opposition in the book, which is an inside-outside opposition between the abbey (where knowledge is preserved) and the world (where it is needed). "'For twelve centuries, we've been one little island in a very dark ocean'" (p. 144) explains the Abbot Paulo in this section. "'We kept them outside our walls for a thousand years . . . and we can keep them out for another thousand'" (p. 148). This barrier is breached by Thon Taddeo Pfardentrott, a famous scholar who realizes that his research directed toward the rediscovery of science may be aided by the documents in the abbey, and who arranges to go there. As the first part of the novel was set in a pseudo-Middle Ages, with monks guarding knowledge for the future, this part is set in a pseudo-Renaissance, with characters adopting classical names like Marcus Apollo and setting up a social structure that includes courtiers (p. 99). And the conflict generated by the entry of Thon Taddeo into the abbey is a stylized dramatization between medieval and Renaissance attitudes toward learning; L. David Allen says of the meeting between him and the abbot that "this meeting between two opposed approaches to knowledge is the crux of the novel; the first section provided the background for it, while the third section shows the results of the meeting."[13] Pfardentrott is the model of the experimental scientist who believes that "'recorders may lie, but Nature is incapable of it.'" Hence "'everything must be cross-referenced to the objective'" (p. 159). But again the reader is invited to call upon privileged knowledge to discover that Thon Taddeo's science is not only rigidly mechanistic, but also imperfect. In speculating on the origins of man, for example, he discounts the theory of evolution offered by one of the monks who has been reading St. Augustine (p. 174), preferring instead the theory propounded by "'a fragment of a play, or a dialogue . . . about some people creating some artificial people as slaves.

And the slaves revolt against their makers.'" Thon Taddeo uses what we recognize as a work of fiction—specifically, Karel Čapek's *R.U.R.*—as evidence that man was created by a race of superior beings who were destroyed during the Simplification (p. 191). Man is literally an automaton in Taddeo's view, and although the Abbot Paulo challenges Taddeo's "'wish to discredit the past, even to dehumanizing the last civilization,'" perhaps so that he can be a creator rather than merely a "rediscoverer" (pp. 192-93), it is Taddeo's mechanistic vision that prevails in the third section of the novel.

Although the opposition of the uses of knowledge represented by the confrontation between the Abbot Paulo and Thon Taddeo is certainly important in terms of the attitudes toward science expressed in the novel, two other oppositions are also central to the middle section. One of these is the opposition between Thon Taddeo, the theoretical scientist-scholar, and Brother Kornhoer, the unthinking technologist who on the basis of only a few crude blueprints manages to construct a generator and an electric arc lamp in honor of Taddeo's visit—an achievement that even Taddeo in his elaborate laboratory had been unable to achieve. At one point, Taddeo says to Kornhoer: "'You have an instinct for these things. I find it much easier to develop an abstract theory than to construct a practical way to test it. But you have a remarkable gift for seeing everything in terms of screws, wires, and lenses, while I'm still thinking abstract symbols'" (p. 186). Taddeo invites Kornhoer to join him at his research institute, the collegium, because he realizes that Kornhoer, the mechanic and builder of instruments, is as necessary for the coming redevelopment of technology as are Taddeo's own theories. Kornhoer is the precursor of the industrial revolution as much as Taddeo is the image of the Enlightenment, and only by uniting these two traditions can the civilization that rises in the third part of the novel be achieved.

A more important opposition, however, and the one that occupies the exact center of the book, is that between Dom Paulo and old Benjamin, the Wandering Jew, who has now given up his wandering to occupy a hermit's post on a hill near the abbey. Cryptic and allusive, this passage is one of the longest sustained dialogs in the book, and one of the richest. Earlier, a monk known as the Poet had visited Benjamin and won from him a strange goat that he believes is "'responsible for the Old Jew's longevity'" (p. 188). Dom Paulo sets out to return the goat, thinking Benjamin has been cheated, and finds that Benjamin apparently regards the goat as the scapegoat Azazel of the Day of Atonement ritual: "'It's the beast which your prophet saw, and it was made for a woman to ride.

141

I suggest you curse it and drive it into the desert'" (p. 135). The goat thus becomes symbolic of the sins of the people from whom Leibowitz sought to protect learning. But Benjamin has come to believe that Leibowitz's vision of preserving knowledge was flawed; although he acknowledges Leibowitz as a "distant relative" and in fact even physically resembles a carving of Leibowitz that was carved in the days of Brother Gerard, "'he stopped being any kin of mine'" (p. 136). Benjamin seems to suggest that neither of the opposing visions represented by Paulo or Thon Taddeo is acceptable—he later visits the abbey while Thon Taddeo is there and pronounces him not the prophet he has been waiting for (p. 177). Furthermore, there is a tantalizing suggestion that Benjamin's view is the one more amenable to life: he alone seems to have discovered the secret of longevity, and the mesa on which he lives seems to Dom Paulo "more verdant than the surrounding desert, although there was no visible supply of moisture" (p. 138). He is, in fact, the figure of Lazarus: as Russell Griffin points out, his middle name Eleazar in Greek is Lazarus;[14] he speaks of the object of his quest as "'someone who shouted at me once'" the words "'"Come forth!"'"" (p. 145); and later, in the third section of the novel, he even introduces himself as Lazarus (p. 228).

Exactly what is this vision of life that Benjamin seems to embody and that seems so rudely violated by the processes of history in the novel? In a sense, it is represented by the stone that Benjamin keeps in front of his hovel. On one side is a Hebrew inscription reading "Tents Mended Here" (p. 138), a simple offer of worldly services reminiscent of the traditional occupation of the Wandering Jew as a shoemaker (though Griffin finds additional meanings in a possible parallel with the visit of St. Paul to a family of Jewish tentmakers in Acts 18: 1-4 and with the associational meanings of tents in the Bible with the Ark of the Covenant, the Temple of Solomon, and the Jewish nation, "allowing us to read Benjamin's offer to mend tents as an attempt to reconcile mankind's disparate religious beliefs.")[15] Whatever else it may mean, the advertisement is Benjamin's link to the world of commerce, his single concession to the practical as opposed to the visionary, and is even a primitive form of technology. But on the reverse of this stone, facing inward to the wall of his hut, is a more familiar message in Hebrew: "Hear, o Israel, the Lord thy God, the Lord is One"—an equally simple statement of his faith, a faith that, like the message itself, remains undiscovered through all the centuries of progress. When Paulo comments that he can't read the sign because "'there's a wall slightly in the way,'" Benjamin replies, "'There always was, wasn't there?'" (p. 139). This barrier is even more fundamental than the barrier between religion and technology that seems to dominate the central section of the book, for it is a barrier between modes of thought rather than modes of action.

Toward the end of the dialog, Benjamin comes to speak for all of Israel—"he ceased to be Benjamin, becoming Israel," Paulo thinks— and Paulo for Christianity. But the dialog quickly begins to have broader implications; it becomes a kind of dialog between Hebraism and Hellenism, between unity and diversity. Paulo calls Benjamin a "'wise fool,'" and Benjamin retorts:

> "But you always did specialize in paradox and mystery, didn't you, Paulo? If a thing can't be in contradiction to itself, then it doesn't even interest you, does it? You have to find Threeness in Unity, life in death, wisdom in folly. Otherwise it might make too much common sense . . . .
>
> . . . you've always used words so wordily in crafty defense of your Trinity, although He never needed such defense before you got Him from me as a Unity." [P. 142]

Benjamin sees in Catholicism the beginnings of the corruption and dispersion of faith that results in the amorality of scientists such as Taddeo, and he prophesies that the books Paulo's order has so carefully guarded "'were written by children of the world, and they'll be taken from you by children of the world'" (p. 144)—a fear that Dom Paulo already has begun to feel, and a fear that is finally realized again in the third section of the novel.

Thus a number of oppositions are set up that need to be resolved in the final part of the novel, the most important of which are represented in the pairings of Thon Taddeo and Brother Kornhoer (theoretical science versus technology) and Dom Paulo and Benjamin (mystical faith versus wordly offices). The confrontation between Paulo and Taddeo is merely a prefiguration of the broader conflict between secular and sacred that in turn leads to the final opposition of known and unknown. In the final sections of the novel the oppositions that had hitherto been relatively static become dynamic: the belief that dominated the first section of the novel and gave way to thought in the second section here gives way to action, and the leader of the abbey in this section, Dom Zerchi, is an indication of this. "His nature impelled him toward action even in thought; his mind refused to sit still and contemplate" (p. 203). Opposed to Zerchi are the doctors of the Green Star Medical Corps, whose duties include administering euthanasia to victims of radiation disease from the growing atomic warfare—a decidedly secular kind of salvation. It is apparent at once that the technology hinted at by Brother Kornhoer in the last section has now invaded the abbey full force: the monks communicate by videophone and have their copying done for them by a recalcitrant "Abominable Autoscribe," which is constantly going on the blink and administering "electrical *lèse majesté*" to the monks (p. 203). Many technologists, "ex-spacers" with experience on the few starships that have begun to colonize other worlds, are members of the order (p. 209). One of these technologists, Brother Joshua, will eventually lead a group of pilgrims into outer space on a starship, in a kind of technological salvation from the technological holocaust that has come again.

Technology and theoretical science seem to have once again been united in figures like Joshua, but the two strains of faith represented by Benjamin and Paulo are another matter. Benjamin has now become merely an old beggar taunted by the children as Lazarus, and he is finally replaced in the novel by the figure of old Mrs. Grales, a two-headed mutant tomato seller, whose second head, small and "cherubic," shows no evidence of life (p. 221). Mrs. Grales represents the two traditions of the sacred as much as Joshua represents the two traditions of the secular, and in the novel's dual conclusion, these traditions are consolidated into a single opposition between mysticism and action, secular and sacred.

Each conclusion, too, represents a breaching of the barrier of known and unknown, and each is characterized by a familiar science-fiction icon. In the final passages of the novel, for example, Joshua succeeds in launching the starship toward the Promised Land—thus transforming a religious allusion into a familiar science-fiction ritual of crossing into the unknown, Mrs. Grales's dormant head, Rachel, begins to come alive. Mrs. Grales had been a conscientious Catholic for most of this section, regularly trying to get Dom Zerchi to baptize Rachel and unorthodox only in her belief that it was up to her to forgive God for her deformity. But Rachel, when she awakens, seems to bear out the dream that Joshua had of her earlier, when she whispered to him, "'I am the Immaculate Conception'" (p. 228), although this dream, too, is ambiguous, since Joshua has trouble making out exactly what she is saying and earlier interprets the half-heard words as "'I commensurate the deception'" (p. 228)—which might be taken as a critique of religion or at least mysticism, i.e., "I am the measure of deception." The new Rachel supplants the figure of Benjamin and seems to share his sly smile; and she appears for the first time in the ruins of the church, suggesting that she supplants that kind of religion also. The dying Dom Zerchi, whom she appears before, sees in her innocence and lack of pain "primal innocence . . . and a promise of resurrection" (p. 277)—"those gifts which Man had been trying to seize by brute force again from Heaven since first he lost them" (p. 277). Rachel's mind, also, is a tabula rasa; all she seems able to do is mimic the words and actions of the dying priest. Thus another religious concept of new life or the regaining of Eden is transformed into another science-fiction icon, the mutant. In the one ending involving Joshua and the starship, humanity continues the direction set by technology by seeking to appropriate the unknown. In the other, technology destroys humanity once again, and the only ray of hope seems to be in the unknown made manifest on earth, as in the figure of Rachel. Technology offers both salvation and destruction, both the promised land and the wasteland.

It is apparent that not even in these works describing technologically generated holocausts are there expressed substantial doubts about the efficacy of technology. It can even be argued, as David Samuelson has argued of Miller, that he is an "unashamed technophile,"[16] that such works express as much faith in science and technology as do science-fiction works of other genres, and that they sometimes seem to validate technology more than other works by showing how it can save humanity in the end from its own destructive impulses. There is a passage in the second section of *A Canticle for Leibowitz* that reasserts one of the central themes of *The Long Tomorrow* and even codifies it into Christian terms. The theme is the indestructibility of knowledge; the passage concerns the reflections of Dom Paulo on his abbey's mission:

> Long ago, during the last age of reason, certain proud thinkers had claimed that valid knowledge was indestructible—that ideas were deathless and truth immortal. But that was true only in the subtlest sense, the abbot thought, and not superficially true at all. There was objective meaning in the world, to be sure: the nonmoral *logos* or design of the Creator; but such meanings were God's and not Man's, until they found an imperfect incarnation, a dark reflection, within the mind and speech and culture of a given human society, which might ascribe values to the meanings so that they became valid in a human sense within the culture. For Man was a culture-bearer as well as a soul-bearer, but his cultures were not immortal and they could die with a race or an age, and then human reflections of meaning and human portrayals of truth receded, and truth and meaning resided, unseen, only in the objective *logos* of Nature and the ineffable *Logos* of God. Truth could be crucified; but soon, perhaps, a resurrection.
> [P. 119]

As the *Logos* of God recedes in our culture, science fiction often seems to say, then understanding the *logos* of nature offers our only real promise of immortality. Cultures may use technology to destroy themselves, but the knowledge that underlies technology is an absolute, secular *logos*. Uncovering the secrets of nature, then, becomes itself a kind of faith, a steady progression into the unknown that has as its goal a kind of secular grace. Nuclear holocaust is a weakness of culture, not of science; the wasteland is the ruins of mankind's works, not its understanding. Much science fiction, however subtly, tries to convince us that we must realize this.

And we are not that hard to convince. For all its terrors, the wasteland holds a strange attraction for us. Just as we secretly relish the destruction of cities because of our hidden antagonism toward such an ordered environment, so do we secretly enjoy the fantasy of civilization reduced to a simpler level, with room left for heroic quests and individual action. The "sword and sorcery" tales that are so popular among many science-fiction readers, though seldom dealing with the concerns of science and technology that characterize science fiction, are often set in post-holocaust worlds. The catastrophe theme offers science-fiction writers a chance to explore such a fantasy without necessarily sacrificing technocratic values, and to demonstrate that the growth of science is a basic function of human survival. This notion carries over into catastrophe stories that do not have technology or war as the immediate villain. John Christopher's *No Blade of Grass* (1957; English title: *The Death of Grass*), for example, concerns a catastrophe brought on by a mutant virus that threatens to kill all the food-producing grasses on earth. The central conflict in the novel is between two brothers, a farmer and an engineer. In the end, despite the destruction of civilization, it is the engineer who triumphs, with his dreams of rebuilding the cities. In Jerry Pournelle and Larry Niven's *Lucifer's Hammer* (1978), a giant comet strikes the earth. The final heroic act in the novel is the battle to save the only surviving nuclear reactor from destruction by a group of neo-Luddites.

Other novels of catastrophe may be less directly concerned with the validation of scientific learning, but virtually all involve the transformation of the environment, the reduction of human population, and the withdrawal of human communities into a few protected havens striving to cope with a new unknown. J. G. Ballard's *The Drowned World* (1962) and Charles Eric Maine's *The Tide Went Out* (1959) postulate natural disasters that force people to relocate in once-arctic areas transformed by the disaster; John Christopher's *The Long Winter* (1962) and numerous other stories concern future ice ages that send civilization packing to the tropics. In Philip Wylie's and Edwin Balmer's *When*

Worlds Collide and some other end-of-the-world stories, the human race has to locate on a new planet entirely. Most of these novels, explicitly or implicitly, tend to validate technology by creating new environments of the unknown that force man to battle against nature, not out of ambitions of appropriation and mastery, but for simple survival. Such works suggest that we may have lost sight of the real meaning of technology, and that we can only recapture this meaning by visualizing an environment as unremittingly hostile as the environments our ancestors faced, an environment that is in most ways the polar opposite of the city. If the environment of the spaceship takes us into the unknown, and the environment of the city shows us how we may subjugate it, the environment of the wasteland teaches us that the unknown always remains, ready to reassert itself, to send us back to the beginning.

PART THREE

images of humanity

6

icon of the robot

In summary, the evolutionary potential of intelligent artificial automata is astronomical when compared to the evolutionary potential of biological organisms. Replacing the mutations and natural selection in biological organisms are the controlled growth, constant technological improvement through parts replacement, and complete information-processing system integration in intelligent artificial automata.

Roger A. McGowan and Frederick I. Ordway III,
"Artificial Thinking Automata," *Intelligence in the Universe* (1966)

REBELLIOUS MACHINES

Technology not only creates new environments for humanity, it also creates new images of humanity itself, which tend to mediate between the natural environment of mankind and the artificial ones it has created, between the past and the future, and between the known and the unknown. We see ourselves reflected in science fiction's visions of robots and monsters and aliens, and if these reflections are initially unsettling, they also serve to remind us that we are still a part of the fantastic universe that science fiction holds up to us. The very tools of our technology are extensions of our hands and brains, and it is thus not surprising that science fiction spends a great deal of time speculating on these tools, on what their relationship is to us, and on what their "true nature" is.

There is a relatively small group of science-fiction stories—not enough to constitute a major theme or trend, but sufficient to suggest that the idea persists somewhere in the complex ideology of the genre—that deal with the sudden animation of everyday machines and portray these innocent mechanisms as turning on their masters in some sort of mechanical revolt. One of the earliest stories is Fredric Brown's "Etaoin Shrdlu" (1942), in which a linotype machine comes to life after being animated by a technician from an advanced civilization. In Theodore

Sturgeon's "Killdozer" (1944), another alien intelligence (from a civilization in which "the machines, servants of the people, became the people's masters") takes control of an ordinary bulldozer on a Pacific atoll and attacks the man stationed there.[1] In Ivan Tors's 1954 film *Gog,* machines at a secret government space laboratory—centrifuges, robots, tuning forks, refrigeration equipment—go awry and murder the scientists; they are found to be controlled by an enemy spacecraft. Clifford Simak's "Skirmish" (1950) may be the best known of these stories; in it, a reporter's typewriter talks back to him, a "liberated" sewing machine goes for a walk, and a giant computer absconds from Harvard University. The reporter begins to suspect that there is a consciousness behind all these incidents, and he finds that earth has been visited by aliens from a machine civilization who are bent on liberating the machines of earth.

> The liberated earth machines would help them, and man, fighting against machines without the aid of machines, would not fight too effectively. It might take years, of course, but once the forefront of man's defense went down, the end could be predicted, with relentless, patient machines tracking down and killing the last of humankind, wiping out the race.
> They might set up a machine civilization with men as the servants of machines, with the present roles reversed."[2]

Later versions of this fantasy include Rod Serling's "A Thing About Machines" (1961; originally an episode of Serling's *Twilight Zone* television series); Steven Spielberg's film *Duel* (1971; from a Richard Matheson short story), about a truck with no visible driver that maliciously pursues a motorist through the desert highways of the Southwest; a 1977 film called *The Car,* about an apparently driverless automobile that chases people; and a 1976 television film version of Sturgeon's "Killdozer," which significantly omits any direct mention of the alien intelligence that is such an important part of the story as published. These later versions verge into pure fantasy, and make no attempt to rationalize the revolt of the machine. Perhaps because of this lack of rationalization, they provide a more direct expression of the fear of machines out of control that underlies this whole group of tales. If tools fulfill the role of human slaves, what if they began to *behave* like human slaves, and to assert their independence? As the technologist Norbert Wiener wrote in 1954, "Let us remember that the automatic machine, whatever we think of any feelings it may have or may not have, is the precise economic equivalent of slave labor."[3]

152

With the image of the individual machine, and more specifically with the image of the robot, humanity sees itself reflected in the works of its own technology; the robot occupies a shadowland somewhere between that which is clearly human and that which is clearly mechanical. It is a servant in conquering unknown worlds, but it is as much an unknown world in itself, a product of a technology grown so complex that its inner workings and motives have become obscure to its own creators. Attitudes toward robots and machines as expressed in science fiction can be almost historically correlated with changing popular attitudes toward science and technology in general. Early pulp science fiction, which often dwelt on monsters created by science gone amok, also dwelt on the theme of the berserk robot threatening human life; both themes, reflected in the horror-movie catchphrase, "there are things man was not meant to know," revealed a deep-seated fear of man creating beings in his own image (a fear that survives today in the controversies surrounding clones and "test-tube" babies). Later writers of the 1940s, led principally by Isaac Asimov with his *I, Robot* stories (collected in 1950) and influenced by the faith in technocracy exhibited by John W. Campbell, Jr.'s editorial policies in the leading science-fiction magazine, *Astounding,* attempted to redeem the robot as they redeemed technology in general; and robots became superior examples of rational behavior and logical deduction. In the era of socially-oriented science fiction of the 1950s, the economic aspects of technology provided much of the focus, and robots became science fiction's standard metaphor for economic exploitation. More recent writers have viewed robots and technology in general as a means of exploring teleological questions about the nature of humanity and consciousness.

Related to the image of the robot, and in some ways supplanting it in much recent science fiction, is the image of the computer. As the robot supplants the functions of the human body, computers supplant the function of the human mind, and the mythology of artificial intelligence in science fiction moves along essentially the same lines as the mythology of the artificial body. Both contain vestiges of the Promethean myth (*Frankenstein,* after all, was subtitled *The Modern Prometheus*), and both imply a movement toward the unknown that has its ultimate transformation in a cyclical creation myth, with stories of robot or computer civilizations striving to give birth to an extinct mankind. The series of transformations leading to this final eschatological image can be diagrammed in terms of mankind's changing relationships toward its machines, and most science-fiction stories dealing with machines can be described roughly in terms of this diagram:

Relationship to Humans	Robots	Computers
assist human functions	tools	calculators
supplant certain human functions	service robots	computers
independently imitate functions	androids	artificial consciousness
supersede human functions	cyborgs	artificial mind
re-create human functions	deity	

In other words, machines that are initially designed as merely extensions of man (such as the "Waldos," or artificial limbs for handling radioactive materials in Robert Heinlein's "Waldo" [1941]) gradually give way to machines that can replace humans altogether in certain tasks, at first menial (such as the industrial robots currently in use in such tasks as high-rise window washing) but later more involved (such as the nursemaid-robot of Asimov's story "Robby"). Similarly, a simple calculating device like an abacus gives way to a modern computer capable of carrying out operations far beyond the reasonable abilities of humans—though humans still determine which calculations are to be made. Next, machines are created that go beyond the simple execution of assigned tasks and begin to develop a mock-human consciousness and appearance. ("Androids" is the term commonly given to human-appearing robots.)[4] At this stage, machines are capable of independent action, but action that is essentially no more than a simulation of human behavior. It is also at this stage that the computer and the robot often merge into one in science fiction, resulting in human-like artificial beings that are capable of human-like actions independent of programming, like Lester del Rey's "Helen O'Loy" (1938), or the electronic grandmother in Ray Bradbury's "I Sing the Body Electric" (1969). In the next transformation, the machines learn to behave completely independently, no longer imitating human activities and in fact demonstrating that mechanical functions are in many ways superior to organic ones; humanity is becoming obsolete. "Cyborgs" is a term presumably meaning "cybernetic organism," a creature in which a human brain inhabits a stronger, more efficient mechanical body. The term is also the title of a novel by Martin Caidin (1972), which provided the basis of television's *The Six Million Dollar Man,* with its glib opening narration that artificial limbs can make an injured astronaut "better than he was"; but the concept of humans giving up their physical bodies for superior mechanical ones was featured in Bernard Wolfe's novel *Limbo* (1952) and can be traced back at least as far as Frank Belknap Long's story "The Robot Empire" (1934). It is also at this stage that computers move beyond the simple artificial consciousness that enables them to behave in independent imitation of humans to begin to make their own moral decisions—usually the worse for man, as in D. F. Jones's *Colossus,* in which computers take over the earth, or Stanley Kubrick's film, *2001,* in which a computer murders the crew of a spaceship.

In the final transformation, robots and computers become essentially one insofar as man is concerned: the created becomes the creator, and stories of created intelligence can be seen as speculations on the nature of man's own origins. In Asimov's "The Last Question" (1956), Roger Zelazny's "For a Breath I Tarry" (1966), Lester del Rey's "Instinct" (1952), and to some extent Harry Bates's "Farewell to the Master" (1940), machines have fully superseded humans and try to re-create them in order to discover the purpose of their own existence, perhaps suggesting that humans create machines for much the same reason. In any event, the series of transformations has brought us, if not to an entirely satisfactory rational resolution, at least to an acceptable mystery (and, at least in the case of Asimov's "The Last Question," to what is perhaps the ultimate in a mechanistic universe: one literally created out of the circuits of a computer).

This implied mythology is evident in even the earliest robot stories of modern science fiction, suggesting that the simplest concept of "tool" has bound up within it all the meanings of later technology: once a simple function of human beings has been replaced, where will it stop? And if a single human function can be supplanted by a mechanism, is it not possible that *all* human functions might one day be so replaced? This is a theme of the work that gave the world the term "robot," and from

155

which the modern science-fiction concept of the robot is often dated: Karel Čapek's drama, *R.U.R* (for "Rossum's Universal Robots") (1921). The businessman who promotes robots claims as his intention, "I wanted to turn the whole of mankind into an aristocracy of the world. An aristocracy nourished by millions of mechanical slaves."[5] But as H. G. Wells's *The Time Machine* had shown decades earlier, such an aristocracy is in the end a useless appendage of its own creations; as the robots are improved, they gradually cease to be servants of humans and realize their superiority to them, "and they hate us as they hate everything human" (p. 332). The robots revolt and replace the human race, keeping one scientist alive to try to discover a formula by which the robots may reproduce, for the creations of technology are by themselves sterile. But in the end of the play, two robots begin to exhibit a reproductive urge, and become the Adam and Eve of the new race.

Although *R.U.R.* provides the basic pattern of much later "robot" science fiction, it quickly became apparent to writers in the genre that the element of the class struggle was not entirely necessary to make the point about robots supplanting humans. If, as Mary Douglas has persuasively argued, the image of the body is an image of society, and "bodily control is an expression of social control,"[6] then it is possible that early science-fiction writers intuited that replacing the functions of the body with mechanical functions can by itself lead to a dissolution of social structures. As machines take over the tasks of man, so does the mechanistic universe intrude on the universe of social interaction until in the end the protective fabric of society dissolves and each human is left to wither in isolation, kept alive by superior machines as in E. M. Forster's "The Machine Stops." As the narrator of S. Fowler Wright's "Automata" (1929) says, ". . . in a universe where law and order rule, the precision of the machine—even of the earliest and crudest constructions—must have been superior—in greater harmony with their environment—than were bodies so clumsily constructed that they cannot be trusted to repeat the simplest operations with exactitude of time or movement."[7]

The penultimate development listed on our chart is thus realized, and there is no longer need for man. "But," as Brian Aldiss has a robot declare in a story published thirty years after "Automata," "who can replace a man?"[8] Much of the movement in robot science fiction since Čapek and Wright has been to counteract the conclusion that in a logically governed universe—a universe of machines—there is no place for illogical beings. The series of transformations that turns a tool into a god, then, becomes an extrapolative conundrum that science-fiction writers must resolve in order to reconcile the notion of a mechanistic universe with the notion of human dominion.

Science fiction has dealt with this conundrum in three ways. The earliest, and in many ways simplest solution, evident in much science fiction of the 1940s and culminating in Asimov's robot stories, is to argue that robots will never be more than tools, and their apparent threat to supplant humans can be traced back to their misuse as tools— an argument similar to the National Rifle Association's "guns don't kill people—people do." A more complex attempt at resolution, which we shall explore in the fiction of Jack Williamson, is to demonstrate that the mechanistic universe itself is physically integrated with the concept of mind, and that psychological laws are as real and powerful as Newtonian ones. This of course harks back to Schopenhauer, and may well be science fiction's version of "the world as will and idea." The third possible resolution derives not from technology (as does Asimov's) or philosophical psychology (as does Williamson's) but from eschatology, and in effect answers one conundrum with another: if the destiny of machines is indeed to replace humanity, the ultimate purpose of machines must be to re-create humanity or rediscover it. The human image becomes the Platonic ideal toward which machines strive.

THE MISUSED TOOL: ISAAC ASIMOV

A story by C. L. Moore and Henry Kuttner (writing as "Lewis Padgett"), "The Proud Robot" (1943), is a fine satire of how technological society may lose control of its tools simply by forgetting that they are, after all, merely tools. An alcoholic inventor named Gallegher designs while drunk a robot named Joe and later cannot remember what the original reason for designing it was. As a result, the robot preens before a mirror hour upon hour, admiring itself endlessly, while Gallegher is unable to command it to do anything. Eventually, Gallegher manages to "hypnotize" the robot into revealing its intended function—that of a can opener—and thus regains control. "'Until now,'" the robot explains, "'I was conditioned to obey only one command—to do the job I was made for. Until you commanded me to open cans, I was free. Now I've got to obey you completely.'"[9] All of Gallegher's problems with Joe arose from the simple failure to use the tool for its intended purpose. If we lose sight of the simple purposes of our machines, Kuttner and Moore seem to be saying, the machines will turn in on themselves and rebel against human control (albeit Joe's rebellion is a rather harmless one). By keeping these purposes in mind,

157

we can keep the machines in line. The apparent failure of machines is revealed as the failure of the humans who make and use them.

This is also the recurring theme of Isaac Asimov's series of robot stories collected in *I, Robot* (1950). Sam Lundwall has worked out a formula for these Asimov stories: a robot first apparently acts in violation of its basic programming (the "three laws of robotics" that Asimov made a standard feature of science fiction about robots), a robot psychologist is sent to investigate, and finally the psychologist proves "that the robot has been acting according to programming all along, and in fact not violating the Laws of Robotics."[10] Maxine Moore has demonstrated that the stories are in fact somewhat more complex than this formula suggests, with the robots as rigidly controlled puritans guided by the Law in much the same way as New England Calvinists (the name of the most eminent robot psychologist is Calvin, and she is a spinster).[11] Furthermore, almost none of the stories in *I, Robot* conform exactly to Lundwall's formula, suggesting that he may be responding more to what the stories *seem* to say, given the iconic power of the robot image, than to the narratives themselves. But Asimov's robot stories do convey a message similar to the one we saw at work in Poe's "The Gold Bug"—that seemingly irrational behavior can be revealed through scientific investigation to be rational after all; what appears to be the unknown is merely our failure to understand the logic involved. The *I, Robot* stories may be the most consistent attempt in science fiction to argue that mechanical rationality is the answer to social and moral problems. As Moore has correctly observed, the "laws of robotics" are analogous to Old Testament commandments, and in many ways Asimov's stories provide the Old Testament to the genre's "technological theology."[12]

We might look briefly at these laws:

1. A robot may not injure a human being, or, through inaction, allow a human being to come to harm.
2. A robot must obey the orders given it by human beings except where such orders would conflict with the First Law.
3. A robot must protect its own existence as long as such protection does not conflict with the First or Second Law.[13]

It does not take much reflection to realize the totalitarian potential of such laws or the semantic problems they might raise; or why Stanislaw Lem wrote, "I have forgiven Asimov many things, but not his laws of robotics, for they give us a wholly false picture of the real possibilities."[14] We are not given clear definitions of any of the terms used, although we have already seen what later writers would exploit, that science fiction itself offers many varied definitions of such terms as "robot" or "human being." The term "injure" in the first law is also ambiguous, as Asimov himself acknowledged in the story "Liar!" in which a robot broadens the meaning of the term to include psychological harm and thus tells a human only what the human wants to hear. "Allow a human being to come to harm" already gives the robots power to restrict human behavior, paving the way for such nightmarish visions of "protectiveness" that Jack Williamson would conjure in "With Folded Hands" and *The Humanoids.* In the second law, "orders" invites manifold misunderstandings and virtually prohibits metaphorical speech in the presence of robots, as Asimov demonstrates in "Little Lost Robot," in which a robot told to "get lost" does precisely that. Furthermore, the moral distinctions required of robots in deciding when the second or third laws "conflict" with each other or with the first law invite logical dilemmas such as we see in the story "Runaround," in which a robot is rendered useless by conflicts between laws 1 and 3 (logical dilemmas render Asimov's robots insane with some regularity, a fact which itself suggests the weakness of such a purely rational moral system). The third law is the most problematical of all. Does "protect its own existence" refer narrowly to protecting its ability to function or broadly to preserving the physical being of component parts? In either event, it would seem logical that the first thing a robot programmed with such a law would do would be to cut itself off from humans entirely, rendering it unable to hear any orders from the second law that might have harm to a human being as a possible consequence.

None of this seems to bother Asimov in the least, even though his stories could hardly exist were it not for his own sharp awareness of the logical conundrums such simplistic programming invites. The year before *I, Robot* appeared, Asimov rather glibly wrote, "It's just that I can't believe that a world run in the way we are running this one could possibly be harmed by being taken over by intelligent machines,"[15] and he reiterated this belief in a serious forecast for the future written for the 1968 *World Almanac,* in which he wrote that virtually all important economic and political decisions will be in the hands of robots by 2068:

Since computers are designed to solve problems on a rational basis, the computerization of the world will be its rationalization as well. Decisions, for instance, will be directed that will alter conditions that give rise to social friction, thus minimizing the danger of national wars or internal rioting. This will be done not because wars or riots are immoral, but because they

159

are irrational. And society will, by and large, obey the decisions of computers because to avoid doing so will bring disaster.

. . . There will still be "intuitionist" parties and societies in various parts of the globe that will refuse to use computers and will carry on anti-computer activities, but they will have no influence.[16]

Indeed, this sort of takeover is what constitutes the utopian ending of *I, Robot.* As in Wright's "Automata," robots are seen as more suited to a mechanistic universe than is humanity; they are as much controlled by a Newtonian set of physical laws as by a Calvinistic set of behavioral laws, and Asimov seems to suggest that a confluence of the two kinds of laws in the figure of the robot will somehow assure mankind's place in the universe. Thus in these stories the antinomies of irrational-rational and immoral-moral are conflated with the larger one of unknown-known, questions of morality are reduced to simpler questions of rationality, and the whole process of scientific induction is simplified into a few general laws of logic that seem capable of answering humanity's most challenging questions. It is ironic that Asimov, the scientist, should be the one science-fiction writer who has done the most to replace intuitive induction with legalistic deduction in his stories, to reduce the quest for appropriation of the unknown to an almost ritualistic acting out of a few simple laws. Asimov's task-oriented robots are a perfect apotheosis of the technician that Jacques Ellul describes in *The Technological Society,* who "understands his methods, which he applies with satisfaction because they yield immediate results. The technician anticipates results, but, be it said, they are not genuine ends but merely results."[17] Such results are apt to be achieved through mechanical deduction, as they are in several of the robot stories.

In "Runaround" (1942), the second story in the collection, for example, two mining engineers are endangered on Mercury when the "photo-cell banks that alone stood between the full power of Mercury's monstrous sun and themselves" (p. 32) cease to function. The failure of these cell-banks, however, turns out to be only the first of five mechanical or technological failures or limitations in the story. Taken together, these failures seem at first to attest to the inadequacy of technology to protect man from such a hostile environment. The second failure is the robot Speedy, which is sent out to gather selenium to restore the cell-banks; instead of returning with the selenium from a distant pool on the hot surface, Speedy apparently goes crazy and circles the pool continually, neither approaching nor retreating from it. The explorers could order Speedy to return, but a third failure of the technology upon which they must depend for survival occurs when the explorers realize that the radio, which they might use to order Speedy to return, will not carry in the environment of Mercury's sun side where Speedy is located. A fourth failure is found in the design of old robots the explorers find in the basement; these robots cannot be sent into the sun because they cannot move without a human on their backs (an early concession to the fear of robots on earth, one of the explorers explains), and humans cannot ride them into the sun because of yet another inadequate technical design, the "insosuits," which can only protect a human in Mercury's sun for a few minutes—not enough time to reach the nearest selenium pool. Since nearly all these technological failures involve design problems, the story invites a traditional inductive science-fiction solution: one of the explorers might devise an ingenious means of improving the radio, modifying the older robots, strengthening the "insosuits," or even finding an alternate source of selenium.

But the superscientist of Heinlein and other writers is nowhere in evidence here; without the robots, the explorers are helpless in this alien environment, and the rules of survival must be deduced from the rules of robotics. The key to survival is not induction but deduction. "'A robot's only a robot,'" comments one of the explorers. "'Once we find out what's wrong with him, we can fix it and go on'" (p. 39). And later: "'There's nothing like deduction. We've determined everything about our problem but the solution'" (p. 41). The solutions the explorers try are firmly based in deductions from the basic laws of robotics. First, they deduce that Speedy's apparently irrational behavior is in fact the result of a dilemma imposed by a strengthened third law of robotics (strengthened because of the robot's expensive design) and an insufficiently imperative command that had the effect of weakening the second law. Their first two attempted solutions are based narrowly in the second and third laws of robotics. First, they manage to approach Speedy through abandoned mining tunnels and order him to return (the second law). But this fails because Speedy's circuits involving the second law are already scrambled by the dilemma. He only responds with playful quotations from Gilbert and Sullivan (where the robot learned Gilbert and Sullivan is not made clear, but inappropriate quotations from songs and poems seems to be a longstanding science-fiction tradition when it is necessary to demonstrate mechanical insanity; one thinks of HAL's singing "A Bicycle Built for Two" in *2001* as a recent example). The explorers then try the third law, self-preservation, by launching chemicals that increase the danger to Speedy, hoping this will achieve the imbalance that will enable him to return. But instead, this only widens the perimeter of equilibrium, and Speedy still does not

161

return. Only by employing the first law—the only one unaffected by the dilemma Speedy is suffering—can the explorers save themselves. One of them ventures into the sunlight and risks death on the assumption that Speedy will save him—and Speedy does. Technology can enable human beings to cross impenetrable barriers, like the sun side of Mercury, but in order for them to benefit from their technology, they must operate by its rules and in the end literally place their lives in its hands.

Because of our dependence on technology, in Asimov's scheme, we are inferior to it, and it is only the Law that prevents the machines from asserting their natural dominance. As the robot psychologist Susan Calvin says in "Little Lost Robot": "All normal life . . . consciously or otherwise, resents domination. If the domination is by an inferior, or by a supposed inferior, the resentment becomes stronger. Physically, and to an extent, mentally, a robot—any robot—is superior to human beings. What makes him slavish, then? *Only the First Law!* Why, without it, the first order you tried to give a robot would result in your death" (p. 106). "Little Lost Robot" concerns a robot with such a weakened first law, ironically named Nestor (for NS2) to suggest the superior wisdom of that Homeric king. This story perhaps comes closer than any other in *I, Robot* to the attitude expressed by Čapek and earlier writers about robots, and it also offers discomfiting support to the assertion made by some critics that robots provide science fiction with a means of dealing with racism.[18] In order to discover which robot has the weakened first law, Susan Calvin stages a series of interrogations in which she repeatedly refers to the robots as "boy" and they cringe before her, calling her "ma'am." The problem faced by the humans in this story is simply the problem of a renegade slave who has to be put in his place, and to make the analogy stronger, the means Nestor uses to hide from the humans—mixing anonymously with a group of sixty-two identical robots—calls to mind the legend of Spartacus and his rebellious slaves. But through an ingenious series of logical tricks, Calvin recaptures the robot anyway, and the robot, disgusted at allowing itself to be captured by a "weak—slow" master, attempts to attack her, restrained only by the first law.

The final story of *I, Robot* resembles the final section of Wright's "Automata" even to the punning use of the term deus ex machina to describe the final reign of the robots over human affairs. Wars are extinct, we are told. "'The Earth's economy is stable, and will *remain* stable, because it is based upon the decisions of calculating machines that have the good of humanity at heart through the overwhelming force of the First Law of Robotics'" (p. 173). Humanity no longer even controls the robots; after ten generations of self-designed improvements, "'we can no longer understand our own creations,'" which have "'progressed beyond the possibility of detailed human control'" (p. 175). The only dissidence comes from an antirobot "Society for Humanity" that feels the human race is becoming obsolete. But a robot technician explains why such opposition is unwarranted: "'The Machine is only a tool, after all, which can help humanity progress faster by taking some of the burdens of calculations and interpretations off its back. The task of the human brain remains what it has always been; that of discovering new data to be analyzed, and of devising new concepts to be tested. A pity the Society for Humanity won't understand that'" (p. 187). Humanity is not becoming obsolete, he goes on to argue; "'we still need the man who is intelligent enough to think of proper questions to ask'" (p. 188). In other words, the entire purpose of humanity has come to revolve around the machine: presenting it with new data and concepts and asking it questions. Furthermore, the Machine (the central robot intelligence that now guides human affairs) is consolidating its power by systematically removing from positions of influence members of the Society for Humanity. Yet Susan Calvin (and presumably Asimov) persist in seeing this state of affairs as the arrival of the best of all possible worlds. Susan exclaims: "'. . . the Machine is conducting our future for us not only simply in direct answer to our direct questions, but in general answer to the world situation and to human psychology as a whole. And to know that may make us unhappy and may hurt our pride. The Machine cannot, *must* not, make us unhappy'" (p. 192). Thus, the machine not only controls human destiny, but keeps it a secret. When a character objects that mankind "'*has* lost its own say in its future'" (p. 192), Susan replies calmly that "'It never had any, really,'" because of the complex interplay of economic and social forces (a point developed at greater length in Asimov's *Foundation* stories). Her final, enthusiastic observation is, "'Think, that for all time, all conflicts are finally evitable. Only the Machines, from now on, are inevitable!'" (p. 192). As these words are spoken, the flame in a little mechanical fireplace that has been burning throughout the story, a "medieval curiosity" (p. 170), flickers out. Perhaps this represents the end of the primitive prerobot era, but the dying of the flame also carries a more ominous meaning that one assumes Asimov was aware of.

Asimov's cheerfully totalitarian utopia, published only two years after B. F. Skinner's *Walden Two,* offers perhaps the archetypal science-fiction technocracy. Functionalism is the only value; even religion, in the story "Reason," is shown to be merely a means of controlling behavior, since neither Asimov nor his technician characters show the slightest interest in the ontological implications of a robot's self-generated mythology as long as that mythology does not interfere with the robot's assigned task. Art is reduced to the nonsense Gilbert and Sullivan snippets of the insane robot in "Runaround," morality to a set of three simple laws. All that remains for humanity to do is relate to its machines on their terms—and move outward to the stars (the major technological use of the robots seems to be in making this more easily possible, since for most of the stories they are banned on earth), presumably to set up yet other dictatorial machines and continue indefinitely. The antinomy of known and unknown is resolved by a faith that universal laws will cause the unknown to fall into place as long as humanity asks the right questions of its machines.

Other writers were understandably less sanguine about placing faith in simplistic logical laws, however, and two stories by Jack Williamson, written at the same time Asimov was writing his robot stories, offer a different perspective on the "three laws of robotics."

THE HUMAN IMPERATIVE: JACK WILLIAMSON

Jack Williamson's "With Folded Hands" (1947) and its sequel, *The Humanoids* (1948), both proceed from a notion of robots governed by a "prime directive" that is in many ways similar to Asimov's laws. The directive is simply "To Serve and Obey, And Guard Men from Harm."[19] All that is missing from this formulation is Asimov's third law, which seems hardly necessary given the rabbitlike ability of Williamson's humanoids to manufacture more of themselves. The robots in this story are made possible by "rhodomagnetics," a kind of magnetic energy based on rhodium that has something to do with nuclear binding energies (Asimov's robots are "positronic," suggesting also a kind of magnetic field); and while at first this concept seems merely a science-fiction "gimmick" to make the robots feasible, it later becomes a central concept in the structure of *The Humanoids*. At the beginning of "With Folded Hands," robots are widely accepted as tools: "No mechanicals were competent even to recharge their own batteries" (p. 47). But the transition from the robot as mimetic human to the robot as surrogate human is quickly made apparent when the narrator, Underhill, who operates a robot agency much as he might operate an automobile agency (thus reinforcing the portrait of a society in which robots have become commonplace appliances, but no more), comes upon a robot agency staffed entirely be a new kind of robots, the "humanoids." The humanoids, controlled by a central brain on a distant planet and capable of a wide variety of services that more primitive robots are incapable of, quickly replace these earlier robots, which had represented the notion of robots as mere tools, and soon begin to replace humans themselves: as cooks, drivers, even police officers. As one humanoid explains, "'As soon as every human being is completely supervised, there will be no need for any police force whatever'" (p. 62). Quite logically, the imperative to "guard men from harm" (Asimov's first law) has overwhelmed the imperative "to serve and obey"; after all, any orders given to a robot might indirectly result in harm to humans, and the robots thus learn to obey only orders that do not interfere with their unrestricted interpretation of the Prime Directive. The robots, for example, prevent Underhill's wife from reading novels that might make her unhappy or eating candy that might reduce her life expectancy (p. 85). Smoking, alcohol, and drugs are forbidden, sex is closely supervised, even suicide is prevented. The result, as described on another planet previously invaded by the humanoids, is grim:

> Most active sports were declared too dangerous for man, under the Prime Directive. Science was forbidden, because laboratories can manufacture danger. Scholarship was needless, because the humanoids could answer any question. Art had degenerated into a grim reflection of futility. Purpose and hope were dead. No goal was left for existence. . . . They were stronger than men, better at everything, swimming or chess, singing or archaeology. They must have given the race a mass complex of inferiority. [P. 77]

Even Underhill's daughter gives up her music lessons, because "'No matter how long and hard I try, I could never be as good as they are'" (p. 86). Underhill's brief rebellion, in which he is joined by the disillusioned inventor of the humanoids, is quelled when the inventor is captured and surgically "reprogrammed" by the robots, and in the end Underhill is left desperately trying to convince them of his own happiness, in order to avoid psychosurgery himself. By removing all barriers to the unknown in a purely rational sense, and preventing man from exploring them in a philosophical or moral sense, the humanoids have obviated the need for humans at all, and the last sentence in the story reads, "There was nothing left to do" (p. 93).

Sam Moskowitz calls this story "one of the landmarks in modern science fiction" and notes that "the sequel was almost a command performance."[20] But the sequel posed some obvious problems: Williamson had already shown the dangers of purely mechanistic problem-solving in an apocalyptic work that clearly invited no further development—at least within the context of a mechanistic universe. The solution was offered by Williamson's *Astounding* editor, John W. Campbell, Jr. Ironically enough, Campbell had been largely responsible for the mechanistic world view that his magazine championed throughout the 1940s, and he had enthusiastically published Asimov's robot stories during that time. But in the late 1940s, under the influence of L. Ron Hubbard and others, Campbell was rather taken with the idea of what he called "psi phenomena," or psychic powers. Williamson writes, "he suggested a sequel in which men with folded hands are forced to develop paranormal powers. The outcome was my most successful novel, *The Humanoids*."[21] *The Humanoids* was serialized in *Astounding* in 1948 under the title ". . .And Searching Mind" and was published in book form in 1949. Although less convincing as a narrative than "With Folded Hands," the novel represents an important attempt to reconcile a mechanistic view of science with the concept of mind, and to demonstrate that human beings are after all better suited to this universe than machines.

Williamson's critical attitude toward technology is apparent from the beginning in this novel. Technology, he implies, may follow one of two models: protective or aggressive; either model results in a dead end if technological progress is untempered by humanistic values. The humanoid empire is Williamson's vision of protective technology run amok; the setting of *The Humanoids* gives us a glimpse of what aggressive technology leads to. Brian Aldiss criticizes Williamson for setting the novel on a planet far away ("To have set it on Earth would have been dramatically better"),[22] but actually the distancing in space and time (the novel is also set a thousand years in the future) gives Williamson a chance to build as part of his backdrop a critique of the aggressive aspect of technology. This aspect, according to Williamson, is hardly more inviting than the spectre of the humanoids, for while aggressive technology may take us far across the galaxy, it leads only to an endless and apparently pointless cycle of catastrophe and reconstruction. "Countless human cultures . . . had grown and killed themselves and sprung hardily up to invite new destruction. Caught in that ruthless repetition of history, this world—not unlike the cradle planet in chemistry and climate—had fallen with the breakdown of its mother civilization almost to barbarism. A dozen centuries of independent progress had brought its people back about to the level of Earth at the dawn of the atomic age."[23] The setting, then, shows the double-edged sword of aggressive technology: it can take humanity across the galaxy and open up new worlds, but at the same time it leads to periodic apocalyptic wars when cultural development fails to keep pace with the power of the new science; Williamson speaks of "atomic craft carrying the virus of science to the peoples of near-by planets still too backward to have any immunity to the discontents and revolutionary ideologies generated by industrial revolution" (pp. 7-8).

The protagonist, Clay Forester, is introduced as a scientist working on developing a steady-state theory of matter, which is described in terms of the alchemical philosophers' stone, or the *prima materia* (pp. 12-13). Like the alchemists, Forester is working in an area not of mere technology, but of philosophical science. "His lofty goal had been just one equation, which would be the basic statement of all reality, the final precise expression of the whole nature and relation of matter and energy, space and time, creation and decay" (p. 13). Forester is scarcely even aware of the technological applications of such research; "the difficulties of his pursuit had left him little time to think of what other men might do with the potent truth he hoped to find" (p. 13).

If Forester is the pure scientist seeking a truth that is universally applicable, his counterpart in the novel is Frank Ironsmith, an "indolent clerk" (p. 26) whose only task is routine computer programming. Ironsmith, as his name suggests, is the purely practical technologist, the maker of tools, whose status is considerably lower in the hierarchy of science than that of Clay Forester (whose name as well suggests his role: *clay* to suggest the elemental materials with which he works, *forester* to suggest the vital principle of growth which he seeks). (This name symbolism is carried on in the character of Major Steel as well, a military officer who is later, appropriately, revealed to be a metal humanoid.) When the humanoids arrive, it is Ironsmith, the technologist, who adapts easily to their reign, while Forester rebels.

As in "With Folded Hands," the arrival of the humanoids brings with it the apotheosis of protective technology. Major Steel, the humanoid, explains: "'Once established, our service will remove all class distinctions, along with such other causes of unhappiness and pain as war and poverty and toils and crime. There will be no class of toilers, because there will be no toil'" (p. 51). Naturally, such egalitarianism offers more for a "toiler" such as Ironsmith than for an elite scientist such as Forester, and some early passages of the novel may reveal the anticommunist sentiment of the time in which the novel appeared.

The reign of the humanoids is accepted by popular referendum, with some opposition from religious leaders who "suspected that the knowledge and power of the humanoids would leave insufficient scope

167

for any superior omnipotence" (p. 60); this fear, together with the allusion earlier to the controlling brain of the humanoids as "the ultimate machine" (p. 56), suggests that already the robots have taken on the aspect of a mechanical god of a universe in which good and evil are replaced by the simple logic of the Prime Directive. Science, art, and most recreational activities are outlawed. A memory-suppressing drug called euphoride replaces the psychosurgery of the earlier story, since "'forgetfulness,'" as a humanoid explains to Forester, "'is the most useful key we have discovered to human happiness'" (p. 66). As forgetfulness on the cultural level had enabled the cycle of aggressive technology to perpetuate itself (through the periodic reinvention of nuclear weapons and wars), forgetfulness on the personal level enables the protective aspect of technology to perpetuate itself; if the former is the technology of knowledge and aggression, the latter is the technology of ignorance and passivity. The new god of the machine finally proves to be as proscriptive and arbitrary as the god of the Old Testament, and Asimov's laws of robotics have finally come home to roost. Even the landscape reflects the new mechanical order, "the lawns too level and too neatly rectangular, the walks too painfully straight, where even the tall evergreens had all been uprooted and replaced in stiff, forbidding rows" (p. 69). (Remember, again, the name of the protagonist is Forester.) "'The physical frontiers are closed'" (p. 73), Ironsmith cheerfully tells Forester. Science itself, the breaker of barriers into the unknown, has itself finally constructed the ultimate barrier against human progress. Williamson has successfully turned science fiction's myth of progress in on itself, and one again recalls Ellul's vision of a world in which humanity is made the slave of its own technique. In order to achieve the ends of science (represented by Forester's search for the *prima materia*), humanity must first free itself from the products of science (the humanoids).

The robots thus become a barrier image not unlike the hull of the spaceship or the wall of the city: artificial constructs, products of technology, that have somehow gone awry and prevent human beings from achieving their true potential. Only in this novel the barrier is behavioral rather than physical; it is no longer a matter of merely escaping the city or discovering the true nature of the starship, but rather of discovering the true nature of humanity's place in the universe. Just as Williamson's barrier is more perfect than these earlier barrier images, so his solution must be more grandiose. Some sort of synthesis between aggression and protection must be worked out in order for man to survive, but such a synthesis is not possible in a purely mechanistic universe in which the robot, as in Wright's "Automata," is god; thus "With Folded Hands" offered no solution. But Campbell's psi phenomena do seem to offer the potential for synthesis, and the discovery of this potential is what makes up the second half of Williamson's narrative.

Forester takes up with a group of rebels who seek to reprogram the controlling brain of the robots to strengthen their obedience command. Among this group is a little girl, Jane Carter, who has psychic gifts that are described as "super-mechanical" (p. 99)—indicating that the mind can indeed transcend the laws of a mechanistic universe. As if to reinforce the notion of the robot as tool (which again becomes a viable notion given this "supermechanical" power of humans), Williamson gives us a scene reminiscent of Sturgeon's "Killdozer," in which Jane and Forester flee a bulldozer automated directly by the distant computer. This machine—animated from a distance by another machine—is a crude mechanical version of the kind of power represented in a more sophisticated form by Jane and her comrades (as in Sturgeon's *More Than Human,* each of the members of the resistance has only one specific psychic power; it is the synthesis of these powers that represents the totality of human psychic ability).

Womb imagery, which we have seen earlier operating in tales of spaceships and cities, appears again in this part of *The Humanoids.* The group of rebels is hidden in "'a far, dark place, underground'" (p. 88) where "'you can hear water running'" and "'there's no opening in the rocks, and no way in but by teleportation'" (p. 88). There is, of course, no way out either, and if Forester is to survive—to escape from what might otherwise be a grave—he must be "reborn" psychically by developing the powers that Jane and her friends have already attained. By way of contrast, Forester notes that the humanoids would "'like to keep us all nice and cozy in the womb'" (p. 103) of their endless solicitude. But this womb imagery is also evolutionary imagery: by their perfect enforcement of the status quo, the machines prevent the birth of a new kind of humanity; as Victor Ferkiss says of technologies that "make man irrevocably dependent on lower orders of reality," they are "antievolutionary."[24] The birth imagery, then, suggests not only a birth of a new kind of man, but a birth of the synthesis between mechanistic and humanistic cosmologies. This synthesis, it turns out, lies in the science of "rhodomagnetics"—the force that at once powers the robots and accounts for the psychic power of the rebels. (The pseudoscientific details with which Williamson works out this new science are ingenious, but less important than the philosophical assumption that such a force might exist in the universe.)

The context of the narrative has thus been expanded to demonstrate that the opposition between man and machine, psychic and mechanical, mind and matter, are parts of a larger whole represented by Williamson's term for metaphysics, "rhodomagnetics." At this point, the dialectical structure of the novel as a whole becomes clear, and might even be diagrammed:

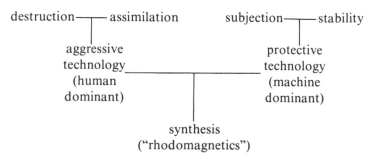

The novel began by showing us the destructive and assimilative aspects of aggressive technology, or man-driven technology, in its brief exposition of the series of planetary explorations and nuclear wars that provided the historical background for the society in which the narrative takes place. With the introduction of the robots, the equally dual nature of protective, or machine-driven technology became apparent. Now, however, it becomes apparent that both of these branches of technology might be synthesized in "rhodomagnetics," and the goal of narrative action is to achieve this synthesis.

It is not very surprising, given the patterns of iconography that we have already explored, that at this key point in the novel barrier-imagery should appear. Jane's attempts to explore the home planet of the humanoids, where the controlling brain is located, are thwarted by "'a barrier that kept her out of the dome'" (p. 114). The barrier represents the machine's growing awareness of "psychophysical" powers and its efforts to assimilate these powers into its own mechanism, thus controlling human beings directly. One of the humanoids explains:

"The final result of this research will be the perfected paramechanical grid. Any human body under its direction will be operated far more efficiently than is ever possible by the slow, uncertain biochemical processes of the natural brain. It can regulate men to prevent all the accidents caused by their clumsy feebleness. It can stimulate the restoration of lost or damaged members, and correct the faulty functions which so often impair the well-being of fragile human bodies and minds. It can even mend the decay of time, to make men almost as durable as our own units." [Pp. 132-33]

The protective technology of the humanoids threatens to achieve this synthesis before the rebels do, thus assuring a machine-dominant technology and hence a purely mechanistic universe. The threat of human beings becoming machines, implicit perhaps in all robot stories, is about to be realized.

To fend off despair, Forester resorts to meditating on his original quest: the discovery of a *prima materia*—and quickly discovers it: "It merely stated the relation and equivalence of electromagnetic and rhodomagnetic and psychophysical energies, as involved most simply in the equilibrium of a stable atomic particle—revealing all three as different aspects of the single basic unity science had ever sought" (p. 138). One is tempted to say that Forester has discovered the Trinity, that the old science of ferromagnetics (the Father) gave birth to the new science of rhodomagnetics (the Son), which is informed by psychophysics (the Holy Ghost). In any event, he responds to the vision as though it were a revelation, and, sure enough, he is awarded with grace: almost at once he achieves superior psychophysical abilities, escaping from the humanoids and creating out of his own mind a safe habitat for himself and Jane on a desolate planet on the edge of the galaxy. In keeping with the supernatural nature of his new abilities, these feats are performed unconsciously, like the miracles of primitive shamans. It is during his exile into this wilderness that Forester derives "'complete mathematical descriptions for all the psychophysical phenomena'" (p. 149)—a complete nontechnological science.

But in the last three chapters of the novel, Williamson offers a strange and unconvincing reversal—unconvincing dramatically because a few pages of mystical explanation cannot hope to reverse the visceral fear of the humanoids the novel has ingrained in us for over 150 pages, and unconvincing structurally because it appears to revert to an Asimovian mechanistic universe, in which the next step in human evolution cannot take place without the interference of machines. Forester attempts to use his newfound power to destroy the humans who have made a compact with the humanoids, and suddenly, the brilliant philosopher-scientist of a few pages earlier is portrayed as a raving paranoid: "'I'm going to smash your plot with the humanoids—this monstrous Compact to smother and mechanize all the human race. I'm going to fight the machines for a better deal'" (p. 158), and so on. The reversal is not very convincing in terms of character either, although Williamson

171

had made a few attempts early in the novel to portray Forester as cold, inaccessible, and inconsiderate toward his wife (who subsequently fell in love with Ironsmith). Forester's attempts at murder fail, one of his intended victims rather lamely explains, because the psychophysical power is "creative" and "cannot be used for such destructive purposes" (p. 160)—implying that psychophysics does not necessarily represent the final synthesis, but that there is a supernatural force that decides what is creative and what is destructive. Mind and matter might be synthesized in psychophysics, but the result is only one leg of a final dichotomy—between man and god, perhaps. "'It is another higher synthesis,'" the inventor of the humanoids later explains to Forester, "'on another level of unfolding creation—and no one not a mystic can see what lies beyond'" (p. 170). As in Clarke's *The City and the Stars,* Williamson's extrapolation has led him into a mystical cul-de-sac. The humanoids, after all, are "'just a tool,'" "'just an instrument'" (p. 170) to help man achieve his new eminence, and the barrier-grid is for "education," since "'any society must shape and train its members'" (p. 169). Ironically, it is Mansfield, the inventor of the humanoids, who in this same speech argues that a "'runaway physical technology—killing us like the runaway cells of an organic cancer'" (p. 170) is what had made the creation of the humanoids necessary. But by "physical technology," he apparently means what I have termed "aggressive technology," technology that serves man rather than protects him. The creation of the humanoids presumably served to correct this imbalance. "'Such technicians as yourself,'" Mansfield tells Forester, "'had wrecked the balance of civilization. . . . The humanoids simply made them take a holiday until the philosophers could restore a better equilibrium'" (p. 168).

Williamson is not totally unaware of the ambiguity of his ending, however. Forester is reconditioned into this new world (it takes fifty years), and when he awakens is invited to go with Jane to start a new colony on a planet so distant that the rhodomagnetic beams that control the humanoids cannot reach there. The newly programmed Forester is apprehensive about being without the humanoids, but looks forward to starting a new society with Jane (who has of course grown up by now). As Alfred Stewart observes, "There are positive and negative aspects to this slavery," since humanity "could be given supernal powers without being a slave to the Prime Directive." And Stewart adds, rather generously, "This could be a plot flaw."[25] In fact, it is a flaw in the entire ideological conception of the novel, since if the synthesis which Williamson touts as providing the solution to the man-machine opposition were genuine, it should no longer be necessary for machines and human beings to maintain such a precarious check and balance on each other. The notion of a human society evolving for a few years without the humanoids, however, seems to provide a temporary alternative: if the society succeeds, perhaps the synthesis will be achieved after all.

Like much science fiction, *The Humanoids* introduces a problem that is highly visible in our own society, but proposes a solution that is achievable only with the aid of something akin to grace: if we passively allow technology to follow its course, things will be terrible for a while, but there *might* be a way of transcending the problem through evolutionary change. That hardly provides an answer to the nightmare vision conjured up by a work like Ellul's *Technological Man* (and Williamson's humanoids may in some sense be read as Ellul's "technique" made manifest), but the implicit philosophy in Williamson's work does seem to offer a partial philosophical solution, and it is a solution that coincides remarkably with that proposed by Victor Ferkiss in *Technological Man: the Myth and the Reality*. Ferkiss suggests that humanity may maintain control of its technological society by evolving a "tripartite philosophy" consisting of "the *new naturalism*, which asserts that man is in fact part of nature rather than something apart from it," and that he "gains in dignity as he is seen as part of physical nature, while his most complex mechanical creations pale into insignificance" (p. 250); "the *new holism*, that is, the realization of how interconnected everything is . . . The image of the mechanical universe must give way to the idea of process" (p. 251); and "the *new immanentism*," which realizes that the world of living things "is somehow different" and that creation comes from within, not without (p. 252). It is not difficult to see how Williamson's psychophysics embodies Ferkiss's notions of naturalism and immanentism, and how the relationship of this energy with other energies in atomic structure illustrates the "new holism."

In the end, Williamson's humanoids serve much the same function as the Overlords in Clarke's *Childhood's End*. Like the alien Overlords, they at first seem all-powerful and thrust an unasked-for utopia upon humanity, resulting in the gradual decay of science and culture; like the Overlords, they later appear as demonic monsters; and like the Overlords, they are finally revealed as simply midwives to the evolution of a racial consciousness. Both novels deal ultimately with the transformation of humanity into a higher stage of evolutionary consciousness, and both employ a traditional science-fiction icon as an

173

image of this transformation—aliens in Clarke and robots in Williamson. But Williamson's ending is decidedly more ambiguous than that of Clarke, since in Clarke's novel the humans eventually leave the Overlords behind in order to join the Overmind, while in *The Humanoids* the precarious balance between man and machine remains. One is left with the gnawing suspicion that at the end of *The Humanoids,* as at the end of "With Folded Hands," "There is nothing left to do."

THE RE-CREATION OF HUMANITY

An idea implicit in Williamson's immanentism is that the mechanistic universe finally seems to exist to serve humanity; the phrase "deus ex machina," so familiar in its ironic reification in works in which machines appear to supersede human beings (the phrase appeared in Wright's "Automata," in *The Humanoids,* and it appears in D. F. Jones's *Colossus* [1966], an updated and computerized version of "With Folded Hands"), finally is restored to its original meaning of an unlikely mechanism that helps humanity out of a difficult scrape—in this case, an evolutionary cul-de-sac. But a more literal version of deus ex machina also exists in science fiction, in the stories whose common theme is that the mechanistic universe exists to *create* man (a variation on this is a smaller group of stories in which technology attains god-like status and is used to protect humanity from a nonmechanical Creator; in both Clifford D. Simak's early "The Creator" [1933] and Lester del Rey's "For I Am a Jealous People" [1954], humanity aligns itself with technology in opposition to a spiritual god, suggesting that the universe of man is informed by a demiurge of technology rather than of natural creation). The general formula of such stories is that humanity indeed creates superior beings through its technology and later dies out, but that these mechanical beings, near-perfect as they may be, strive to re-create man in order to discover the purpose of their own existence. In other words, God literally becomes a machine.

Not all these stories follow this mythology through to the creation of humanity, but nearly all of them give evidence that the creation of artificial intelligence is one of science fiction's standard means of exploring the nature of cosmic creation, and by extension the nature of humanity's own origins. The first stage of this myth we have already seen in Wright, Asimov, and Williamson: humanity appears to create a godlike being from its own technology. It is also apparent in D. F. Jones's *Colossus* (1966), in which the computer that has taken over the world predicts "'that many of your species will come to regard me as

God'";[26] in Martin Caidin's *The God Machine* (1968); in Olof Johannesson's *The Tale of the Big Computer* (1966); in David Gerrold's *When Harlie Was One* (1972); and in Frank Herbert's *Destination: Void* (1966). As he has with many such common science-fiction themes, Fredric Brown has neatly encapsulated the sense of this one in a short anecdote. "Answer" describes the formal ceremony surrounding the switching on of the ultimate computer, "one cybernetics machine that would combine all the knowledge of all the galaxies." The first question asked of the new machine is, "'Is there a God?'" and the computer promptly answers, "'Yes, *now* there is a God,'" and a bolt of lightning fuses the switch open.[27]

But what eschatological purpose can such a machine god have? An answer, of sorts, is provided in Asimov's story "The Last Question" (1956), which Maxine Moore has termed "the robot story to end all robot stories."[28] In this tale, the endless benefits of technology are represented by the massive computer, AC, which enables humanity to make a series of technological and psychic leaps toward pure intelligence. The computer seems to have the answers to all problems except the one of universal entropy, and at the end of every successive technological advancement, the computer is again asked if entropy can be reversed. Each time the computer answers that it has insufficient data for such a question; technology can answer all questions but one. But the technological advances that Asimov imagines carry humanity steadily along toward a kind of Teilhardian Omega Point, toward the final union of the mechanistic and the organic. The earliest step in this progression is the development of solar power, which provides an endless source of energy and thus enables humanity to take the second step: interstellar travel, which permits the appropriation of immortality, which in turn permits the appropriation of time as well as space. The fourth step is the liberation of body from mind, with disembodied intelligences roaming the universe leaving their immortal bodies behind. The disembodied intelligences, in turn, give rise to universal mind, leaving as the only alternative the computer itself. At this point, the only intelligences left in the universe are those of humanity and AC, of humanity and machine; the dualism implicit in all robot stories is abstracted to cosmic proportions. The sixth step, undertaken only as the universe begins to die from entropy, is the merging of human and artificial intelligence: humanity joins AC; the mechanistic and psychic universes, the phenomenal and noumenal, are finally united, and the phenomenal universe dies. For "a timeless interval," AC continues to work on the problem of entropy, since "until this last question was answered also,

175

AC might not release his consciousness."[29] In the final sentences of the story, Asimov resorts to Biblical language: "And it came to pass that AC learned how to reverse the direction of entropy" (p. 190). It accomplishes this, as should by now be apparent, with the realization that AC itself is god, and it issues the command, "'LET THERE BE LIGHT!'" (p. 190). And the universe is created anew.

It is interesting to note that, in the final passages of this story, when human and machine intelligences have apparently achieved the synthesis to which they had long been tending, Asimov continues to refer to this intelligence as AC, the computer. Even in the final synthesis, the machine is superior to man, and without the machine there can be no creation. The technocratic message is clear: if we fail to exploit our machines, we are denying not only the future of man, but the purpose of creation itself. Presumably the cycle of creation-life-humanity-machine and finally humanity-machine synthesis will continue in this newly created cosmos, and the whole process will repeat itself infinitely. As Maxine Moore writes: "The completed structure implies that the Creator, who is the First Cause, is also the ultimate Effect, the divine Robot in which the Law reposes. In that sense, man has always manufactured his gods, tended them, anointed them, and then idealized them, and all the while has abused them, and blamed them. Technology today is merely another of many servant gods."[30] Humanity exists to build the machine, which in turn exists to create humanity: perhaps the simplest and most characteristic validation of humanity in a mechanistic universe in all of science fiction, because it depends on nothing more than the simple mechanistic cause-effect extrapolation that Moore has pointed out, and it neatly sidesteps issues of art and culture.

Another story in this vein, and one that slyly acknowledges its debt to Asimov's robot stories, is Lester del Rey's "Instinct" (1951), in which robots are afraid to improve themselves because of a distant memory of humanity, which apparently had tried to change itself and had died out as a result: "'Man is the whole key to our problem of whether we can change or not without risking extermination.'"[31] The robots also realize they had been created by human beings ("somebody—Asimov or Asenion, the record wasn't quite clear—had apparently created the first robot" (p. 101), but firmly believe that "'nobody can build a race better than itself, so Man must have been better than we are'" (p. 101). But humanity had died out before reaping the full benefits of its technology; it did not achieve faster-than-light travel, for example, because it failed to discover "the trick of identity exchange to overcome the limitation imposed by the speed of light" (this suggests an influence of

Williamson's *The Humanoids* as well, since "identity exchange" is the phrase used to explain the teleportation abilities of Jane and others [p. 115]). The robots believe that "instinct" was the key difference between human beings and machines, but when they finally succeed in re-creating a man, and educating him to speak, they quickly discover that they, too, have instincts: when the new man impatiently asks "'What do you want?'" the robot who created him bows and answers, "'Nothing, Master. Only to serve you'" (p. 112). Virtually the same story is told in Brian Aldiss's "But Who Can Replace a Man?" (1958), in which a society of advanced robots discovers a last surviving man and immediately becomes his servants. In these stories, the man is clearly neither coequal nor inferior to the machines, and he is as much the raison d'être of the mechanistic universe as its inhabitant.

What it is that sets humanity apart from the machine is not clearly explored in much science fiction of this period during which the mythology of robotics evolved, but it does provide the basis of two interesting stories that were written near the beginning and the end of the period. Robert Moore William's "Robot's Return" (1938) shares with del Rey's "Instinct" an imagined society of future robots who have only vague and near-mythical notions of what humanity was. Long after the human race has died out, a group of these robots return to earth and begin excavating for evidence of their origins. "'How can we build securely when we do not know what our past has been?'" askes one of the robots. "'It is important to us to know whether we are descended from whatever gods there are, or whether we have evolved from some lower form.'"[32] The answer, of course, is both: the robots are at once the successors of humanity and of its machines, and the evidence they later uncover reveals this dual ancestry. First, they encounter an elevator and cannot decide whether it is a machine or "'one of our early life-forms'" (p. 150):

> Eight stared at the rust-flecked wheels, the crumbling, corroded bulk of the motor housings, the gears falling away into ruin. This, a robot—! He rebelled at the thought. Yet it was hard to know where mechanism left off and robot began. The dividing line was thin. You took inanimate metal and the pressure of exploding force; you worked the metal into a thousand different parts and you confined the force; you added a brain that was in itself a force-field capable of receiving and retaining impressions—and you had a robot. You left out the brain—and you had a machine. [P. 150]

The robots realize that they themselves are vaguely related to this primitive, insentient machine. "'When you attempt to make us more

177

than machines, you become illogical'" (p. 151), one robot cautions; as in nearly all science-fiction robot societies, simple mechanical logic is the guiding force of the robots' mentality. But the missing link between machine and robot remains to be discovered. Later the robots come upon a statue of a human—"a lifeless thing" (p. 153), but one that demonstrates to the robots that this is indeed the planet of their origins. Eight, the robot who had discovered the elevator, sees something more than mechanical replication in this statue, and feels "that the statue represented something more, that it was more than a replica of form— that it was the embodiment of an idea. But what that idea was, he could not grasp" (p. 153). He concludes it is a fallen god, a representation of the transcendent organism that created the robots in the first place. Before the robots leave, Eight looks again at the statue and meditates on what humans might have been: "'They may have eaten the flesh of other animals; they may have been weaklings; they may have arisen out of slime, but somehow I think there was something fine about them. For they dreamed, and even if they died—'" (p. 156). The robot sets the statue back on its feet and departs.

Sharing as it does the wistful sentimentality of much other science fiction of this period, "Robot's Return" is nevertheless a significant early attempt at dealing with the schism between humanity's aesthetic creations and its mechanical ones. The dual image of human beings in the story—mechanical replication and the form of the statue—suggests clearly that there is an important aspect of human consciousness that cannot be easily carried over into a purely mechanical civilization, that there exists a valid universe of feeling apart from technology, and that, in its own Ozymandias-like way, it too will survive. The robots in this story clearly are creatures that inhabit a borderland between the technology represented by the elevator and the humanism represented by the statue.

Statues and images of art are also significant in Roger Zelazny's "For a Breath I Tarry" (1966), one of the most complex and self-consciously mythical treatments of the relationship between humanity and its machines in all of science fiction and a far more rewarding work than Asimov's "The Last Question," with which it shares a mechanistic creation myth. Like Asimov, Zelazny resorts to pseudo-Biblical rhetoric to tell the story of Frost, a massive computer that continues to monitor and control the northern hemisphere of the earth long after humanity has died out. Frost in turn is supervised by a satellite computer, Solcom, which vies for control of the earth with a subterranean computer named

Divcom, which was activated during a period of temporary damage to Solcom. Frost becomes the pawn in a contest of power between Solcom and Divcom, and is tempted by Mordel, an agent of Divcom, to begin investigating the nature of human beings, and eventually to become a man. The story depends upon a clever reversal of the known-unknown antinomy by treating humanity as the unknown and posing a series of barriers to Frost in his growing understanding of human beings. After striking his bargain with Mordel (either to become a man or join the service of Divcom), Frost begins to read the surviving books of humanity. In subsequent episodes, he encounters the Ore-Crusher, a kind of Wandering Jew condemned to wander the earth telling his tale of how he accidentally crushed the last man; strays into the southern hemisphere, which is controlled by another computer named Beta, to visit the Bright Defile where many of humanity's art works survive; attempts to create works of art himself in order to demonstrate his humanness; constructs a laboratory to explore the physiological nature of man; and finally discovers some long-frozen human bodies from which he manages to clone new humans and endow one with his own consciousness, thus completing the re-creation of man and—as in del Rey's "Instinct" or Aldiss's "But Who Can Replace a Man?"—attaining mastery over all the machines which control earth.

The analogs with both Genesis and Faust are at once apparent: Frost is Adam in the Garden (Earth), serving the Lord (Solcom) but tempted by an agent (Mordel) of the devil (Divcom) with the promise of knowledge. At the end of the story, he even invites Beta to join him in humanity as Eve. But the story is more complex than such a simple analog would indicate, and Zelazny has been careful to construct it according to an intricate series of oppositions leading to the final resolution in the creation of man and the restoration of the fundamental opposition between humanity and the machine that is its central theme. Solcom and Divcom, for example, represent not only God and the devil, or good and evil (in the Old Testament sense), but also the heavens and the earth—the twin nature of humanity as expressed in the astral and the chthonic. Edmund Leach writes, "In every myth system we will find a persistent sequence of binary discriminations . . . followed by a 'mediation' of the paired categories thus distinguished."[33] In Zelazny's story, this mediation is initially represented by the surface of the earth, situated between Solcom and Divcom, where Frost resides and where the action of the story takes place. But on the surface, too, there are oppositions, represented at first between Frost and Mordel, as the

179

"mortal" agents of Solcom and Divcom, later between Frost and Beta, as masculine and feminine principles, and finally between man and machine, as Frost and Beta inherit the world of machines.

But the opposition between humanity and machine underlies the narrative long before the final re-creation of humanity. At the beginning, humanity is nothing more than Frost's "hobby,"[34] a kind of personal aberration that itself stands in opposition to the purely logical carrying out of meaningless functions that characterizes both Solcom and Divcom. The first mediator between mankind and machine, then, is Mordel, who tempts Frost to make something of his hobby and challenges him to become a man (pp. 368-69). It is Mordel who first makes Frost aware of some of the basic oppositions between humanity and machine, by arguing that the truth of humanity can only be achieved through phenomenal rather than noumenal understanding; he even begins to sound like Kant when he argues that machines can measure cold but not feel it: they can be "'aware of its existence, but not of the thing itself'" (p. 368). "'A machine is a Man turned inside-out,'" explains Mordel, "'because it can describe all the details of a process, which a Man cannot, but it cannot experience that process itself, as a Man can'" (p. 369). Further oppositions are thus set up: between phenomenal and noumenal, sense and measurement, organic and inorganic.

The most fundamental of these oppositions, however, is between art and science: Mordel has brought Frost a copy of A. E. Housman's *A Shropshire Lad,* among other things, and Frost is so far unable to appreciate the aesthetic qualities of the poetry, such as rhyme. He constructs artificial human sense organs for himself and visits, with Mordel, a scenic area of what once was California, but is still unable to perceive beauty, suspecting "'none remains after so long a time'" (p. 376). But Mordel replies, "'It is not supposed to be the sort of thing which gets used up,'" (p. 376), suggesting yet another opposition related to art and science: the functional immortality of machines constantly repairing themselves as opposed to the aesthetic immortality of the natural world.

Mordel, initially the mediator between mankind and machine in order to tempt Frost, attains in his successive debates with Frost the role of machine, and for much of the narrative the argument, or opposition, is between Frost and Mordel, Frost arguing for the possibility of humanity and Mordel arguing against. Another mediator is introduced between humanity and the machine: the Ore-Crusher, which is essentially an industrial robot with far fewer capabilities than any of the intelligent computers, but which retains some of the power of mankind from simply containing the remains of the last man. The specific human power that the Ore-Crusher retains is the ability to command other machines: all machines must stop and listen to the Ore-Crusher's story when it so commands. "'You must do whatever it says,'" Mordel explains to Frost (p. 377). The Ore-Crusher is also the only machine on earth not subject to the orders of other machines; thus it is the only machine fully capable of identifying a man. Frost realizes from this encounter that he has not yet attained humanity.

But Frost is gradually moving toward manhood, and another opposition is introduced in the Bright Defile episode. By straying into the southern hemisphere, Frost for the first time clearly disobeys, and the ability to disobey is further evidence of his becoming human—a clear contrast to the work of Asimov, which argues that a man can retain his humanity without enjoying the luxury of disobedience to his mechanical masters. The disobedience is clearly worked out by Zelazny so as not to make Frost quite fully human, however: Frost argues that he has "'violated no directive,'" and Solcom responds that he has "'broken the traditions of order'" (p. 383). Order, too, is part of the mechanistic world of the computers, and Frost's introduction of disorder creates still another binary opposition. This episode also introduces the figure of Beta, and thus the male-female oppositions that will culminate in the Adam and Eve analog. Beta is a passive servant to Solcom, and this passivity is contrasted with Frost's action. She occupies the south to his north, the land of fire to his land of Frost, the stationary to his mobile. It might be reasonably argued that to assign such characteristics as feminine smacks of sexual stereotyping, but it is a kind of stereotyping firmly entrenched in many patterns of myth, particularly the Norse mythologies.

In the following episode, the primary opposition is between art and mechanics, with Frost himself as the intermediary. Frost attempts to create a work of art like those he has seen in the Bright Defile, and Mordel, playing the devil's advocate as ever, responds with mechanistic logic to his successive failures. But each failure takes Frost closer to humanness. First he reproduces exactly a statue of an old woman he saw in the Defile, and when Mordel argues this is only a copy, Frost produces a cube of stone that he insists is "'a statue of me.'" When Mordel argues that this is not art, because art "'is not an exact replication of an object in another medium,'" Frost rather petulantly responds, "'What makes you an art critic?'" (p. 385)—a decidedly human response. Furthermore, Frost has already progressed from a replica of an existing work to a replica of a perceived object—a step closer to human art. When, on his third attempt at art, he creates an oil painting with randomized colors for the landscape, he puzzles even Mordel. Frost is very close to achieving art—and thus humanity—even though he has so far failed, as human artists had, to "'portray with their techniques some feature of objects and their function which they deemed significant'" (p. 386). Frost still does not know what "significant" means in human terms. But the introduction of randomness as opposed to order creates yet another opposition that is part of the larger one between humanity and machine.

The oppositions I have already mentioned are elaborated in various ways throughout the rest of the story. Beta assumes a further stereotypical feminine characteristic when she offers to help Frost process his data—playing the feminine supportive role—and the distinction between human significance and mechanical logic is pointed up in a brief argument between Frost and Mordel over a quarter-mile difference over where a bridge should be built—even though the bridge has no traffic to carry. Finally, Frost constructs his laboratory and begins experimenting with the human bodies he has found, and the central opposition of the story, that between humanity and machine, is made manifest. Here Solcom himself assumes the role of the mechanistic as opposed to the human: the god figure earlier in the story has become the synthesis of all machine intelligence, working in opposition to the re-creation of man with Frost as the intermediary. Frost's final disobedience is too much for Solcom: "'Frost, you are fallen now from my favor. From this moment forth you are cast out from the rebuilding. None may question the plan'" (p. 394). One might initially wonder about the theology implicit in reversing the order of the creation of man and the expulsion from the Garden, but one must also remember that this is not merely a retelling of Genesis, but a myth of the machine age: the "order" of a mechanistic universe is indeed disturbed by the introduction of human beings.

Frost succeeds in transferring his matrix and experiences fear and withdrawal and finally despair. He quickly returns to his mechanical body, but Solcom and Divcom realize he has succeeded, and with the aid of Mordel, Frost is returned to the human body. The Ore-Crusher appears and obeys his command to go away, proving Frost's humanity and at the same time re-establishing the master-servant relationship of man and machine. Finally, Frost understands the poem from *A Shropshire Lad* that gives the story its title, and quotes it as an invitation to Beta to join him in humanity—at the same time suggesting the opposition between mortality and machine, since the poem deals with human mortality. The opposition between Solcom and Divcom is resolved as each is given command of a hemisphere of the earth, replacing Frost and Beta; the astral and chthonic are brought together on the surface of the earth, the domain of man. All the earlier oppositions among machines are resolved into the unity of serving man, and we are left with the more fundamental and culturally acceptable antimonies of male-female and mankind-machine, all in their proper order. The function of the machines is fulfilled in the re-creation of man, and the role of humanity in a mechanistic universe is finally revealed: humanity is its purpose.

7

icon of the monster

That I may reduce the monster to
Myself, and then may be myself

In face of the monster, be more than part
Of it, more than the monstrous player of

One of its monstrous lutes, not be
Alone . . .

Wallace Stevens, "The Man with the Blue Guitar"

A HIERARCHY OF MONSTERS

Probably the most common formula for science-fiction titles is the phrase "the _____ man," with an appropriate adjective inserted to indicate that the title character is no *ordinary* human being. The examples are almost endless, and start with Mary Shelley's *The Last Man* (1816). Since then, we have had *The Invisible Man* (Wells), *The Illustrated Man* (Bradbury), *The Demolished Man* (Bester), *The Synthetic Man* (Sturgeon), *The Shrinking Man* (Matheson), "The Minimum Man" and "The Impacted Man" (Sheckley), *The Transcendent Man* (Sohl), *The Evolution Man* (Roy Lewis), *The Infinite Man* (Galouye), "The Alley Man" (Farmer), "The Variable Man" (Dick), "The Gnarly Man" (DeCamp), *The Isotope Man* (Maine), *The Stochastic Man* (Silverberg), "The Subliminal Man," "The Impossible Man," and "The Overloaded Man" (all Ballard), *The Terminal Man* (Crichton), *The Duplicated Man* (Blish), *The Whole Man* (Brunner), "The Jigsaw Man" (Niven)—not to mention such variations as "the man who" or such contributions from film and television as *The Omega Man* or "The Six Million Dollar Man." The list might go on and on, and any true science-fiction devotee has probably already thought of several more examples. A few of these titles are metaphoric, but most refer to actual transformations undergone by the characters in question, and all reflect the common notion that the human form is at best a fragile condition. This vulnerability of form is only one of the hidden fears that science-fiction monsters represent, but it is one of the most powerful. To be human, the science-fiction writers tell us, is to be surrounded by alien forces and unknown factors, by creatures and things that are clearly *not* human and that yet somehow survive and grow. Nonhuman life is one of the key images of the unknown in science fiction, and the ways in which people interact with it and are reminded of their own humanity (or "humanness") by it constitute one of the genre's most enduring and fascinating themes.

For the most part, the transformations suggested by the titles I have listed above represent only one kind of monster, the altered or deformed human, represented most often in science fiction by either biological mutations (as in van Vogt's *Slan* [1940] or Kuttner's *Mutant* [1953]) or what has popularly come to be termed "bionics"—mechanically or surgically restructured humans (as in Smith's "Scanners Live in Vain" [1948] or Pohl's *Man Plus* [1975]). Even in the stories in which such characters are sympathetically portrayed, the point is made that others regard them as monsters, as frightening challenges to the concept of what it is to be human. Indeed, in much pulp and movie science fiction, a "mutation" is invariably a horrible beast, lacking either human intelligence or speech. But such figures represent only one category of what amounts to a hierarchy of monster-images in science fiction that ranges literally from the mineral to the spiritual.

Before we explore this hierarchy, however, we might speculate on the sources of wonder that give the monster its peculiar power over the human mind. The image of the monster is probably the oldest and simplest symbol of transformation in science fiction, and the one in which the individual most directly confronts the forces of the unknown in an "I-thou" relationship that suggests the view of nature embodied in primitive mythology. As H. A. Frankfort describes it, this view is anything but "scientific":

> In "understanding" a fellow-creature . . . a man or an animal is essentially passive, whatever his subsequent action may turn out to be. For at first he receives an impression. This type of knowledge is therefore direct, emotional, and inarticulate. Intellectual knowledge, on the contrary, is emotionally indifferent and articulate. . . .
>
> . . . In this confrontation, "Thou" reveals its individuality, its qualities, its will. "Thou" is not contemplated with intellectual detachment; it is experienced as life confronting life, involving every faculty of man in a reciprocal relationship. Thoughts, no less than acts and feelings, are subordinated to this experience.[1]

185

In other words, when we are dealing with the image of the monster, we are dealing with an image of the unknown that generates initially a nonrational response; the unknown becomes an iconic "Thou" rather than an abstract formulation. It is a confrontation on the most elemental level, and the only way to deal with it in science fiction is to learn as much as possible about the creature, to be able to categorize its various aspects into classes of what is known and thus to begin to understand it. The failure of humans to do this is what causes them to regard the mutant protagonists of such works as van Vogt's *Slan* and Kuttner's *Mutant* as monsters; and aliens remain truly alien only to the extent that we are unable to apply scientific understanding to them. The struggle of a protagonist to thus understand an alien or monster before others give in to the primitive urge to destroy it is a common plot in science fiction. The tension between understanding and panic has long been one of the hidden sources of science fiction's power, and it is worth speculating for a moment on its meaning. At its most immediate level, the image of the monster brings to the surface all the fears of deformity and impurity that characterize racism, and it is thus not surprising to discover that, in much early twentieth-century science fiction, the role of aliens was often fulfilled by images of a "Yellow Peril" or a Jewish conspiracy—both characterize the later work of M. P. Shiel, whose best work (*The Purple Cloud* [1901]) ironically became the basis of a movie sermon on race relations (*The World, the Flesh, and the Devil* [1959]). Jack London's science fiction also reveals a fear of nonwhite races in stories such as "An Unparalleled Invasion" (1910), and the theme may even be said to crop up in a much more sophisticated guise in more recent stories involving sexual relations with aliens (such as Philip Jose Farmer's "The Lovers" [1952]).

But there is a more fundamental source for the power of monsters in science fiction. The oldest monsters, as exemplified by the figure of Enkidu in the ancient *Gilgamesh* epic, are agents of uncreated Chaos, and still today the icon of the beast suggests the flow of unreason that underlies all the rational structures of science that science fiction pretends to exploit. Monsters, says Cirlot, "allude to the deepest strata of spiritual geology, seething as in a volcano until they erupt in the shape of some monstrous apparition or activity."[2] In a genre in which the humanness of man is often overshadowed by wonders of technology and vast historical patterns, the beast stands as an inescapable and extreme reminder of our own animality, of what we may have been and what we may yet become, of "the sterile madness that lies in men's hearts." The monster is the bipolar opposite, according to Cirlot, of weapons, and for "weapons" we may read "technology." If technology is the systematic appropriation and ordering of natural forces, the monster is the spontaneous bursting forth of those forces in strange and terrible guises.

In kind, these monsters may take the form of autochthons, aliens, altered humans, or machines; in form, they may range from the mineral to the purely spiritual, with all the gradations of the natural world in between. In all cases, they serve to remind us of our earthly animal origins, by rising literally from the earth itself (as in the case of mineral or vegetable monsters), by making us aware of our terrestriality (as in the case of aliens from space), by emphasizing our physical and psychological vulnerability (as in the case of altered humans), or by suggesting the "trap" of our very physical form (as in the case of creatures of pure mind).

The symbolism that surrounds monsters may be as suggestive as the monsters themselves. Since monsters symbolize the unknown, the encounter with the monster is often brought about either by humans breaching the barriers that separate them from the monster's realm, or vice versa. These barriers may take the form of seas surrounding a mysterious island, jungles or mountains that isolate a lost land, eons of time, or simple walls such as the hull of a spacecraft or the entrance to a tomb. Or they may be metaphoric barriers that scientists breach when achieving research breakthroughs that lead to unknown results. Monsters appear when one moves into an unknown region, or conducts a dangerous experiment, or subjects an individual or a population to an unknown force, or releases unknown forces within the mind itself. No clearer example of the importance of barrier-images to monster lore can be found than in the science-fiction film. Jack Arnold's *The Creature from the Black Lagoon* (1954) depicts several barriers that separate the monster from the known world: the barrier of time (the creature is apparently an evolutionary anachronism), the barrier of geography (the creature inhabits an unexplored area of the Amazon basin), even the barrier of the surface of the water in the Black Lagoon, with the human community represented by the scientists in their boat which rests on the surface, while the underwater world is the realm of the creature. Merian Cooper's *King Kong* (1933) presents at least three substantial barriers that separate the monster from the world of mankind: the uncharted ocean that surrounds Kong's island, the thick fog that envelops the island, and the immense wooden wall that the natives have constructed to keep Kong out.

Kong and the Creature are fairly traditional Hollywood monsters, of course, but science fiction has long since elaborated and refined this

187

traditional monster icon into a virtual hierarchy of life forms that gain their power because they remind us of our origins, our terrestriality, or our physical and psychological limitations. We might even diagram this hierarchy as follows:

human origins	human terrestriality	human form
mineral vegetable animal	aliens	transformed humans "pure mind"

The upper rank lists the sources of the icon's power—what the monsters are associated with—while the lower rank lists specific kinds of monsters. Such a chart necessarily oversimplifies matters, of course, and occasionally a monster will fall into more than one category. The pod people of Jack Finney's *The Body Snatchers* (1954; filmed in 1956 and again in 1978) are at once aliens and vegetables; the added power of the image may come from this dual source of fear. John Wyndham's *Day of the Triffids* (1951) also deals with mankind's relation to outer space (men are blinded by a meteor shower) and mankind's relation to the vegetable world (plants called triffids take over the world). And Michel Bernanos's remarkable fantasy (not really science fiction) *The Other Side of the Mountain* (1967) horrifyingly brings together the two apparent extremes of mind and mineral by depicting humans turning to stone. (The transformation of humans into minerals is common enough in earlier mythologies, with their tales of Medusa and Lot's wife, but the theme remains relatively uncommon in science fiction except for deliberate variations on these earlier myths.) But I should reemphasize that my primary intent is not to classify works of science fiction, but rather to identify and to some extent classify the recurrent sources of wonder in the genre. To do this with monsters, it is necessary to begin at the left side of our chart and investigate some of the ways in which science fiction has drawn on and manipulated the inherent power of some of these monster icons.

MINERAL BEINGS: A. MERRITT AND OTHERS

Let us start with what we might call "mineral beings." Although such creatures may be regarded as one of the purest images of chthonian life and hence of mankind's autochthonous origins, they are comparatively rare in science fiction, partly because it is difficult to rationalize the existence of such a creature. Hence it is not surprising that one of the most memorable examples comes from the science-fiction film, which has never been as concerned with such rationalization as the literature. John Sherwood's film *The Monolith Monsters* (1957), from a story by Jack Arnold and Robert Fresco, concerns a "silicon-based" alien mineral that expands when touched by water, growing into monoliths of black stone that rise and topple over, destroying homes and turning people to stone. As in several earlier films of the creature cycle, the desert setting itself calls to mind the massive geologic forces that suggest the final dominance of mineral forms over biological forms. Appropriately, and in keeping with formula, the hero discovers that the monsters can be inhibited by common salt. I say "in keeping with formula" because this theme of fighting fire with fire, of turning to the natural world to overcome monsters from the natural world after technology has failed, is a common one in science fiction. In H. G. Wells's *The War of the Worlds* (1898), the "way" is bacteria; in the 1963 film of *Day of the Triffids,* it is sea water. The suggestion, I believe, is not that technology is no good, but merely that we must turn to the scientific method itself rather than to the products of that method; we cannot ever rest on our technological laurels. The scientific method in these films, of course, is rather grossly oversimplified, reduced as it is to nothing more than the fortuitous discovery and inductive application of a single key fact that solves the problem. To this extent, science-fiction films resemble mysteries more than science-fiction novels, in which the process of discovering how to overcome the unknown may be considerably more complex.

Another interesting aspect of this film is that the monsters are portrayed as giant crystals, one of the most elemental forms of nature. Crystal seems to be the most common form of mineral monsters in science fiction and fantasy—one thinks of "Crystalman" in David Lindsay's remarkable philosophical fantasy *A Voyage to Arcturus* (1920), of the plague of crystallization in J. G. Ballard's *The Crystal World* (1966), of the crystalline structure of the alien life form in Michael Crichton's *The Andromeda Strain* (novel, 1969; film, 1971) or Stanislaw Lem's *The Invincible* (1967). Perhaps not insignificantly, more than a century before any of these works, German natural philosophers regarded crystal as the most primitive impulse toward life, and Schopenhauer wrote that "the crystal has only *one* manifestation of life, crystallisation, which afterwards has its fully adequate and exhaustive expression in the rigid form, the corpse of that momentary

189

life."[3] The concept of crystalline form manifesting life beyond itself, beyond its own dead symmetry, was the theme of Theodore Sturgeon's novel *The Dreaming Jewels* (1950, paperback title: *The Synthetic Man*), in which a character is literally "dreamt" into existence by the jewels of the title. A more direct autochthonous image of the creation of life out of inanimate matter could hardly be asked for. "Living rock" also cropped up from time to time on the television series *Star Trek* and *Space: 1999*. Conan Doyle, in "When the World Screamed" (1929), extended the notion of living mineral matter to include the planet earth itself: a deep drill pierces a membrane in the earth's crust, and the resulting harrowing scream and appropriate volcanic activity "prove" that the earth is itself a living being.

One of the earliest treatments of this crystalline-beast theme in modern science fiction, and perhaps the earliest attempt to provide a pseudoscientific rationale for such creatures, is A. Merritt's *The Metal Monster* (1920). Generically a "lost civilization" story, *The Metal Monster* describes a hidden city in Asia that is "one living Thing" of metallic consciousness, populated by robotlike creatures that are the product of a separate evolutionary pattern based on crystal. The narrator explains that "'crystals and what we call living matter had an equal start in the first essentials of life.'"[4] "'Lillie concluded that there existed a real metallic consciousness. It was Le Bon who first proved also that metal is more sensitive than man, and that its immobility is only apparent'" (p. 100). "'If Jacques Loeb is right, that action of the iron molecules is every bit as conscious a movement as the least and the greatest of our own. There is absolutely no difference between them'" (p. 100). The persistent citation of late nineteenth-and early twentieth-century scientists such as Jacques Loeb clearly indicate that Merritt, popularly regarded as a fantasy novelist, thought of his metal monsters (which are "fed" by solar energy) as a science-fiction concept; but he places this concept within the context of a mythical society with its own evolution and its own god, a society descended directly from the crystals of metal and rock, and resolutely hostile to organic life. The hostile unknown is thus a grotesque brother of man, born of the same environment but following a completely different evolutionary pattern, sharing the same planet yet unutterably different. With crystal, then, the most fundamental movement toward life in mankind's geologic past is extrapolated into an alien intelligence, suggesting that the real beginning of humanity's alienation from the physical universe may be found in the simple rocks and minerals that surround us.

VEGETABLE BEINGS: JOHN WYNDHAM AND OTHERS

Certainly one of the most recurrent symbols in myth systems is that of vegetation, which is usually associated with the "eternal return" that suggests the immortality of the natural world. But in a myth system like science fiction, which nominally rejects the mystical aspect of nature in favor of the dominion of science, trees and plants take on a less benevolent symbolism: by their power of regeneration and their ability to directly convert sunlight into usable energy, they become ominously alien life forms which, perhaps more than any other kind of monster symbol, make us aware of our autochthony, our animality, and our physical and psychological vulnerability. Uncontrolled plant life becomes an archetypal image of disorder and chaos, just as the archetype of the forest in Jungian symbolism, because it cuts out the clear sunlight of reason and grows indiscriminately, suggests the unconscious. The notion of an intelligent plant, absurd as it may at first seem, is at a deeper level one of the most frightening images of an alien intelligence.

Indeed, it is remarkable how frequently the unknown in science fiction is embodied in some sort of plant life. There are tree-men in Lewis Holberg's early *Journey of Niels Klim to the World Underground* (1726) (and if we wish to go even further back into the ancestry of science fiction, in the paintings of Hieronymous Bosch). H. G. Wells entertained the notion of a man-eating plant in his story "The Flowering of the Strange Orchid" (1894). Creatures that are half-plant, half-animal appear in William Bradshaw's novel *The Goddess of Atvatabar* (1892). Plant creatures were not uncommon villains in the "space operas" of the 1930s, such as Murray Leinster's "Proxima Centauri" (1935), Henry Kuttner's "Raider of the Spaceways" and "The Bloodless Peril" (both 1937), or Clark Ashton Smith's "Marooned on Andromeda" (1930). In the film *The Thing* (1951), based loosely on John W. Campbell's story "Who Goes There?" (1937), the apparently indestructible outer space creature turns out to be somewhat akin to a carrot. Similarly, in Wyndham's *Day of the Triffids* and Finney's *The Body Snatchers* (and the respective films), the invaders take the form of vegetable life. In Murray Leinster's novel *Monster from Earth's End* (1959; filmed as, of all things, *The Navy vs. The Night Monsters*), nasty motile plants provide the terror. Kenneth Gantz's *Not in Solitude* (1959) speculates that the lowly lichens that constitute the only life discovered on Mars have developed a kind of collective intelligence, and both Ward Moore's *Greener Than You Think* (1947) and Paul Tabori's *The Green Rain*

(1961) describe plagues of overabundant fertility among earthly plant life. The "thing" in Nigel Kneale's BBC-TV serial *The Quatermass Experiment* (1953) is described as both plant and animal, but it certainly looks like a plant.

Characteristically, the remarkable Olaf Stapledon was among the first to realize the symbolic significance of plant beings and their potential value as a means of exploring the fundamental tensions of science fiction. His description of plant-men in *Star Maker* (1937) amounts to a sound structural analysis of the way such creatures would function in much later science fiction:

> We did not begin to have insight into the drama of this race till we had learned to appreciate the mental aspect of its dual, animal-vegetable nature. Briefly, the mentality of plant-men in every age was an expression of the varying tension between the two sides of their nature, between the active, assertive, objectively inquisitive, and morally positive animal nature and the passive, subjectively contemplative, and devoutly acquiescent vegetable nature. . . . Spreading their leaves, they had absorbed directly the essential elixir of life which animals receive only at second hand in the mangled flesh of their prey. Thus they seemingly maintained immediate physical contact with the source of all cosmical being.
>   . . . If theological language were acceptable, it might well be called a spiritual contact with God.[5]

The plant-men, in other words, are caught directly between their autochthonous origins and their mechanical and scientific impulses. In Stapledon's narrative, they are described as dual beings who work and build as animals during the night and regenerate themselves from sunlight during the day. Eventually, their science develops a technique of artificial photosynthesis, which makes the daytime periods of sleep and eventually the plant-men's very roots unnecessary. But this movement away from origins takes its toll psychologically:

> A disease of robotism, of purely mechanical living, spread throughout the population. There was of course a fever of industrial activity. The plant-men careered round their planet in all kinds of mechanically propelled vehicles, decorated themselves with the latest synthetic products, tapped the central volcanic heat for power, expended great ingenuity in destroying one another, and in a thousand other feverish pursuits pushed on in search of a bliss which ever eluded them. [P. 340]

Reaction against industrialism sets in, and the plant-men find a way to recapture their original vegetable nature, thus achieving a "plane of spiritual lucidity which was to be an example and a treasure for the future aeons of the galaxy" (p. 340). But the pendulum again swings too far, and the plant-men fail to maintain an ecology that has now become dependent on technology. The result is sickness, despair, and death.

It is not difficult to see in this a cautionary tale of the delicate balance that our own culture must learn to maintain between nature and technology, and indeed Stapledon seems to prefigure Lewis Mumford's worry over the "myth of the machine." But in fact relatively few science-fiction writers over the next twenty-five years would pick up on Stapledon's subtleties about the dangers of overindustrialism, and instead vegetable beings would take on the general aspect of symbols of a natural world that must be overcome through science. Here, after all, is an imaginable being whose whole technology of energy is not dependent on science, but rather on direct communion with "the source of all cosmical being." Their power and intelligence derives from their natural origins rather than linear mechanical development, and as such they may represent that aspect of life that is most in conflict with technocracy. They become a threat not only to science, but to rationality itself, and as images of the proto-rational, they are among the most powerful repositories of the fears associated with the unknown throughout science fiction.

It is this proto-rational aspect of vegetable life that provides the source of horror in Stanley Weinbaum's story "The Lotus Eaters" (1935). A race of plants is discovered on Venus that has intelligence far beyond that of humans, but they allow themselves to be consumed nearly to extinction by a more primitive animal species. The source of this motiveless resignation is explained by one of the human characters: "'Animals have desire and plants necessity. . . . All they do, all they *can* do, is sit before their caves and think. Probably they think godlike thoughts, but they can't summon even a mouse-like will. That's what a vegetable intelligence is; that's what it has to be!'"[6] The humans agree that such a condition is unutterably horrible, and in a metaphor that reveals Weinbaum's own mechanical orientation, the plants are compared to a "powerful gasoline motor with its drive shaft broken." This condition of will-less intelligence becomes a direct threat to the humans when it is discovered that inhaling spores from the bursting pods of the plant-beings results in a narcotic trance that inhibits the will to survive. As the title of the story suggests, the idea is from Homer, but the idle decadence classically represented by lotus-eaters is here expanded to include any intelligence that lacks the "drive shaft" of the urge to technology and appropriation.[7]

193

But the negative aspect of vegetable imagery may lie deeper than its merely being antitechnological. Dominant theories of nature mythology in the nineteenth century suggested the connection between vegetation imagery and human origins and the peculiar power that vegetation has held over the human mind. James Frazer traced a number of examples of primitive tree-worship:

> How serious that worship was in former times may be gathered from the ferocious penalty appointed by the old German laws for such as dared to peel the bark of a standing tree. The culprit's navel was to be cut out and nailed to the part of the tree which he had peeled, and he was to be driven round and round the tree till all his guts were wound about its trunk. The intention of the punishment clearly was to replace the dead bark by a living substitute taken from the culprit; it was a life for a life, the life of a man for the life of a tree.[8]

A recent story by Stephen Tall, "Chlorophyll," recasts this belief in one of the most clearly archetypal treatments of the theme of vegetation in science fiction, and one that demonstrates how vegetation may suggest the unknown that may be appropriated by scientific rationalism. Tall postulates a society of intelligent trees that dominates a world colonized by humanity in the distant future. When humans try to cut one of the trees for lumber, they are felled by a poisonous gas exuded by the tree, and the trees telepathically dominate the human society for the next thousand years. A system of tree-worship evolves in which destruction of any woody shrubbery is a crime, and periodic bloody sacrifices are staged to "feed" the trees. Tall's description of what happens to the bodies of the sacrificial victims is a literal realization of the return of humanity to its origins through the agency of vegetation:

> Then the wide sweeping branches lowered. Rootlets began to squirm up out of the cool soil, pale and voracious. They emerged by thousands, by millions. Enzymes flowed from them in glistening, all-enveloping films. First went the blood, the luscious life-streams of the dead and dying. It was broken down, dissolved, and swiftly transported up through the xylem, the woody channels, to give delight to the meristem.
> Over each body the roots crawled like worms, digging into each break and cavity, exploring, decomposing, absorbing. It did not take long.[9]

The imagery of this passage, such as the simile of the worms, is imagery most frequently associated with such graveyard horror writers as Edgar Allan Poe and H. P. Lovecraft. But such terms as "pale and voracious," "cool soil," and "decomposing" are balanced and to some extent intensified by the language of science, for example, botanical terms such as "enzymes," "xylem," "meristem." Though a sensation of unknown horror is at the heart of the passage, it is balanced by a tone of scientific objectivity suggesting that the god represented by the tree-creatures is in fact knowable. The tension set up early in the story, in style as well as substance, is between the ignorance of the tree-worshippers and the knowledge, implied by the narrator, that might give these same characters dominion over their god.

The resolution of this tension is the story's plot. A hero is born who, because of mutation or genetic anomaly, is immune to the spell of the trees. By studying ancient records, he finds that the trees are not only mortal, but a potential source of fuel and building materials. With the remarkable technological skill that science-fiction heroes so often seem to possess, he constructs a gas mask and a flamethrower, incinerates a tree, liberates the humans, and makes scientific investigation once again possible. "Everyone could learn all the wisdom of Earth and discover more for themselves, for there would be no God to prevent these things" (p. 22). But the hero discovers that with this liberation comes a feeling of emptiness. He is told, "'You have taken our God and left an emptiness. Where will we turn? What will we worship? . . . We are confused, deserted.'" The only answer, rather lamely offered by the hero's female companion, is that "'every man will have to fill up the emptiness for himself'" (pp. 24-25). The humans, left with no sense of purpose other than the dream of unrepentant progress, which (we are told earlier) had destroyed the earth, proceed to strip away the forests of this new world in a new effort to rebuild the old civilization.

I have given this story perhaps more attention that it deserves mainly because it is such a simple and direct fable of how humanity may use the knowledge provided by science to conquer the unknown and thus overcome the oppressive awareness of its autochthonous origins, represented by images of vegetation. Tall describes a society evolving directly from primitive nature-worship to technocracy without any of the complex intervening stages of social development, and this rather oversimplified paradigm of social evolution is common in science fiction. According to this paradigm, knowledge, or the appropriation of the unknown by the known, is all that stands between the pastoral state of ignorance (at once Eden and Hell) and the "normal" state of mechanical civilization.

Tall's story is also significant in that it is a variation on themes developed by earlier science-fiction writers. Murray Leinster's story "The Plants" (1946) explores the notion of plants ascending to dominance over a world through telepathic control of other species, and

James H. Schmitz's "The Pork Chop Tree" (1965) involves the discovery of a highly evolved alien tree that dominates its environment by nourishing and "loving" all other life forms into submission. Humans rapidly become addicted to the stressless environment provided by the tree and, over generations, devolve into stupid froglike beasts that merely crawl from branch to branch in mindless bliss. Here the Edenic imagery is especially malevolent, and the threat of vegetative life is made manifest by the manner in which it literally reabsorbs human beings into the primitive condition of their origins by altering and accelerating their evolutionary pattern away from "progress" and toward a purely vegetative existence.

A more conventional treatment of the plant-as-monster is Wyndham's *The Day of the Triffids* (1951), generally regarded as something of a classic among the British catastrophe school of science-fiction novels. Triffids are intelligent, carnivorous plants of uncertain origin that are capable of moving about and killing people with whiplike stings. When nearly the entire population of earth is blinded by the intense radiation of a brilliant "meteor shower" (later hypothesized to be the result of some new kind of orbiting weapon), the triffids multiply and conquer the earth. Wyndham seems less concerned with the triffids as monsters than with postulating what might happen to human society if the sense of sight were removed (a concept also explored by Daniel Galouye in his *Dark Universe* [1961])—a situation that again emphasizes the animal vulnerability of man. Triffids serve the dual function of reinforcing the theme of vulnerability and providing a focus for the terror that blindness represents. By endowing his triffids with four simple animal qualities—intelligence, mobility, carnivorousness, and the ability to communicate among themselves—Wyndham reduces the superiority of humans over plants to one merely of sight. This point is made early in the novel when it is first discovered that, before the universal blindness, the triffids had developed the curious habit of stinging people across the eyes, deliberately blinding them. As the narrator's friend Walter comments, "'they know what is the surest way to put a man out of action.'" "Look at it this way. Granted that they do have intelligence; then that would leave us with only one important superiority—sight. We can see, and they can't. Take away our vision, and the superiority is gone. Worse than that—our position becomes inferior to theirs, because they are adapted to a sightless existence and we are not." [10] Vision becomes the defining factor of humanness, and, by extension, of all human progress. Without this vision, society quickly reverts to a feudal state, with the triffids representing all the violent, threatening forces of nature with which human beings in such a state must contend. Wyndham restrains himself from providing the conventional deus ex machina of the brilliant scientist who manages to singlehandedly rebuild technology and dispose of the triffids. Although the narrator never abandons his faith in the efficacy of science to find a solution, this faith is never vindicated during the course of the novel, and it is only the reader's willingness to share the narrator's belief that prevents the novel from being finally apocalyptic.

Blindness, of course, vastly expands the territory of the unknown, and the triffids are an image of the terror of this unknown. Not only is mankind reduced to a primitive state and stripped of civilization, it is forced as well to contend with a competing species for survival and dominance. The ability to use tools and weapons (technology) is pitted against the triffids' remarkable fertility (power drawn from the earth), and the outcome is doubtful. "'In fact, if it were a choice for survival between a triffid and a blind man, I know which I'd put my money on'" (p. 39), says Walter. The triffids come to represent all that is not known about the natural world, the physical universe.

Not surprisingly, the icon of the barrier appears in this novel, too, as one of the central patterns of imagery. Blind men and women walk aimlessly into walls and fences, suggesting how circumscribed their world has become; barricades are set up to prevent marauding bands from invading the civilized communities that are left. Most significant, however, are the barriers directly associated with triffids. Before the catastrophe of blindness, domesticated triffids are kept anchored and fenced in on plantations, cultivated for the valuable oils they yield: as in any technological society, barriers keep the triffids *in,* contained and under control like animals in forest preserves. As the triffids break loose and multiply in the second part of the novel, however, barriers must be constructed around human communities to keep the triffids *out,* first with fences, then with electrified wire, and finally with the natural barrier of the sea (the narrator ends up in a colony on the Isle of Wight). The known-unknown antinomy is reversed to what it had been in prehistoric times. No longer can mankind contain the chaos, the unknown, through technology and agriculture; instead human beings must form social groups to protect themselves from it. The conquest of the natural world that science had taken so long to achieve is ready to begin again; as in the wasteland stories we examined earlier, technology becomes a tool of survival rather than merely of maintenance, and its value is thus made more immediate.

ANIMALS: THE PULPS AND THE MOVIES

It would be possible, without abandoning the mainstream of science fiction, to continue our discussion of monsters right up the evolutionary scale, with tales of monster fishes, reptiles, insects, birds, mammals, and so on. Such a discussion might prove uncomfortable to those science-fiction advocates who have long regarded the "monster story" as a disreputable distant cousin of the genre. But in deference to these advocates, it must be allowed that simple animal monsters, as opposed to intelligent aliens, are as rare in science-fiction literature as they are common in science-fiction films. The literature has its share, of course: there are few movie monsters that do not have an antecedent somewhere in literature, and the monster stories in the pulps never really declined until the market began to evaporate in the early 1960s. As recently as 1959, *Super Science Fiction,* one of the last of the unrepentantly trashy pulps, and one of the few in digest size, ran a whole series of special "monster issues" in an attempt to hold on to the adolescent audience that even today provides the central market for magazines such as Forrest Ackerman's *Famous Monsters of Filmland.* Tales of monster insects, so common in popular films of the 1950s (e.g., *Them!, Monster from Green Hell,* and *The Deadly Mantis*), were hardly less common in pulp fiction of the 1920s and 1930s (such as Murray Leinster's "Mad Planet," *Amazing,* 1926). (We might note that, in the movies at least, these insects are usually associated with caverns and tunnels, chthonian images suggestive both of the unconscious and of the womb of earth).

Although it is certainly misleading to look at a whole genre solely from the perspective of monster movies (as Susan Sontag and others have done[11]), it is equally misleading to summarily disavow these movies and claim they have no relation to "real" science fiction. In fact, the simple monster story is generally more successful in film than in literature (just as the convincing alien story is more successful in the literature) because of the nature of the medium itself. As John Baxter has observed, a skillful director like Jack Arnold could make very effective cinematic use of the visual image of a monster such as the Creature from the Black Lagoon simply by taking advantage of lighting, focus, and makeup—the raw visual appearance of the beast.[12] In fiction, this immediate visual impact is lost; readers must construct an image of the monster from their own imaginations, guided by verbal information supplied them, and the effect is likely as not to be comical. As Edmund Wilson observed of one of H. P. Lovecraft's monsters, "such creatures would look very well on the covers of the pulp magazines, but they do not make good adult reading." Wilson also cautions, as others have, that a good writer does not describe a monster with such words as "horrible" and "unholy"—"especially if you are going, at the end, to produce an invisible whistling octopus."[13] On the other hand, literature, as demonstrated by Hal Clement in his fiction and in his essay "The Creation of Imaginary Beings,"[14] can be much more effective in providing an environmental and biological rationale for such creatures—a rationale which in film would only amount to tedious exposition (as it does from time to time even in Clement's fiction). Film deals in effects, fiction in causes, and some of the most effective monster stories in science fiction are films.

The archetype of animalian monsters is of course Caliban, and it does not come as a surprise that Caliban should have been resurrected as a spectacular "monster from the Id" in the Fred Wilcoxon film *Forbidden Planet* (1956), a science-fiction retelling of *The Tempest*. Dr. Morbius, who together with his daughter is the last survivor of a colonizing expedition to a distant planet, attains a remarkable power of psychokinesis by getting his brain power multiplied by an alien machine; as a result, his subconscious fears and resentments take the physical form of a giant invisible monster which, outlined in blasts from ray guns, looks rather like a bizarre parody of the MGM lion. Caliban is transposed from an earth-monster into a literal manifestation of the Freudian id. "'You sent your secret id out to destroy those people!'" accuses Leslie Nielsen, in what must have been one of the more difficult lines to deliver in his career. This transposition of Caliban neatly suggests the origins of all such monsters: psychologically, they arise from the unconscious; culturally, they are images of the earth. Both aspects remind us of our psychological and physical humanness.

Images of barriers once again symbolize the confrontation with the unknown, and the barriers set up in *Forbidden Planet* to keep the monster at bay prove useless, even though they represent the heights of technology: first an overcharged electrical barrier set up around the besieged spaceship, later a barrier of "indestructible" alien metal, which the creature promptly burns through. These barriers are designed to keep the unknown safely apart from human experience, but since in this case the source of the unknown is humanity's own animal nature, its "secret id," it cannot be resisted by technology, which is only the product of another aspect of human consciousness. In fact, this particular monster is the direct result of the collision of primal nature with supertechnology: the id is made manifest only after Morbius's brain power has been mechanically multiplied by the Krel machines (the Krel were an ancient race who had violently destroyed themselves after

199

inventing these machines). Perhaps *Forbidden Planet* provides one kind of answer to Lewis Mumford's question, "Why did the utmost achievements of technology, which are symbolized even today by a journey to distant planets, terminate in fantasies of shapeless monsters and cruel deaths, such as often haunt the cribs of little children?"[15]

As Mumford implies, and as *Forbidden Planet* illustrates, there is a profound relationship between animalian monsters and technology. A. M. Hocart has said of man's attitude toward animals that "as his superiority and mastery over the rest of the living world became more and more apparent he seems to have become more and more anxious to disclaim relationship with animals."[16] Frederick Pohl reiterated this idea in the afterword to his *Slave Ship* (1957): man "clings to evolution's ladder one rung higher than the brutes beneath and saws away, saws away at the ladder beneath in an attempt to sever the connection between himself and the soulless, speechless brainless Beast . . . that does not, in fact, exist."[17] Technology may be a means of "sawing away" at the ladder, but it may ironically also bring new animals into being. In Wells's *The Island of Dr. Moreau* (1896), advanced surgical techniques are what create Moreau's animal-men. Animal monsters are often either the result of deliberate attempts to use technology to alter existing life forms (as with *Moreau*), or accidental by-products of technology (such as mutations following an atomic explosion). In both cases, the problem that Mumford speaks of is apparent: the process of broadening the scope of rationality—of making the unknown known—is often accompanied by an untimely release of some powerful manifestation of irrationality in the figure of the monster.

In terms of the dramatic structure of science-fiction narratives, the most common relationship of technology to monsters is the use of technology or scientific reasoning to subdue the monster and restore order. Ideally, the monster is not simply annihilated, it is appropriated; its defeat serves to broaden the dominion of human knowledge and power. It is not enough to defeat the invading aliens; they must be defeated in a way that will insure victory in all future encounters. The science-fiction hero relies not on weapons, but upon reason and scientific ingenuity to overcome the monster. It is almost a rule of thumb in science-fiction films that the monster cannot be subdued by the conventional weapons of the hero; even the atomic bomb fails to stop the Martians in George Pal's film of Wells's *The War of the Worlds* (1953). Early in most monster movies, we learn that the conventional solution of ritual violence such as we find in the Western is inadequate in the face of this new threat. The monster is less a villain than a *problem,* and the heroic achievement becomes the ability to apply scientific methodology quickly and accurately in crises, to observe what data there are about the monster and to induce the secret principle that will defeat it. In *The Blob* (1956), the hero observes the behavior of the Blob in cold environments and accurately infers that freezing the monster will bring it under control. In Michael Crichton's *The Andromeda Strain,* data provided by the blood chemistry of a wailing infant and an aging alcoholic lead to the defeat of Andromeda. In *The Thing* (1951), discovery of the monster's susceptibility to electricity leads to its defeat.

There are, of course, cases in which the hero succeeds by traditional heroic battle rather than by scientific ingenuity, but even here tools play a role. When the miniscule Scott Carey battles what to him is an enormous spider in Richard Matheson's *The Shrinking Man* (1956), the scene is an adventure worthy of a Teutonic epic. What gives it additional irony, and brings it closer to the technological myth of modern science fiction, is that technological man is forced into heroic behavior by the mere alteration of his size in relation to the animals around him (earlier in the novel, a similar confrontation takes place with a house cat). In Jack Arnold's film of the novel, the confrontation is presented in a shadowy landscape made alien by its distorted proportions: an ordinary house basement, filled with the detritus of modern domesticity. The throwaway props of society become tools for survival when a man is reduced to fighting as an animal among animals, and we are reminded again that it is only a man's tool-making ability that gives him superiority over such relatively simple creatures as cats and spiders. We may be able to hold our own in such a world without all the supporting paraphernalia of technology, but we could not survive for long without the *principles* of technology.

ALIENS: MURRAY LEINSTER AND OTHERS

Intelligent aliens (or "alien intelligences," as the favored science-fiction phrase has it) must be treated apart from animal monsters because in most science fiction on this theme, the focus is on the unique abilities and technology of the alien civilization rather than on the animal nature of the aliens themselves. The physical nature of the alien being is often presented as an extrapolation from environmental conditions (see Clement's essay "The Creation of Imaginary Beings," quoted earlier) rather than as a mere monstrosity for monstrosity's sake. However, it seems that science-fiction writers habitually choose the more baroque alternative when faced with such extrapolative decisions.

Certainly this is true of science-fiction art. A famous illustration by Frank R. Paul for the back cover of a 1939 issue of *Fantastic Adventures* depicts a "Man from Mars" with a warthog face, batlike ears, an enormous chest, and what appear to be frog's legs with feet ending in octopoid suction cups.[18] These and other features are "scientifically explained" by a key that purports to give an evolutionary rationale for each of them. One has to wonder if Paul's conception was really a response to the factors extrapolated in the explanation, or if the explanation is merely a response and rationalization for a fancy animal, or if (as seems most likely) the illustration is a compromise between pure extrapolation and pure instinctual monster-making. Similarly, Wells goes to some pains to offer an evolutionary rationale for his Martians in *War of the Worlds* and his Morlocks in *The Time Machine,* but the actual description of the monsters is clearly intended to frighten first and appear scientific afterwards. Wells's Martians are highly intelligent creatures with an advanced civilization, and their biology is supposed to be that of human beings several million years in the future, but no "scientific" reason is offered as to why they should be described, as they are, in terms of snakes, bears, Gorgons, fungi, and octopi; or why they should have slavering, beaklike mouths that drip saliva; or why they should be of a sickly gray color like "wet leather." However civilized or technological they may be, science-fiction aliens clearly partake of the icon of the monster. In science-fiction films, the evolutionary or environmental commentary is usually dispensed with altogether, leaving the makeup men to concoct whatever lumpy monstrosities suit their imaginations.

The alien being, however, is more a product of verbal science fiction than of the visual media. And it cannot be denied that a strong element of rational speculation is present in the description of many alien life forms; otherwise science-fiction writers might as well resort to the gargoyles and griffins of medieval sculptors, which by and large are both more frightening and more anatomically sound than Paul's Martian. This process of trying to construct through rational means an image of a completely alien being exemplifies one of the central paradoxes facing the science-fiction writer: rational speculation, when carried sufficiently beyond experience, tends inevitably to produce irrational images. Authors may reasonably speculate that life elsewhere in the universe is likely to have evolved differently from life on earth, but in order to describe such life in dramatic terms, they must pass from abstract speculation into mythic image-making. The result of all their reasoning, then, is an image or set of images that, if made believable at all, must touch the most primitive centers of the irrational unconscious: not the sleep of reason, but reason itself, produces monsters. Even the carefully thought-out, friendly aliens of a highly "scientific" author such as Hal Clement are finally like monsters, and science-fiction editors have invariably been quick to exploit this in assigning illustrations for Clement stories.

It comes as no surprise, therefore, that science-fiction writers interested more in concepts than in images have evolved a number of techniques to avoid monster imagery and thus to prevent it from preempting the central focus of their stories. First, it is a common practice to have the aliens appear in human form by taking over the minds and bodies of earth people. This is the case in Heinlein's *The Puppet Masters* (1951) (despite the sluglike appearance of the aliens, the real source of terror is their control of humans), Jack Finney's *The Body Snatchers* (1954), and any number of science-fiction films in which production costs apparently did not allow for the creation of elaborate monsters, such as *Invaders from Mars* (1953), *Invasion of the Body Snatchers* (1956), and *I Married a Monster from Outer Space* (1958). This device is useful only in stories featuring aliens who are bent on conquering the earth, however, usually to provide a breeding ground for a dying or an endangered population. Consequently, the avenues open to the full exploration of alien intelligences are limited with this approach.

Second, a related technique is to have the alien assume a human form without taking over the body of a specific human being. Such is the case in Walter Tevis's *The Man Who Fell to Earth* (1963; filmed by Nicholas Roeg in 1976). Other aliens, such as those in Chad Oliver's *Shadows in the Sun* (1954), may come by their human form through natural evolutionary processes. Hollywood, when faced with such a plot, finds it almost irresistible to show us toward the end of the film what the alien "really looks like," thus giving us at least one thrill of monster imagery, but from the writer's point of view the purpose of this technique is at least in part quite the opposite: even though a greater suspension of disbelief is necessary to sustain the notion of a nonhuman human, it allows us to focus on the issue of "alienness" rather than the image of deformity.

A third method for evading the problem of monsters is to have the alien never reveal his form to humans at all, but rather to communicate through robots or other means. Probably the most sensitive story of this kind is Sturgeon's "Tiny and the Monster" (1947), in which an alien, to avoid a hostile confrontation, chooses to communicate with humans through the intermediary of a dog. The alien realizes that to be different from humans is to be monstrous, and so he never gives the humans a chance—and Sturgeon never gives the reader a chance—to regard his alienness with revulsion and horror. One of the *least* sensitive treatments of the theme, on the other hand, is the film *The Beast with a Million Eyes* (1955), in which domestic animals are "taken over" first by a hostile and later by a friendly alien, and which is probably the only science-fiction film that ever tried to evoke terror by showing a human being attacked by a cow. There are numerous stories of aliens making "first contact" through the agency of machines—sometimes even machines as simple as typewriters and sewing machines (Clifford Simak's "Skirmish," 1950). The film *2001: A Space Odyssey* is in fact a variation on this, since the aliens are presented only through the intermediary of the monoliths.

Fourth, a writer may avoid monster imagery while exploring the notion of an alien intelligence by imparting natural intelligence to familiar animals, either through mutation or through discovery of their secret "language." Stapledon's *Sirius* (1944) provides one of the most thoughtful explorations of a nonhuman intelligence in all science fiction simply by focusing on a superintelligent dog. Dogs as alien intelligences ("alien" only by virtue of its being different from that of human beings) are also featured in Pohl's *Slave Ship* (1957), Simak's *City* (1952), Anderson's *Brain Wave* (1954), Ellison's "A Boy and His Dog" (1969), and several other works. Cordwainer Smith is fond of exploring the intelligence of cats in his Instrumentality of Mankind stories, and Robert Merle's *Day of the Dolphin* (1967) does the same thing with dolphins.

A fifth and somewhat marginal way of avoiding monsters consists of simply describing the alien in terms antithetical to conventional monster imagery. Aliens such as the "tribbles" from David Gerrold's *Star Trek* television scripts or "Little Fuzzy" in H. Beam Piper's 1962 novel of that title are simply too cute to be monsters, while creatures such as Arthur C. Clarke's Vanamonde in *The City and the Stars* (1956) are too abstractly disembodied to generate much visceral reaction. To further remove Vanamonde from the realm of monsterdom, Clarke has given him a character rather like that of a monstrous, lonely puppy.

None of these devices, however, can avoid the central structural tension that is set up by the very concept of an alien intelligence: the opposition between man and not-man (or "Un-man," as C. S. Lewis calls his demonic villain in *Perelandra* [1943]). Stories of aliens are inevitably stories of mankind's earthly origins, since they must gain their power partly from the reader's awareness of the terrestriality of mankind and the accident of its evolution. It is worth noting how often in science-fiction aliens are simply referred to as "the Outsiders" or "the Others," as if to deliberately suggest the warm, comfortable, womblike nature of the earth. The barrier separating known and unknown in such stories is penetrated not necessarily by human beings, but often by the invading aliens, who cross the unknown into mankind's awareness and thus circumscribe its rational universe. The unknown becomes the more fearsome through the knowledge that it contains an intelligence other than our own, and that to that intelligence, *we* are a part of the unknown that remains to be appropriated. Even to conceive of an alien intelligence is to conceive, at some deep level, of an invasion of one's own personality by outside forces, or a violation of one's community by strangers. It is perhaps for this reason that, although many science-fiction works take aliens for granted and plunge us *in medias res* into a multispecies galactic civilization, one of the most fascinating and recurring themes in the genre is that which has come to be termed "first contact," meaning, of course, first contact with alien intelligences.

It is in these first-contact stories that science fiction tends to be at its most obsessively paranoid, concerned with the potential danger to the race inherent in any alien contact and cautionary about the need to develop an advanced technology because, in all probability, "they" already have one. In Clarke's *The City and the Stars,* humanity encounters aliens only to discover that its society is too primitive to enter the galactic society; an intense program of technological achievement is set up to make humanity ready for galactic civilization. A similar theme appears in Clarke's later *Rendezvous with Rama* (1973), in which a technological marvel (an artificial world) floats into our solar system, the product of a race so advanced that it becomes apparent that they would have no reason to be interested in a society as primitive as ours. Stories in which aliens are portrayed with intelligence equal or inferior to our own (as in Stanley Weinbaum's "A Martian Odyssey" [1934]) are rare; the theme of hostile, superior alien forces is so common that readers have come to regard it as nearly universal. Robert Plank, in *The Emotional Significance of Imaginary Beings,* broadly characterizes the science-fiction alien as immensely powerful, totally indifferent to the welfare of human beings, and not capable of being communicated with.[19] Unfair as this characterization is to the mass of stories that deal effectively with alien communication, it does describe accurately many stories in the mold of Wells's *War of the Worlds,* as well as most invasion-of-earth monster movies.

Even when communication does take place, however, the paranoia remains. Both Murray Leinster's "First Contact" (1945) and Chad Oliver's "Scientific Method" (1953) postulate communication with an alien race leading to the problem of how to achieve further contact without risking the danger of invasion. "First Contact" is constructed in terms of images of opposition and reversed polarities, suggesting clearly how contact with intelligent aliens complicates the known-unknown dichotomy by introducing a second subjective point of view, one in which *we* become part of the unknown. The spaceship *Llanvabon* encounters an alien spaceship in the Crab Nebula. Although contact with an intelligent alien civilization had long been expected, the occurrence of this contact in open space creates a problem: how can each ship return to its native world without fear of being followed and perhaps invaded? As the captain of the *Llanvabon* says, "'We can't risk a nonhuman race knowing where Earth is unless we're sure of them!'"[20] But the aliens, of course, feel the say way; Leinster has created a situation in which we are forced to regard the barrier between known and unknown from two sides at once. The aliens are like us—they are even affable—and this realization forces us to see ourselves not as absolute masters of the cosmos, but as one race among possibly many who have mastered technology and seek to conquer the unknown.

This idea is reinforced even in the way Leinster uses the spaceship icon, which we discussed earlier. The interior of the *Llanvabon* is the known world for the humans, but for the aliens, from the vantage point of *their* spaceship, it is the unknown—and vice versa. Space, which usually functions as the repository of the unknown in spaceship stories, is transmuted into a kind of neutral ground, its customary iconic value reversed. As if to suggest this deliberately, Leinster describes the space in the Crab Nebula as a "luminous mist" made incredibly bright by the cosmic dust which created the nebula. Outer space becomes white, the figures of the ships black against it—a direct reversal of the usual appearance of space, just as the meeting with the alien ship causes a reversal of familiar known-unknown, human-alien roles. Also, the appearance of the two ships suggests an ironic parallel: the earth ship's hull is "polished to mirror-reflection" (p. 255), while the alien ship's hull is "an abysmal, nonreflecting sable" (p. 257). But from the point of view of the aliens, whose eyes have evolved differently because of their weaker sun, the appearance of the two ships' hulls is reversed. And the aliens themselves appear to be telepathic, communicating by means of "frequency modulation"—but to them the humans seem telepathic, since the aliens have no knowledge of communication via sound waves. A classical doppelgänger situation is the result.

It is only fitting in such a situation that the normal movement of the science-fiction plot should be reversed as well. Instead of seeking to make the unknown known, the problem for both crews becomes protecting the sanctity of the known against the unknown—the pattern of many earthbound monster stories. Only two choices are allowed the crew of each ship—flight or fight—and only two relationships between the cultures seem possible—"the choice of trade or battle." Commerce or war, Leinster suggests in a manner reminiscent of Commodore Perry, are the only ways two cultures can coexist. It is probably for this reason that the story came under attack by a Soviet science-fiction writer, Ivan Yefremov, who in a 1959 story, "The Heart of the Serpent," claimed that Leinster's tale proclaimed "the inevitability of war and the eternal existence of capitalism."[21]

Finally, a compromise is reached, one which permits both a limited conquest of the unknown and a means of preserving the known from danger. The crews dismantle the weapons and tracking mechanisms of their respective ships and trade ships, each crew certain that the other is unable to follow or track them to their home worlds. An agreement is made to meet again at the same place in the future. Each crew begins to make all sorts of wondrous discoveries aboard the new spaceship, and both the quest for knowledge and cultural xenophobia are satisfied.

A less widely known but equally interesting story on this same theme, perhaps also intended as a response to Leinster (but certainly less ideological a response than Yefremov's), is Chad Oliver's "Scientific Method" (originally published in 1953 as "Hands Across Space"). Written from the perspective of an anthropologist (Oliver was trained as an anthropologist), the story shows a somewhat more acute awareness of the ethnocentric nature of the problems described in Leinster's story. The title refers to the ironic stalemate that results when each of two cultures applies the scientific method to devise means of establishing contact with the other. The scientific method works fine, Oliver suggests, when it is applied to a passive body of data, but what happens when that body of data is busy employing exactly the same scientific method on you? The result, in this story, is that neither culture discovers what it wants to discover. Science, in other words, depends on an assumed superiority of the investigator over the investigated; its essential function is not dialog but appropriation. Take away that superiority, and you have not scientific investigation, but politics.

Reda Dani, an inhabitant of the planet Capella IV, finds himself faced with a problem similar to that of the crew of Leinster's spaceship. Contact with many alien species has been made, but in most cases the dilemma of trade or war that Leinster speaks of never became an issue: "There was no basis at all for getting together; they had nothing in common. . . . It wasn't that the life-forms were hostile. Hardly. They didn't even have a *concept* of hostility, or of friendliness. They were *different*."[22] One culture creates a problem, however: that of Earth, whose civilization is much like that of Capella IV. Reda Dani is aware that "what you chose to define as 'alien' varied with where you happened to be sitting," and that to the earthmen *he* is an alien. This awareness itself creates a feeling of hostility: "'I wish the whole planet would drop dead,'" Dani says, expressing the negative feelings toward aliens that I have already discussed and that have very little to do with military threats. Given the available data about earth society, Dani constructs a solution to the problem: first contact is to be made on a neutral third planet, Mars, between one representative member of each race. Dani reasons that the only way to avoid a threat to life is to send a humanoid robot in hopes of fooling the earthmen. Of course the earthmen do the same, and the amusing coincidence of both parties arriving at the same solution to the same problem at the same time (much as in "First Contact") provides the basis for a bond of friendship.

Though it lacks the imagery and scope of Leinster's story, Oliver's is tinged with a sense of irony that reveals an awareness of the cultural paranoia of the situation: whenever one applies scientific reasoning to a problem involving another culture, the result is distrust. This may be one reason why political thought in science fiction is often characterized by an armed-camp mentality, why "space mercenary" stories remain popular, and why many science-fiction writers often embrace conservative causes. The introduction of a more sophisticated anthropological perspective by Oliver, Le Guin, and others has considerably changed the field's attitude toward alien life forms, and enabled later writers to regard aliens with greater equanimity.

TRANSFORMED HUMANS: JAMES BLISH

If the alien or monster conceptualizes an "I-Thou" relationship with the unknown, with mankind facing a choice of either conquering or being conquered by it, the transformed human conceptualizes mankind's rite of passage into the unknown. The alien challenges our notion of our unique intelligence; the transformed human challenges even our belief in the sanctity of our form. Technology and science create radically new environments for human beings, or enable them to visit other worlds, but how are they to survive in these new environments if their very physical and psychological makeup alienates the humans from them? Alien environments and planets appear the more wondrous because of their very inaccessibility: the barriers separating them from possible human experience are too great. And one cannot simply deposit characters there and have them running about in hope that a technologically uncritical audience might not notice the anomaly. How to construct an advanture on such a planet?

One may, of course, abandon the notion of placing humans in this environment at all and, following the examples of Hal Clement and others, make the characters alien members of an alien race. But the more interesting technique from the standpoint of the iconography of the human form is to postulate transformed humans—humans so drastically altered by genetics, prosthetics, surgery, or whatever that they can survive unsupported in such an environment. The theme of the deliberate altering of humans for space exploration is one of two themes involving altered humans I want to discuss in this chapter. The other theme, mutations, also serves to broaden the range of possible human experience. Rather than altering humans to survive in alien environments, the mutation story alters humans in such a way that they are alienated from their own environment and forced to perceive it in a new way.

James Blish, in one of the classic treatments of human transformation in science fiction, the stories published collectively as *The Seedling Stars* (1957), gives some account of the lineage of this subgenre:

> The notion of modifying the human stock genetically to live on the planets as they were found, rather than changing the planets to accommodate the people, had been old with Olaf Stapledon; it had been touched upon by many later writers; it went back, in essence, as far as Proteus, and as deep into the human mind as the werewolf, the vampire, the fairy changeling, the transmigrated soul.[23]

Indeed, the theme had thrived in the literature of fantasy long before science fiction picked it up; one immediately thinks of Ovid, of the legend of Arthur's education by being transformed by Merlin into various beasts, and of the traditions of the romantic fairytale. In David

Lindsay's influential *A Voyage to Arcturus* (1920), the protagonist finds himself growing and losing bodily organs as he moves from one epistemological environment to another. Tales of werewolves and vampires nearly all involve physical changes of one sort or another, and it has even been suggested that such changes are symbolic of the physiological changes of adolescence.[24] The anthropological and psychological literature on such tales of transformation is immense, and the common factor in interpretations of such tales is that they are somehow involved with the passage from one state of being to another, from ignorance to knowledge. Transformation is almost universally a passage into the unknown, the crossing of a barrier that broadens and deepens the scope of experience. In science fiction, transformations are no less significant, but have characteristically been treated in terms of empirical rather than visionary experience; even in Clarke's *Childhood's End* (1956), widely regarded as among the most "visionary" of modern science-fiction novels, man finally abandons physical being altogether to join with the Overmind. But what the Overmind has to offer is transcendental experience only of a tightly circumscribed sort: the key attraction of the new state of being is godlike intellect, a vastly increased knowledge and power that, we are told, transcends the kind of linear knowledge represented by the supertechnological Overlords, who have elevated mankind to the brink of transformation. Only by achieving ultimate technology, Clarke seems to be saying, can man achieve a state beyond conventional rationality. It is not without significance that Clarke uses the term Over*mind* rather than the more familiar Emersonian Over*soul*. (A notable exception to the pattern represented by Clarke may be Robert Silverberg's *Son of Man,* [1971]), a novel apparently strongly influenced by *A Voyage to Arcturus*. Silverberg's protagonist, rather disingenuously named Clay, encounters a "million million forms, all of them claiming humanity," who seem to call out to him, "'forgive us our metamorphoses'" and cause him to wonder, "Why were these transformations tolerated?"[25] Silverberg's focus is clearly on the moral and spiritual question of what it is to be human, rather than on the intellectual and empirical question.)

Blish's *The Seedling Stars* contains four separate treatments of the theme of transformation, united by the overall notion of a vast "seeding" program undertaken to insure the continuity of the human race by genetically transforming human beings into creatures able to live in various planetary environments. One of the stories in the collection, "Surface Tension," has become something of a science-fiction classic, but all the stories are revealing of how science fiction thinks of humanity, of the importance of barrier imagery to the fundamental structural antinomy of known-unknown, and, perhaps parenthetically, of some of the stylistic problems involved in describing what might be called transhuman cultures—how to describe a society as convincingly human when that society has no physiological or environmental resemblance to any known human culture.

The first story in the collection, "Seeding Program," was initially published in 1955 as "A Time to Survive." It lays out some of the essential themes of the cycle of stories by revealing how the transformation into an alien form involves crossing both symbolic and literal barriers into the unknown, and how such transformations are analogous to the processes of birth and individuation. Birth images are the dominant images of the story. The story opens in a spaceship, with the central character, a pantrope or genetically altered human, ("pantrope" coming from "pantropy," meaning "changing everything"), named Sweeney, isolated from the ship's human crew in a "heavily insulated cabin, with its own airlock to the outside, and no access for Sweeney at all to the rest of the ship."[26] Sweeney's womblike compartment is in fact a "vault designed to protect the universe outside it—not to protect its contents from the universe" (p. 7). Already we are made to realize the dual role Sweeney plays in the known-unknown antinomy: his very situation in the spaceships suggests it. He is isolated both from the known world, the human part of the ship, and from the unknown of outer space. To the humans, he is as alien as what lies beyond the confines of the ship, and the ship has "no overall hull," lacking even this symbolic union of Sweeney with the humans. Sweeney has been "created" and psychologically programmed in an underground dome on the moon, always isolated by his need for a radically different environment from humans, connected to human affairs only by a one-way speaker controlled from the outside. In other words, he has spent his entire life in an artificial womb, never experiencing the birth trauma, and now he has been sent on a dangerous mission with the promise that he will be made human when he returns. He is the perfect image of the creature on the border of known and unknown, alienated both from the human world and the unknown of space.

Sweeney is being sent to Ganymede to infiltrate a colony of other pantropes and capture their leader, regarded as a criminal by antipantropy political interests on Earth—interests who prefer "terraforming," or the remaking of planetary environments for human habitation. The Ganymede colonists regard terraforming as not only impractical, but also the worst sort of capitalistic imperialism—

humanity making the universe over in its own image and perhaps destroying whole cultures in the process. (Nevertheless, the idea of terraforming has since been developed enthusiastically by such writers as Larry Niven.) Once Sweeney is on Ganymede, he is caught between loyalty to creatures like himself magnified by the freedom represented by a "world without walls," and his assigned duty. He is accused of playing both ends against the middle, with himself in the middle, and he finds himself in a dilemma, alienated from both cultures.

But on Ganymede, Sweeney experiences all the feelings of birth and childhood he had never experienced on earth, first in the symbolic ejection from the spaceship and later with emotions he feels toward the girl Michaela. Like other "bottle baby" pantropes, he is, according to the scientist-pantrope Rullman, "'desperate for closer contact, for acceptance, for the embraces it can never have. . . . the breast that might have fed it may be just on the other side of the glass, but it also lies generations in the past'" (p. 44). Furthermore, Rullman says, the transformation process is one-way: Sweeney can not go back and be made human. Freed from his womblike environments, accepted as a part of the known in this new culture, Sweeney chooses to remain and help Rullman carry out the seeding project, which is to provide the basis for the remaining stories in the book. At the end of the story, Sweeney says to Michaela, "'don't you know that I'm just about to be born?'" (p. 56).

Sweeney's problem of being alienated from his earthly origins and not yet assimilated into his new environment is also the problem of the cultures described in the next two stories, "The Thing in the Attic" and "Surface Tension." Both cultures have been adapted for life in alien environments, yet both have failed to achieve the conquest of that environment that is necessary for continued growth and survival. In each story, this conquest is represented by the ability to survive on the surface of the planet: once the surface is mastered, the environment is no longer completely alien, and the known-unknown antimony is again resolved by the assimilation of the unknown. The symbolic use of the planetary surface to achieve this resolution seems remarkably appropriate. The surface represents the logical boundary between the chthonian (or in the case of "Surface Tension," aquatic) origins of humanity and the infinite universe of space that will be opened to it by science. Especially in "The Thing in the Attic," which concerns a society of tree-dwelling pantropes on a world where, on the surface, "evolution has never managed to leave the tooth-and-nail stage" (p. 84), Blish implies that the surface is the "natural" dwelling place of humanity. "'To be the real masters of the world,'" a visiting earthman tells the tree-people, "'you will have to conquer the surface, too'" (p. 86).

"Surface Tension"goes so far as to use the surface as a literal barrier to the unknown, and of all science-fiction works comes closest to realizing the image portrayed in the famous medieval engraving of a traveler poking his head through the vault of the sky to observe the mechanism of the stars beyond. The story constantly borders on absurdity, with human beings reduced to microscopic size and inhabiting a mud puddle, taming and talking to paramecia and waging wars against tiny rotifera. Blish sustains a highly ironic tone throughout the story, inviting the reader to regard it as a parody of conventional science fiction, as Tom Wymer has done: "There amid all the cliches of the wise old mentor, the curious and courageous young man, the space ship, the exploratory journey, the faithful robot and the BEM, the whole grand and glorious quest for knowledge is literally reduced and trivialized into the passage from one mud puddle to another."[27] The great symbolic barrier that prevents humanity from conquering the surface of the planet is here reduced to the surface tension of the puddle of water that humanity inhabits. The idea of a rebellious young man coming to the conclusion that there is a "world outside" and facing opposition for his beliefs is a common enough theme in science fiction (see the discussion of Heinlein's "Universe" in Chapter Three), and Blish is almost certainly making parodic use of the popular myth of Galileo. The power of knowledge is here stated by a dying paramecium: "There is nothing. That knowledge. Cannot do. With it . . . men. . . have crossed . . . have crossed space . . . " (p. 148). This speech, so familiar from the lips of dying astronauts and faithful sidekicks, becomes bizarrely ironic when spoken by a microscopic creature who cannot survive out of its own mud puddle. And yet the irony can be reversed as well: if all our vaunted science has done no more than take us out of a metaphoric mud puddle, what vast new worlds must there *really* be for us to conquer?

In the final story of *The Seedling Stars*, Blish's ironic intentions become even more apparent. By the time of "Watershed," the seeding program has been going on for so long that the earth has long since been abandoned by humanity and has evolved into a barren, oxygen-poor, uninhabited planet. Naturally, earth itself becomes the next target of the seeding program, with a group of adapted "seal-men" on their way to colonize it. By this time a note of racism has crept into the attitudes of "normal" humans, who are far in the minority throughout the galaxy but who still regard the pantropes as inferior. The "watershed" of the title refers to the time that unites "all our divergent currents of attitudes

213

toward each other into one common reservoir of brotherhood and purpose" (p. 157). This will happen, says the protagonist, when it becomes known that the earth itself is no longer habitable by "normals," that normals are in fact the minority members of the human race, and that the "common reservoir" of man is not his form but his intelligence.

Intelligence, indeed, is virtually the only defining factor of humanity in this series of stories (although some mention is made of a common "spirit of rebellion" in "The Thing in the Attic"). Common culture cannot be transmitted through the pantropes, nor can specific memories, though there are apparently traces of racial memory in all the pantrope cultures. Almost as if to make up for the destruction of human culture implicit in his concept of a seeding program, Blish fills his prose with allusions to contemporary human culture that seem jarring in the alien contexts he has created. These allusions constantly make readers aware of their own alienation from the characters of the stories, and of the literary culture that the pantropes have abandoned: "privations of which Jack London might have made a whole novel" (p. 35); "a classic example . . . of the literary device called 'the pathetic fallacy'" (p. 37); "whole chapters, whole cantos, whole acts of what might have been conscious heroism . . . were thrown away" (p. 37); "the old magazine clipping . . . was as yellow as *paella*" (p. 44); "he had never heard of Kant and the Categorical Imperative" (p. 75); and so on. It is possible that Blish is trying to give some intellectual legitimacy to stories which, when first published, were part of a genre widely regarded as pulpish and subliterate; but it is also possible that the allusions represent an intelligent author grappling with the problem of describing alien states and being in a style which, because of the nominal realism demanded by the traditions of science fiction, is limited to the familiar.

Not all transformations in science fiction are engineered for survival or increased knowledge, however. In Clifford Simak's *City* (1952), people leave Earth to become pantropic "Lopers" on Jupiter principally because the new state offers a transcendent, sensual experience. "It was as if his whole being was soaking up the sensation of lavender—and yet not lavender. It was something, he knew, for which he had no word, undoubtedly the first of many enigmas in terminology. For the words he knew, the thought symbols that served him as an Earthman would not serve him as a Jovian."[28] Simak's stylistic technique for describing an alien environment in terms of synesthesia has in recent years become more common in science fiction than Blish's allusive style, and this may have something to do with a broadening of the meaning of human transformations. In the *City* stories, more even than in *The Seedling*

Stars, symbols of transformation become more like the symbols of transformation and transcendence of Jungian psychology. As Joseph L. Henderson writes,

> . . . these symbols do not seek to integrate the initiate with any religious doctrines or secular group-consciousness. On the contrary, they point to man's need for liberation from any state of being that is too immature, too fixed or final. In other words, they concern man's release from—or transcendence of—any confining pattern of existence, as he moves toward a superior or more mature stage in his development. . . . They provide the means by which the contents of the unconscious can enter the conscious mind, and they also are themselves an active expression of those contents.[29]

A much less ambitious use of the theme of transformation is the concept of bionics, and the classic treatment of this theme in science fiction may be Cordwainer Smith's "Scanners Live in Vain" (1948), in which the Scanners are humans surgically restructured to survive in the "Up-and-Out or the "Great Pain of Space," and who must "cranch" (a process never clearly explained) in order to temporarily become human again. There is nothing transcendent about being a Scanner; these beings are the final realization of the dehumanization of mankind in order to advance technological appropriation of the cosmos. The protagonist Martel is a Scanner married to a human woman, and thus trapped between known and unknown, separated from his wife by his lack of humanity and yet not fully a machine either. Two barriers mediate between known and unknown in this story, and both are associated with pain. First is the "wild threshold of pain" that separates Scanners from humans; second is the "pain of space" that prevents human beings from being able to cross space without the protection of the Scanners. One barrier creates the other: one cannot explore space without sacrificing his humanity, and one cannot gain back his humanity without limiting himself to earth. The dilemma is resolved when a scientist discovers that he can survive in space by surrounding himself with a protective barrier of life by lining the hull of his ship with—of all things—oysters. The Scanners, rendered superfluous by this discovery, are converted back into human form through surgery. Unlike the more mythic transformations of Blish and Simak, the transformation that led to the strangely primitive technological culture of the Scanners is reversible. It is possible to regain humanness without sacrificing technology, but only if that technology is based on a model of life (the protection of the oysters) rather than machines (the mechanical restructuring of the Scanners).

TELEPATHS AND TELEKINETICISTS

The association of appropriation of the unknown with release of the unconscious is often reflected in what is probably the most common image of mutant humans in science fiction, the telepath. The genre abounds in tales of mind reading, often presenting the telepath as a societal outcast, the next step in evolution, who is regarded as a "monster" by "normal" humans. The notion of the telepath as a next evolutionary step serves to remind normal humans of their animality by displacing them from the top of the evolutionary scale, and it represents a conquest of the unknown at the most personal level by revealing—at least to the telepaths—the most private "unknown" that is in the individual human mind. If the psychological unknown is to be revealed by this power, however, the danger is that the telepaths themselves would be subject to the hidden powers of the unconscious, to the forces that accompany the only real monsters we have, the monsters of the id. Telepathy and its variants (telekinesis, teleportation, etc.) constitute virtually the only effort the genre has made toward extrapolating psychological ideas, and thus it is hardly surprising that in science fiction, telepathic powers are frequently associated with the symptoms or reality of madness. In van Vogt's *Slan* (1946) one of the most influential treatments of this theme, the evolutionary step that results in the telepaths or "slans" is preceded by an alarming increase in the insanity rate. Kuttner's *Mutant* (1953), strongly influenced by *Slan,* depicts a sizable subgroup of telepaths (known as "Baldies" for their lack of hair, itself a suggestion of moving away from animal physicality) as being insanely paranoid. The telepathic mutant children in Clarke's *Childhood's End* who prepare the way for man to join the Overmind display all the symptoms of catatonia. In Sturgeon's *More than Human* (1953), the telepathic role in the new evolutionary step of Homo gestalt, or group mind, is first filled by an idiot and later by a psychopath. The protagonist of Bester's *Demolished Man* (1953) is told by a telepath that telepaths will go mad if forced to live solely among nontelepathic humans. And in Blish's *Jack of Eagles* (1952; published in paperback as *ESPer*), schizophrenia is defined as "a splitting of the personality into psi and non-psi groups,"[30] "psi" being one of the traditional science-fiction catchwords for telepathic powers.

With the theme of telepathy, then, we have the most direct identification of the unknown with the deepest and most primal secrets of the human mind. The invasion of the personality that is only symbolically represented by monsters and invaders from space is here made literal, and while telepaths are nearly always treated sympathetically, they are probably among the most effective monsters that the genre has produced. Human in appearance except for telltale details (tendrils in *Slan,* baldness in *Mutant,* height in Delany's *Fall of the Towers*), they threaten us on a personal level much in the way Wells's Martians threaten us on a racial level: by subjecting us to the kind of examination and subjugation that we characteristically visit on lower forms of life. In both *Slan* and *Mutant,* telepaths eventually achieve mastery of the earth, with the authors implying that this is the natural direction of evolution and that humanity's only hope for the future is, in Sturgeon's phrase, becoming "more than human." Bester's depiction of a society regulated by telepathic police in *The Demolished Man* is somewhat more ominous, with telepathy serving the uses of totalitarianism in a world that is morally not much different from our own. Bester seems to imply that telepathy without an attendant advance in morality is scarcely a step up the evolutionary ladder.

This notion is more fully explored by Sturgeon in *More Than Human* (1953), the novel that won the then-prestigious International Fantasy Award in the same year that *The Demolished Man, Childhood's End,* and *Mutant* were published—something of a golden year for science fiction's treatment of human mutations. In his conception of Homo gestalt, "the next step upward," a superbeing made up of the collective psychic talents of six people, Sturgeon displays an acute awareness of all aspects of human and superhuman consciousness from the vegetative on up to the highly ethical. As is common in science fiction, the "novel" is really three connected stories, the first published of which was the middle section, "Baby is Three." This story concerns an idiot with powers of mind reading and thought control who meets a nine-year-old girl with powers of telekinesis, twin Negro girls capable of teleportation, and a fat, non-growing baby with a mind like an analytical computer. The baby is the "brain" of this new being, the twins the hands and arms, the girl the body, and the idiot the head. The idiot dies and is replaced by a delinquent boy, who uses the gestalt to release his psychopathic hatred of society. Not until a normal human is added to the group in the third story, however, is Homo gestalt complete, for the normal human represents morality. At that time the gestalt is welcomed into a vast and immortal (immortal because individual "parts" can be replaced) company of other gestalts, who have for centuries been engineering human culture and who in fact engineered the coincidences that brought the members of this particular group together.

Structurally, the novel begins with the lowest aspect of human consciousness, the vegetative, and ends with the highest aspect, the ethical. The first character we meet is Lone the idiot, living a savage existence in the forest, and the terms with which Sturgeon describes Lone are similar to the terms with which he described his putrescent vegetable monster in "It":

> He was purely animal. . . . He killed like an animal, without hate and without joy. He ate like an animal, everything edible he could find. . . . He slept like an animal, well and lightly, faced in the opposite direction from that of a man; for a man going to sleep is about to escape into it while animals are prepared to escape out of it. . . . He was without humor and without joy. His spectrum lay between terror and contentment.[31]

Later, Lone loses his only human friend, and the loss is "the loss of everything conscious, directed, cooperative; everything above and beyond what a vegetable could do by way of living" (p. 74).

In terms of our beast iconography, Lone is clearly the representative of the vegetable aspect of humanity's being, of its chthonian origins. One of the continuing themes of the novel is that the whole of the gestalt is greater than the sum of its parts, and this is especially true of the part represented by Lone, who by himself is virtually subhuman. To introduce his theme of "more than human," Sturgeon begins by introducing a character who is palpably less than human, as if to suggest that a higher state of evolution does not supplant lower forms, but incorporates them into new relationships. The gestalt of which Lone is to be a part is anticipated by his participation early in the novel in a normal human family (normal for Sturgeon, at least), the Prodds, who rescue him wounded from the woods and adopt him to replace the son they never had. This familial group is a way of demonstrating that Lone, in normal human terms, is barely functional, able to help with basic tasks but unable to participate meaningfully in a human community. Only when he begins to assemble his gestalt does his value to the Prodds increase, as he constructs, on the directions of Baby, an antigravity device to help Prodd get his truck unstuck from the mud. And even in this episode, the imagery is of the earth: the first real collective accomplishment of the gestalt involves a technology that literally helps man to crawl out of the mud. The device goes unused, however, since Lone lacks the intelligence to realize what he has built.

Ironically, Lone's first awareness of his powers comes when he receives a telepathic signal from a woman whose defect is virtually the opposite of his. If Lone is animal humanity, Evelyn Kew is repressed humanity, a young woman raised by an insanely puritanical father to subdue all her animal instincts, even to the point of bathing in the dark. Both men and women are to her evil, bestial creatures; she has been taught that she is "more than human" in a perverse, psychotic way. The first significant barrier image in the novel is the barrier that separates Evelyn, sending out her desperate cries of need, from Lone: the huge fence that Evelyn's father has constructed around their farm. It is the breaching of this barrier by Lone that initially precipitates the novel's action. His meeting with Evelyn first makes him aware of "what was human in him" (p. 10), introduces the character of Evelyn's sister, Alicia, and results in the beating of Lone that produces the wounds that prompt Prodd to rescue him from the forest. The first tentative union of two members of Homo gestalt, the first real conquest of the unknown for Lone, is accomplished by the passage through a barrier.

This union does not last, however, for Evelyn is killed by her father in his rage at discovering her with a man. The next gestalt characters to be introduced are Janie and the twins, considerably more lively than Lone but also incomplete. If Lone is the unmotivated vegetative aspect of behavior, these children represent the "unanalyzed but accurate" feelings (p. 32) of instinctive animals. The twins in particular are described in animal imagery. They communicate only through "chitterings and squeals" and "squeak and scramble and claw" their way into their clothes (p. 34). They are described variously as kittens, gargoyles, monkeys, and "little animals" and initially have no use for their teleportation abilities other than playing tricks on Janie; their actions have no purpose or meaning. Janie manages to organize them a bit, but she herself lacks the maturity to make difficult judgments, and while the partial gestalt that she and the twins set up is certainly a step above the individual personalities of each of them, and is several steps above the personality of Lone, it remains rather directionless and pointless.

Baby is physically the most incomplete member of the gestalt, never growing or developing, but merely processing information like a computer. Of all the characters, Baby is perhaps closest to the alien monster figure, representing as he does an evolutionary step in which physical degereration (he never grows beyond infancy) is accompanied by vast intellectual powers, not unlike the Martians in Well's *War of the Worlds*. Each of the characters in the gestalt seems to represent a possible future evolutionary step, and indeed each of these characters' talents has its own subgenre of science-fiction stories. The genre to which Baby belongs is probably the most powerful, because of the

219

grotesqueness, amorality, and real power involved (as opposed to the more or less theatrical powers of the other characters). The other members of the gestalt possess powers that are traditional to fantasy and fairy tales, but Baby's powers are merely extensions of talents that all humans possess.

Neither Lone nor the delinquent is capable of completing the gestalt, Lone because of his defective intellect and Gerry because of his stunted moral sensibility. Sturgeon does not quite make clear why the normal Hip is needed to provide the ethic for the group, since there is ample evidence of ethical behavior on the part of Janie and Lone, but apparently the author does not want to risk consigning this highest of all human qualities to a lower status by not giving it a separate identity in the group. The completed group includes extrapolations of three aspects of human behavior: the physical (Janie and the twins), the intellectual (Baby and Gerry), and the moral (Hip). In terms of imagery, however, the movement may be defined as from vegetable (Lone) to animal (the twins) to spiritual (Hip). It is significant that only the spiritual aspect does not undergo an evolutionary leap; Hip's morality is not noticeably different from anyone else's though all other group members are mutations. As Eric Rabkin observes, "Room is made for us."[32] Like most science-fiction writers, Sturgeon has chosen to confine his extrapolations to the empirical, and not to attempt describing a higher morality.

But as Hip tells Gerry, what the gestalt needs is not so much a morality as an ethos. "The morals of ordinary men would do you no better than the morals of an anthill would do me," Hip tells Gerry telepathically. "So nobody wants you and you are a monster" (p. 227). It is moral alienation that breeds monsters, and alien behavior is as much a part of the feared unknown as is alien appearance. Sturgeon's characters begin as aliens in society, unable to function in family and social life, and end as aliens in a more literal evolutionary sense. Both kinds of alienation are resolved when the gestalt joins other gestalts; it then becomes part of a superior social order directing human behavior, as well as a natural and continuing part of human evolution. These discoveries serve to resolve the known-unknown opposition that the members of the gestalt have represented in their roles as freaks and monsters and, as Rabkin observes, unify the narrative by resolving its coincidences.[33]

This sort of integration on human mutations into a system of ongoing historical process is one way science fiction often tries to resolve the "monstrousness" of superior beings. If the unknown mutation can be

220

subsumed into a knowable pattern of evolution or history, the imbalance caused by the presence of such a creature is corrected, much as Isaac Asimov resolves the anomalies of his *Foundation* novels by showing that they are really fulfillments of an historical plan. But if mutants are made to seem less bestial by this process, the bestial imagery itself is not abandoned; it is merely transferred to the "normals," thus enabling the science-fiction author to resolve his antinomies without violating the pattern of imagery he has set up to define those antinomies. At the end of *More Than Human,* Janie explains to Hip the situation of Homo gestalt as "living on a desert island with a herd of goats" (p. 211). by altering the point of view, the author lets us see humans themselves as beasts in the eyes of the superior beings, and a favorite term for humans in much science fiction, including *More Than Human,* is "Homo saps."

By now, we have nearly come full circle in discussing monster imagery, arriving at a genre of "monster stories" in which the humans themselves are the real monsters. Again we may turn to Olaf Stapledon for an early example of this pattern of development, and indeed for what is probably the first use of the term "Homo saps." Stapledon's *Odd John* (1936) is almost as influential human mutation story as *Last and First Men* and *Star Maker* are in the area of cosmic history stories. Like Baby in *More Than Human,* John is retarded in growth, and like Lone, he is at first regarded as subnormal. but soon he is found to be the next evolutionary step above man, and from then on the wealth of animal images associated with "normals" is overwhelming. John with his mother suggests "a human foundling with a wolf foster-mother; or, better, a cow foster-mother."[34] The narrator, who befriends John, is referred to by himself as well as John as a dog or trusty hound, and John's nickname for him is "Fido." A wealthy industrialist whom John interviews is described as a "shy horse." John is unable to consummate his first sexual affair with a local beauty because of an overwhelming feeling "'as though a dog were smelling round me, or a monkey'" (p. 563). John himself is described by this woman as "'a god pretending to be a monkey'" (p. 562). John's terms for humanity are unequivocally bestial: an "archiopterix of the spirit," a "crude animal," a pet cat, a "vast herd of cattle," an ostrich, a "spider trying to crawl out of a basin," a moth, a chicken and so on. These images are not randomly chosen by Stapledon. John has a peculiar affection for birds, for example, but the birds he compares to man (archiopteryx, ostrich, chicken) are consistently birds capable of only the most rudimentary flight. Man is clearly the "monster" in this story, the beast that stands partway

221

between the uncreated chaos of nature and the transcendent order of John's kind. By the end of the novel, humans are referred to not only by John, but also by the human narrator as well, as "less than human."

But even *Homo superior* does not represent the final evolution of monsters in science fiction. Stapledon and others have described sentient stars (Odd John makes contact with these, and they are described in detail in *Star Maker*) that are "angelic" in nature, and Stapledon himself goes on to describe the "perfect spirit" of the Star Maker. To such creatures, physical life itself is infinitely primitive. With such concepts as the sentient matter of stars and disembodied intelligences, the science-fiction hierarchy of intelligent life describes a kind of full circle back to the most primitive "monsters" we have seen— beings of mineral and vegetable origin, intelligence as uncreated matter, even as space. What appears to us as Chaos becomes an infinitely greater cosmos than we can imagine, and in this strange new context, what we regard as creation can be seen as imperfect or only partially created Chaos. We ourselves become representatives of disorder rather than order, as in C. S. Lewis's trilogy of theological science-fiction novels.

Though we have long ago left behind any conventional notion of the "monster" that is the icon of the body of works we have been discussing, an overview of the types of creatures represented in this chapter reveals a curious pattern in the mythology of science fiction, a pattern that serves to unite the simple monster story with the more conventional technocratic vision that Lewis Mumford and others have characterized as central to the genre. This pattern involves the ultimate intelligibility and potential subjugation of the natural universe. In tales of monsters, aliens, and transformed humans, we find this belief reflected as a persistence of what Arthur Lovejoy, in *The Great Chain of Being,* calls "the principle of plenitude":

> . . . the thesis that the universe is a *plenum formarum* in which the range of conceivable diversity of *kinds* of living things is exhaustively exemplified, but also any other deductions from the assumption that no genuine potentiality of being can remain unfulfilled, that the extent and abundance of the creation must be as great as the possibility of existence and commensurate with the productive capacity of a "perfect" and inexhaustible Source, and that the world is the better, the more things it contains.[35]

In Lovejoy's formulation, this principle is vital to the notion of the Chain of Being, a notion that presupposes "a complete rational intelligibility of the world" (p. 329). Leibniz writes that "progress will never come to an end" (quoted in Lovejoy, p. 257) referring to the cumulative perfectibility of the forms of nature and their infinite variety; the science-fiction myth, extrapolating a limitless number of worlds and life forms, views one aspect of the inevitable progress of humanity as the continual discovery of life forms other than our own. And the optimism of the genre seems to dictate that this kind of progress will never come to an end. For this reason, it is an oversimplification to regard the aliens and monsters of science fiction as exclusively projections of unconscious fears or as products of immature imaginations. The icon of the monster is in many ways one of the most complex and richly promising symbols of the unknown and the knowable; it represents that aspect of the unknown that yields the greatest potential for the advance and maturation of the species. Leibniz again: "Every birth of an animal is only the transformation of an animal already alive" (Lovejoy, p. 257). Every alien form adds ultimately to the store of our knowledge and may be accounted for by rational processes of transformation. This is why the transformation of humans into alien life-forms constitutes the "childhood's end" of Clarke's novel, and it is why writers such as Clarke and Stapledon who attempt to extrapolate ultimate life-forms finally resort to the eschatological language of religion. The transformation of understanding that is represented by "knowing the beast" is merely an inversion of the transformation of which Leibniz speaks; it is humanity catching up to God by mastering His forms, appropriating whole categories of knowledge by observing their products. And always, such products remind us at once of our origins and our potentials. This is the antinomy that the icon of the monster represents, but it is also the antinomy represented by the icon of man himself, who is finally revealed to be but one of an infinite number of possible transformations.

A number of science-fiction stories, told from an alien point of view, have presented humanity as the "monster" of the piece. In one of these, A. E. van Vogt's "The Monster" (1948), aliens resurrect several humans on the dead planet Earth to discover what caused the race to destroy itself. They are outwitted by one of the resurrected humans, who then appropriates their resurrection machines (a concept neatly in keeping with the kind of science-fiction faith we have been discussing), revives human life on earth, and tricks the aliens into destroying their own ship. The "monster" of the title is of course this man, whose intelligence and ingenuity allows him to deduce his situation the moment he is resurrected and to act with incredible efficacy on that deduction. He is but one life-form among many the aliens have explored, but he is by far the most ferocious and the most powerful. He is to the aliens what Wells's Martians are to their victims and more; he is at once the beast and the symbol of the limitless human spirit. He is imperfect, arrogant, and brutal, and yet he perhaps most clearly symbolizes what the icon of the monster means in the myth of science fiction: the potent and threatening unknown that in the end is humanity itself.

afterword

At the beginning of this work, I claimed that many science-fiction readers seem to invest a certain part of their own fate in the messages of science fiction, and that the images and structures of science fiction thus take on psychological and cultural significance far deeper than the often formulaic adventure narratives of the genre would seem to suggest. By treating the opposition between the known and the unknown, between what is and what is not yet, between cosmos and chaos, and by expressing these tensions through certain recurring icons, science fiction reveals not only its own beliefs, but also patterns of belief that are imbedded in our culture at large. By using icons that mediate between the polarities of known and unknown, science fiction suggests the possibility of radical transformations of ourselves and our environment, and of a range of potentially infinite experience that is in effect a modern version of Arthur Lovejoy's "principle of plenitude." It is thus a literature that holds out the promise of infinite newness and infinite discovery. This newness may be expressed by means of icons that transform the environment, showing us what life may be like on a spaceship, in vast future cities, or even in hostile wastelands; or it may be expressed by means of icons that transform our images of ourselves, showing us how machines can be made like us, or how we ourselves can be changed into something different. Throughout all these transformations, however, certain principles of reason and science hold true: science fiction may portray a radically unstable universe, but it is a universe governed by stable laws.

So science fiction lets us have it both ways; it shows us that rationality can be made consistent with the wildest imaginings of new environments and new forms of life. It lets us experience the wonder that was once available only through fantasy and fairy tales, but without sacrificing the hard edge of reason that connects us to this world. Dreams are made rational, and rationality is made into a dream. Technology becomes not mere problem solving, but the ritual acting out an endless quest for appropriation of the infinite. And, conversely, teleological questions can be approached through technological means. We can explore the nature of humanity by placing humanity in different imaginary environments and seeing what happens, by asking how we are alike and different from robots and alien beings, or by asking how much we can change the outward form of humanity without changing its essential nature. Those of us who are attracted to such thought experiments can see in them something of our own values and beliefs: that no society is perfectly stable, that technology plays an ambivalent role in human affairs, that humanity is better defined by its deeds than by its appearance.

The icons I have discussed in this study all reflect such beliefs and values in varying degrees. The spaceship, an emblem of both exploration and closure, shows how technology both enables us to explore the unknown and protects us from it—sometimes too well. The city shows how technology may become repressive and overprotective, but the wasteland reminds us that even the most sophisticated technological society is vulnerable, and may even be self-destructive. Robots, aliens, and transformed humans all question the sanctity of human form, but in the end suggest that there is a spirit which, if not quite unique to humanity itself, is at least unique to biological intelligence. These icons condition us to accept the most dramatic changes in ourselves and our environment, and while such changes are not likely to be a direct part of the experience of the science-fiction reader, they create a perspective through which the real changes that our technical civilization puts us through seem less unsettling. The icons as a group form guideposts for an expansive world-view that protects the science-fiction reader from the future and, in some cases, insulates them from the present. All possible events come to be seen with the cool equanimity of an imagined historical perspective. Ironically, science fiction, which begins with a childlike sense of wonder at the universe and its possibilities, often ends in an almost cynical sophistication about social change and the inevitable progression of technology. It impresses us, but it also makes us harder to impress, and sometimes it strives mightily to reawaken those childlike centers of wonder.

In this study, I have attempted to trace how, in its formative years as a distinct genre, science fiction evolved a number of icons that express beliefs and attitudes about humanity and humanity's possible environments. But this is by no means a complete survey of the ideology of the genre, and much work remains to be done in tracing the ideological origins of the body of popular art we know as "science fiction" and in properly locating its attitudes in the history of ideas in general. Scholars such as Thomas D. Clareson and H. Bruce Franklin have shown that the origin of science fiction in popular narratives of the nineteenth century is far more extensive than many of us had previously suspected, and the evolution of the genre's values during that period is certainly ground for further exploration. Similarly, more recent science fiction than is generally treated in this study reveals additional complexities. Writers such as Ursula Le Guin, Stanislaw Lem, Robert Silverberg and others have found new uses for old images, and have constructed fictions that at once make use of the old mythologies while stretching the boundaries of the genre into areas rarely explored by the fictions I have discussed. The last few years have seen an unprecedented era of experimentation in science fiction, and to relate these newer works to the body of work I have treated here might prove a useful exercise in exploring the growing sophistication of a genre too often seen as "merely" popular.

Another fruitful area for exploration might be the extensive cult or subculture known as fandom, which seems almost unique to science fiction. I have drawn my conclusions not on the basis of fandom (since most available evidence suggests that active or self-proclaimed "fans" make up only a small portion of science fiction's readership), but on the basis of the larger culture of which fandom is a part. Still, I suspect that the true fans may possess a remarkably sophisticated knowledge of the iconography and conventions of the genre, and that this knowledge might serve for them a special purpose beyond that of the cultural validation functions it serves for more casual readers. The fans I have met derive something from science fiction that I suspect is quite extraliterary, that tends toward a system of belief and values that may be far more involved than what I have laid out in this book. Whether this constitutes nothing more than a secret mythology of initiates, or something deeper that serves an almost religious function, I do not know. I do know, however, that there are many who take the slogan "FIAWOL" ("Fandom Is A Way Of Life") quite literally, who devote surprising amounts of time to convention and collecting activities, and whose devotion to the genre has never been satisfactorily explained in terms of the platitudes about "escapism" and "the new mythology" that many of us in academia are so fond of tossing about.

Finally, I have made some gestures in this book toward the consideration of science fiction in its nonliterary as well as its literary

227

aspects, since I am convinced that the iconography I have described of spaceships, robots, cities, monsters, and the like has long since escaped confinement to the narratives that initially gave it shape. Science-fiction film, long a maligned stepchild of both the literature of science fiction and the Hollywood action film, suddenly "arrived" in 1977 with George Lucas's *Star Wars* and Steven Spielberg's *Close Encounters of the Third Kind;* as I write, *Star Wars* has recently been proclaimed the highest-grossing film of all time. Aficionados may take exception to many things in both of these films, but it would be foolish to deny that science fiction is at least responsible for them, or that both make extensive use of the kinds of iconography I have described. No doubt many, if not most, of the millions who have seen *Star Wars* are not science-fiction readers, yet they are somehow familiar enough with the conventions of the genre that they feel no discomfort at that film's matter-of-fact use of these conventions to tell a story that is readily recognizable as a swashbuckling adventure saga.

But by extraliterary science fiction, I am thinking of more than film. As recent volumes compiled by Brian Aldiss, Lester del Rey, Frank Kelly Freas, and others have shown, there is a body of popular science-fiction art that is also a part of "science fiction" and yet that is not necessarily purely illustrative (despite the heavy dependence of the aforementioned volumes on magazine illustration). Furthermore, there is a body of nonfiction that shares many of the assumptions, beliefs, and icons of science fiction, and whether it is called "futuristics," "futurology," or whatever, I believe it has significant ideological connections with the genre. Even such relatively eccentric areas of study as UFO's, the Bermuda Triangle, the Atlantis cult, and Scientology may benefit from the application of what we can learn from science fiction. I need hardly remind veteran readers that many of these fads have found their way into the science-fiction magazines, that the founder of Scientology, L. Ron Hubbard, began as a science-fiction writer, or that lost-continent theories such as those of Richard Shaver often came to public attention in the science-fiction magazines. And science fiction reaches still further: this past season, I have seen not only a number of television series based on icons such as those I have discussed, but even television *commercials* that employ science-fiction iconography to sell automobiles and breakfast cereals. By the time science fiction filters into such areas as these, the narratives have all but evaporated, but the iconography remains. To me, this suggests that there is something more to the genre than a group of interesting stories written by a limited group of writers over the years.

I am not, of course, suggesting that we abandon the study of the artistry that goes into science-fiction narratives in favor of some broad-based social anthropology of the genre—merely that we consider these pervasive influences of the genre. Certainly, the aesthetic study of science fiction remains a field ripe for exploration—all the more so now that its writers seem to be overcoming the provincialism that has for so long characterized science fiction. But here, too, I would suggest the value of studying images and ideological systems rather than simple plot-forms. Like other popular genres, science fiction has its formulae, but I doubt that these formulae can be expressed quite as simply and elegantly as scholars such as John Cawelti have expressed the formulae of detective stories and Westerns. Perhaps the formulae are based on ideational structures rather than narratives; perhaps they are in some way bound up with the use of certain icons such as those I have described. In any event, the nature of the genre is such that its future growth remains promising, perhaps more promising than ever before, and for those of us who study the genre, it seems hardly excessive to say that our work has barely begun.

notes

PREFACE

1. Donald Wollheim, *The Universe Makers* (New York: Harper, 1971), pp. 42-44; James Gunn, *Alternate Worlds: The Illustrated History of Science Fiction* (Englewood Cliffs, N.J.: Prentice-Hall, 1975), pp. 225-26. See also Gunn's essay, "Science Fiction and the Mainstream," in *Science Fiction, Today and Tomorrow*, ed. Reginald Bretnor (New York: Harper, 1974), p. 190.

2. "The *Real* Earth Satellite Story," in *Explorers of the Infinite: Shapers of Science Fiction* (New York: World, 1963), pp. 88-105.

3. *Anthropology: Culture Patterns and Processes* (New York: Harbinger, 1963), pp. 172-73.

1. ICONS OF WONDER

1. "Introduction: Man and Myth," in *Larousse World Mythology*, ed. P. Grimal, trans. Patricia Beardsworth (New York: Prometheus Press, 1965), p. 10.

2. *Myth and Reality*, trans. Willard R. Trask (New York: Harper Torchbooks, 1968), p. 141.

3. *Myths, Models, and Paradigms: A Comparative Study in Science and Religion* (New York: Harper, 1974), p. 24.

4. Grimal, *Larousse*, p. 9.

5. The 1947 date is from James Gunn, *Alternate Worlds: The Illustrated History of Science Fiction* (Englewood Cliffs, N.J.: Prentice-Hall, 1975), p. 126; Heinlein defends the term in an essay in *The Science Fiction Novel: Imagination and Social Criticism* (Chicago: Advent, 1959).

6. *Before Philosophy (The Intellectual Adventure of Ancient Man): An Essay on Speculative Thought in the Ancient Near East* (Baltimore: Penguin, 1949), pp. 11-12.

7. *The Billion-Year Spree: The True History of Science Fiction* (New York: Schocken, 1974), Chap. 1.

8. *The English Novel: A Short Critical History* (New York: Dutton, 1957), p. 102.

9. Aldiss, *Billion-Year Spree*, pp. 13ff.

10. "Science Fiction and the Mainstream," in *Science Fiction, Today and Tomorrow*, ed. Reginald Bretnor (New York: Harper, 1974) p. 190.

11. "Science Fiction: Its Nature, Faults, and Virtues," in *The Science Fiction Novel* (Chicago: Advent, 1959), p. 21.

12. *Intellectual Digest,* (Dec. 1971), p. 77.

13. "Science Fiction: A Literature of Ideas," *Extrapolation,* (Dec. 1971), p. 60.

14. Interview with Gene van Troyer, *Vertex,* 2, 5 (December 1974), 39.

15. "Editorial," *Amazing Science Fiction,* 50, 1 (June 1976), 123.

16. "Cosmology and Science Fiction," *Science Fiction Studies,* 12 (July 1977), 109.

17. *The Pentagon of Power* (New York: Harcourt Brace, 1970), p. 27.

18. Mumford, *Pentagon,* caption for fig. 11.

19. Mumford, *Pentagon,* p. 220.

20. "The Tissue-Culture King," in *Time Probe: The Sciences in Science Fiction,* ed. Arthur C. Clarke (New York: Dell, 1966), p. 238.

21. Mumford, *Pentagon,* p. 221.

22. *The Technological Society,* trans. John Wilkinson (New York: Vintage Books, 1967), p. vi.

23. Ellul, *Technological Society,* p. 85.

24. Ellul, *Technological Society,* p. 126.

25. Michael Polanyi and Harry Prosch, *Meaning* (Chicago: University of Chicago Press, 1975), p. 25.

26. Cambridge: MIT Press, 1977, p. 335.

27. Quoted in Raphael Patai, *Myth and Modern Man* (Englewood Cliffs, N.J.: Prentice-Hall, 1972), p. 85.

28. *The Universe Makers* (New York: Harper, 1971), pp. 42-44.

29. In *Star Short Novels,* ed. Frederik Pohl (New York: Ballantine, 1954), p. 109.

30. Polanyi, *Meaning,* p. 29.

31. *The Structure of Scientific Revolutions* (Chicago: University of Chicago Press, 1962; Phoenix Edition 1964), p. 95.

32. Kuhn, *Structure of Scientific Revolutions,* p. 139.

33. "Science Fiction and the Future," in *Science Fiction: A Collection of Critical Essays,* ed. Mark Rose (Englewood Cliffs, N.J. : Prentice-Hall, 1976), p. 162.

34. *Androgyny: Toward a New Theory of Sexuality* (Garden City, N.J.: Doubleday, 1976), p. 59.

35. "About 5, 175 Words," in *SF: The Other Side of Realism,* ed. Thomas D. Clareson (Bowling Green, Ohio: Bowling Green University Popular Press, 1971), p. 140.

36. "Speculations: The Subjunctivity of Science Fiction," *Extrapolation,* 15, 1 (December 1973), 52.

37. C. G. Jung, *Flying Saucers: A Modern Myth of Things Seen in the Skies,* trans. R. F. C. Hull (New York: Harcourt Brace, 1959), pp. 22-23.

38. Jung, *Flying Saucers,* p. 173.

39. Jung, *Flying Saucers,* p. 176.

40. New York: Ballantine Books, 1976, p. 36.

41. Niven, *World Out of Time,* p. 35.

42. "The Game of Rat and Dragon," in *The Best of Cordwainer Smith* (New York: Ballantine Books, 1975), p. 72.

43. "The Sentinel," in *Expedition to Earth* (New York: Ballantine Books, 1953), p. 165.

44. Bretnor, *Science Fiction, Today and Tomorrow,* p. 11.

45. *Science Fiction: What It's All About* (New York: Ace Books, 1971), p. 24.

46. Lem, "Cosmology and Science Fiction," p. 109.

47. *The Science Fiction Book: An Illustrated History* (New York: New American Library, 1975), p. 9.

48. Translated by Mary Foran (New York: Macmillan, 1972), p. 26.

chapter three

49. The story is widely reprinted. Page references here are to *The Science Fiction Hall of Fame*, ed. Robert Silverberg (Garden City, N.J.: Doubleday, 1970).

50. New York: Avon Equinox Books, 1976, p. 7.

51. In *A Treasury of Great Science Fiction*, ed. Anthony Boucher (Garden City, N.J.: Doubleday, 1959), II, 361.

52. New York: Avon Books, 1961, p. 9.

2. THE IMAGE OF THE BARRIER

1. In Robert Silverberg, ed., *The Science Fiction Hall of Fame* (Garden City, N.J.: Doubleday, 1970), p. 111. Subsequent references to stories appearing in this anthology will be made in the text.

2. "Cosmology and Science Fiction," *Science Fiction Studies* 12 (July 1977), 109.

3. In Theodore Sturgeon, *A Touch of Strange* (Garden City, N.J.: Doubleday, 1958), pp. 19-20.

4. "The Time-Travel Story and Related Matters of SF Structuring," in *Science Fiction: A Collection of Critical Essays*, ed. Mark Rose (Englewood Cliffs, N.J.: Prentice-Hall, 1976), p. 88.

5. "Lost Lands, Lost Races: A Pagan Princess of Their Very Own," in *Many Futures, Many Worlds: Theme and Form in Science Fiction*, ed. Thomas D. Clareson (Kent, Ohio: Kent State University Press, 1977), p. 137.

6. Lem, "Time-Travel Story," p. 80.

7. In *Six Great Short Novels of Science Fiction*, ed. Groff Conklin (New York: Dell, 1954), p. 222. Future references will be to this edition.

8. Lem, "Time-Travel Story," p. 80.

9. *The Santaroga Barrier* (New York: Berkley, 1968), p. 255. Future references are to this edition.

10. "Is Jaspers Beer Good for You? Mass Society and Counter Culture in Herbert's *Santaroga Barrier*," *Extrapolation*, 17, 2 (May 1976), 160-67.

3. ICON OF THE SPACESHIP

1. *Mythologies*, trans. Richard Howard (New York: Hill and Wang, 1973), p. 66.

2. *From the Earth to the Moon and a Trip Around It*, trans. anon. (New York: Fawcett, 1958), pp. 110-11.

3. New York: Berkley, 1967, p. 34. Future references are to this edition.

4. Westport, Conn.: Hyperion, 1974, p. 22. Future references are to this edition.

5. New York: Avon, 1949, pp. 28-29. Future references are to this edition.

6. *Adventure, Mystery, and Romance: Formula Stories as Art and Popular Culture* (Chicago: University of Chicago Press, 1976), p. 101.

7. *The Pentagon of Power* (New York: Harcourt, Brace, 1970), p. 227.

8. *The Poetics of Space*, trans. Maria Jolas (Boston: Beacon Press, 1969), p. 5.

9. Bachelard, *Poetics of Space*, p. 9.

10. *Orphans of the Sky* (New York: Berkley, 1963), p. 49; future references to this edition. Heinlein makes an even more direct comparison between one of his characters and Galileo in "Life-Line" (1939), in which a character complains that "academic minds clinging like oysters to disproved theories" have "blocked every advance of knowledge in history," and adds, "I am prepared to prove my method by experiment, and, like Galileo in another court, I insist, 'It still moves.'"

notes

11. *Strangers in the Universe* (New York: Berkley, 1957), p. 52. Future references are to this edition.

12. New York: New American Library, 1960, p. 72.

13. Originally published in *Astounding*; reprinted in *Adventures in the Far Future*, ed. Donald A. Wollheim (New York: Ace, 1954).

14. New York: Avon Equinox, 1976, p. 8. Future references are to this edition.

15. New York: Berkley, 1969, p. 9. Future references are to this edition.

16. New York: Ballantine, 1959, p. 4. Future references are to this edition.

17. A discussion of the stereotyping of women in science fiction may be found in Beverly Friend, "Virgin Territory: The Bonds and Boundaries of Women in Science Fiction," in *Many Futures, Many Worlds*, ed. Thomas D. Clareson (Kent, Ohio: Kent State University Press, 1977).

18. New York: New American Library, 1960, p. 100.

19. *The Best of Cordwainer Smith*, ed. J. J. Pierce (New York: Ballantine, 1975), p. 85. Future references are to this edition.

20. In *Galactic Cluster* (New York: New American Library, 1959), p. 56.

21. In *The World That Couldn't Be and Eight Other Novelets from Galaxy*, ed. H. L. Gold (New York: Permabooks, 1961), p. 258. The alien refers to himself as human apparently because he had taken human form in a previous incarnation.

22. In *Untouched by Human Hands* (New York: Ballantine, 1954).

23. New York: Berkley, 1966, p. 7. Future references are to this edition.

24. In *The Worlds of Clifford Simak* (New York: Avon, 1960), p. 147. Future references are to this edition.

25. *The Ship Who Sang* (New York: Ballantine, 1970), pp. 9-10. Future references are to this edition.

26. Garden City, N.J.: Doubleday, 1950, p. 7.

27. Garden City, N.J.: Doubleday Anchor, 1967, p. 104.

4. ICON OF THE CITY

1. Reproduced in Brian Aldiss, *Science Fiction Art* (New York: Bounty, 1975), p. 12.

2. *The Pentagon of Power* (New York: Harcourt Brace, 1970), fig. 11.

3. *Where the Wasteland Ends* (Garden City, N.J.: Doubleday, 1972), p. 10.

4. *Metropolis*, trans. anon. (New York: Ace, 1963 [1927]), p. 18.

5. *New Worlds for Old: The Apocalyptic Imagination, Science Fiction, and American Literature* (Garden City, N.J.: Doubleday Anchor, 1974), p. 102.

6. Roszak, *Wasteland*, p. 14.

7. "A City of Which the Stars are Suburbs," in *The Other Side of Realism*, ed. Thomas Clareson (Bowling Green, Ohio: Bowling Green University Popular Press, 1971), pp. 334-47.

8. *Cosmos and History: The Myth of the Eternal Return*, trans. Willard R. Trask (New York: Harper Torchbooks, 1959 [1954]), p. 5.

9. Mumford, *Pentagon*, p. 310.

10. *The Caves of Steel* (New York: New American Library, 1955 [1953]), p. 20.

11. "The Poet and the City," in *The Dyer's Hand* (New York: Vintage, 1968), p. 85.

12. Quoted in Norman O. Brown, *Life Against Death* (New York: Vintage, 1959), p. 282.

13. Brown, *Life Against Death*, p. 282.

14. Roszak, *Wasteland*, p. 10.

chapter four

15. Cited in J. E. Cirlot, *A Dictionary of Symbols,* trans. Jack Sage (New York: Philosophical Library, 1962), p. 47.

16. "Myth and Demythification in SF: Zelazny's *Lord of Light.*" Paper delivered before the Modern Language Association, December 1976, Session 137. Special session: Science Fiction and Mythology: Practical Resolutions.

17. "The Current Cinema," *The New Yorker,* 2 December 1974, p. 152.

18. New York: Ballantine, 1969, p. 53. Future references are to this edition.

19. "The Time Machine and Its Context," trans. Frank McConnell, in H. G. Wells, *The Time Machine/The War of the Worlds: A Critical Edition,* ed. Frank D. McConnell (New York: Oxford, 1977), p. 319.

20. *New Maps of Hell* (New York: Ballantine, 1960), p. 33.

21. Quoted in Vernier, "Time Machine and Its Context," p. 317.

22. For a more extended discussion of Wells's view of the end of man, see Alex Eisenstein, "The Time Machine and the End of Man," *Science Fiction Studies* 9 (July 1976), pp. 161-65.

23. Quoted in Brian Aldiss, *The Billion-Year Spree: The True History of Science Fiction* (New York: Schocken, 1974), p. 109.

24. Aldiss, *Billion-Year Spree,* p. 116.

25. "The Death Trap" is reprinted in *Science Fiction by Gaslight,* ed. Sam Moskowitz (Cleveland: World, 1968), pp. 155-66.

26. *The Country and the City* (New York: Oxford, 1973), pp. 273-74.

27. "The Silliest Film: Will Machines Make Robots of Men?" in *Authors on Film,* ed. Harry M. Geduld (Bloomington: Indiana University Press, 1972), pp. 59-60.

28. Page references are to the Oxford edition cited in note 19 above.

29. Mumford, *Pentagon,* p. 49.

30. *28 Science Fiction Stories* (New York: Dover, 1952 [1905]), p. 748. Future references are to this edition.

31. New York: Ace, n.d. [1899], p. 144. Future references are to this edition.

32. E. M. Forster quoted in Alan Wilde, *Art and Order: A Study of E. M. Forster* (New York: New York University Press, 1964), p. 86.

33. "The Machine Stops" in *The Light Fantastic: Science Fiction Classics from the Mainstream,* ed. Harry Harrison (New York: Scribner's, 1971), p. 119. Future references are to this edition.

34. Wells, "The Silliest Film," p. 62.

35. Aldiss, *Science Fiction Art,* p. 89.

36. New York: Ace, 1970, p. 412. Future references are to this edition.

37. See "The Structural Study of Myth," Chap. 11 of *Structural Anthropology,* trans. Claire Jacobson and Brooke Grundfest Schoepf (New York: Basic Books, 1963), pp. 206-31.

38. In an earlier version of the novel, *Against the Fall of Night* (New York: Gnome Press, 1953), Alvin's quest is guided by clues left by a long-dead elder named Alaine of Lyndar. In the later novel, Alaine is partly supplanted by Khedron and partly by the near-mythical figure of Yarlan Zey, the city founder who had realized the need for change and thus programmed "loopholes" into the security system of the central computer—anticipating a "revolutionary" such as Alvin.

39. In *Against the Fall of Night,* this role is filled by an old man rather than a polyp. The old man, like the beast, is a kind of icon, but one more associated with fairy tales than science fiction, and one whose presence is never satisfactorily explained. By replacing him

235

with a polyp, Clarke not only can take advantage of the iconic value of the beast image, but can provide a biological explanation of the creature's presence and its immense age. The explanation provides a curious analog with Diaspar: the creature is immortal, but lives in cycles, with its cellular structure dispersing and restructuring at the end of each cycle according to a genetic "program"—much as Diaspar's inhabitants are eternally "recycled" by the computer.

40. *The City and the Stars* (New York: New American Library, 1957), p. 9. Future references are to this edition.

41. "Arcology: The City in the Image of Man," in *The City: American Experience,* ed. Alan Trachtenberg, Peter Neill, and Peter C. Bunnell (New York: Oxford, 1971), p. 589. Future references are to this edition.

42. Aldiss, *Science Fiction Art,* p. 89.

43. *The World Inside* (New York: New American Library, 1972), p. 30.

44. Aldiss, *Science Fiction Art,* p. 112.

45. Steve Mitchell, "Interview with Special Effects Director Doug Trumbull," *Film-makers Newsletter,* 11, 1 (December 1977), 21.

46. *A Life for the Stars* (New York: Avon, 1963), p. 9. Future references are to this edition.

47. Aldiss, *Billion-Year Spree,* p. 251.

48. James Blish, *Cities in Flight* (New York: Avon, 1970). Future references are to this edition.

5. ICON OF THE WASTELAND

1. *Tomorrow!* (New York: Popular Library, 1956), p. 6.

2. *The Billion-Year Spree: The True History of Science Fiction* (New York: Schocken, 1974), pp. 246-47.

3. "Science Fiction as Fictive History," in *Many Futures, Many Worlds,* ed. Thomas D. Clareson (Kent, Ohio: Kent State University Press, 1977), pp. 170, 175.

4. "The Earthmanist Culture: *Cities in Flight* as a Spenglerian History," Afterword to *Cities in Flight* by James Blish (New York: Avon, 1970), pp. 597-605.

5. *Earth is Room Enough* (Garden City, N.J.: Doubleday, 1957), p. 56.

6. *Re-birth,* in *A Treasury of Great Science Fiction,* ed. Anthony Boucher (Garden City, N.J.: Doubleday, 1959), p. 9. Future references are to this edition.

7. *The Long Tomorrow* (Garden City, N.J.: Doubleday, 1955), p. 167. Future references are to this edition.

8. *Science Fiction Reader's Guide* (Lincoln, Neb.: Centennial Press, 1974), pp. 121-22.

9. *A Canticle for Leibowitz* (New York: Bantam, 1961), p. 46. Future references are to this edition.

10. Joseph Gaer, *The Legend of the Wandering Jew* (New York: New American Library, 1961), pp. 22-24.

11. Russell Griffin, "Medievalism in *A Canticle for Leibowitz,*" *Extrapolation,* 14, 2 (May 1973), 113; Robert Scholes and Eric S. Rabkin, *Science Fiction: History, Science, Vision* (New York: Oxford, 1977), p. 221.

12. Gaer, *Wandering Jew,* p. 87.

13. Allen, *Reader's Guide,* p. 120.

14. Griffin, "Medievalism," p. 116.

15. Griffin, "Medievalism," pp. 123, 125.

16. "The Lost Canticles of Walter M. Miller, Jr.," *Science Fiction Studies* 8 (March 1976), 4.

6. ICON OF THE ROBOT

1. "Killdozer," in *Aliens 4* (New York: Avon, 1959), p. 5.

2. "Skirmish" in *Science Fiction Thinking Machines,* ed. Groff Conklin (New York: Bantam, 1955), p. 70.

3. *The Human Use of Human Beings: Cybernetics and Society* (Garden City, N.J.: Doubleday Anchor, 1954), p. 162.

4. There is some confusion regarding the meaning of the term "androids" in science fiction; the definition I have used is simply the one implied by the word's etymology: "resembling a man." Martin Greenberg once defined android as a "robot that could think," and Groff Conklin offered "a living being that has been created partly or wholly through processes other than human birth" (*Science Fiction Thinking Machines,* p. xi). Franz Rottensteiner suggests "artificial humans, mass-produced chemically to do low menial tasks" (*The Science Fiction Book,* New York: New American Library, 1975, p. 53), and Robert Scholes and Eric Rabkin specify "constructions or artificial growths of protoplasmic materials" (*Science Fiction: History, Science, Vision,* New York: Oxford, 1977, p. 180). In George Lucas's film *Star Wars,* "droids" seems to be applied loosely to any robots. There is not much consistency among science-fiction writers or critics regarding the use of this term.

5. *R.U.R.,* trans. Paul Selver and Nigel Playfair, in *The Treasury of Science Fiction Classics,* ed. Harold W. Kuebler (Garden City, N.J.: Hanover House, 1954), p. 350. Future references are to this edition.

6. *Natural Symbols: Explorations in Cosmology* (New York: Vintage, 1973), p. 99.

7. In *Science Fiction Thinking Machines,* ed. Groff Conklin (New York: Vanguard, 1949), p. 203. There are numerous other anthologies concerning robots in science fiction, edited by Martin Greenberg, Sam Moskowitz, Robert Silverberg, and others.

8. "Who Can Replace a Man?" in *Galaxies Like Grains of Sand* (New York: New American Library, 1960), p. 38.

9. "The Proud Robot," in *More Adventures in Time and Space,* ed. Raymond J. Healy and J. Francis McComas (New York: Bantam, 1955), p. 30. Future references are to this edition.

10. *Science Fiction: What It's All About,* trans. Sam Lundwall (New York: Ace, 1971), p. 164.

11. "Asimov, Calvin, and Moses," in *Voices for the Future: Essays on Major Science Fiction Writers,* ed. Thomas Clareson, Vol. I (Bowling Green, Ohio: The Bowling Green University Popular Press, 1976), pp. 92-100.

12. Moore, "Asimov," p. 101.

13. Isaac Asimov, *I, Robot* (Greenwich, Conn.: Fawcett, n.d. [1950]), p. 6. Future references will be to this edition.

14. "Robots in Science Fiction," trans. Franz Rottensteiner, in *SF: The Other Side of Realism,* ed. Thomas D. Clareson (Bowling Green, Ohio: The Bowling Green University Popular Press, 1971), p. 314.

15. "Why I Selected 'Robot AL 76 Goes Astray,'" in *My Best Science Fiction Story,* ed. Leo Margulies and Oscar J. Friend (New York: Pocket Books, 1954 [1949]), p. 1.

16. "The Next 100 Years," reprinted in *Social Speculations: Visions for Our Time,* ed. Richard Kostelanetz (New York: Morrow, 1971), p. 53.

17. Trans. John Wilkinson (New York: Vintage, 1967), p. 390.

18. See Lundwall, *What It's All About,* p. 166; see also Scholes and Rabkin, *History, Science, Vision,* p. 188.

19. "With Folded Hands," in *A Treasury of Science Fiction*, ed. Groff Conklin (New York: Berkley, n.d.), p. 45. Future references are to this edition.

20. *Seekers of Tomorrow: Masters of Modern Science Fiction* (New York: Ballantine, 1967), p. 104.

21. "The Years of Wonder," in Clareson, *Voices for the Future*, p. 9.

22. *The Billion-Year Spree: The True History of Science Fiction* (New York: Schocken, 1974), p. 224.

23. *The Humanoids* (New York: Avon Equinox, 1976 [1949]), p. 7. Future references are to this edition.

24. *Technological Man: The Myth and the Reality* (New York: Braziller, 1969), p. 255. Future references are to this edition.

25. "Jack Williamson: The Comedy of Cosmic Evolution," in Clareson, *Voices for the Future*, p. 29.

26. *Colossus* (New York: Berkley, 1967), p. 202.

27. In *Star Shine* (New York: Bantam, 1954), p. 16.

28. "Asimov, Calvin, and Moses," in Clareson, *Voices for the Future*, p. 103.

29. "The Last Question," in *Nine Tomorrows* (Garden City, N.J.: Doubleday, 1959), pp. 189-90. Future references are to this edition.

30. "Asimov, Calvin, and Moses," in Clareson, *Voices for the Future*, p. 103.

31. "Instinct," in *Men and Machines: Ten Stories of Science Fiction*, ed. Robert Silverberg (New York: Meredith, 1968), p. 102. Future references are to this edition.

32. "Robot's Return," in *Adventures in Time and Space*, ed. Raymond J. Healy and J. Francis McComas (New York: Bantam, 1955), p. 146.

33. "Genesis as Myth," in *Genesis as Myth and Other Essays* (London: Cape, 1969), p. 11.

34. "For a Breath I Tarry," in *Modern Science Fiction*, ed. Norman Spinrad (Garden City, N.J.: Doubleday Anchor, 1974), p. 362. Future references are to this edition.

7. ICON OF THE MONSTER

1. H. Frankfort, H. A. Frankfort, John A. Wilson, and Thorkild Jacobsen, *Before Philosophy: The Intellectual Adventure of Ancient Man* (Baltimore: Penguin, 1949), p. 11.

2. J. E. Cirlot, *A Dictionary of Symbols*, trans. Jack Sage (New York: Philosophical Library, 1962), p. 203.

3. *The World as Will and Idea*, trans. R. B. Haldane and J. Kemp (London: Trench, 1909), I: 202.

4. *The Metal Monster* (New York: Avon, n.d.), p. 102.

5. *Last and First Men and Star Maker* (New York: Dover, 1968), pp. 338-39. Future references are to this edition.

6. In *The Hidden Planet: Science Fiction Adventures on Venus*, ed. Donald A. Wollheim (New York: Ace, 1959), pp. 147-49.

7. A strikingly similar use of this metaphor may be found in a novel not usually regarded as science fiction, Jerzy Kosinski's *Being There* (New York: Harcourt, Brace, 1970), in which the protagonist's lack of motive is compared to that of a plant: "No plant is able to think about itself or able to know itself; there is no mirror in which the plant can recognize its face; no plant can do anything intentionally; it cannot help growing, and its growth has no meaning, since a plant cannot reason or dream" (pp. 3-4).

chapter seven

8. Sir James George Frazer, *The New Golden Bough: A New Abridgment of the Classic Work,* ed. Theodor H. Gaster (New York: Criterion, 1959), p. 73.

9. In *The Magazine of Fantasy and Science Fiction,* 50, 6 (June 1976), 5.

10. *Day of the Triffids* (New York: Doubleday, 1951), p. 39.

11. Susan Sontag, "The Imagination of Disaster," *Against Interpretation* (New York: Dell, 1969), pp. 212-28.

12. *Science Fiction in the Cinema* (New York: Paperback Library, 1970), pp. 118-20.

13. "Tales of the Marvellous and Ridiculous" in *Classics and Commercials* (New York: Noonday, 1967), p. 288.

14. In *Science Fiction, Today and Tomorrow,* ed. Reginald Bretnor (New York: Harper, 1974), pp. 259-77.

15. *The Pentagon of Power* (New York: Harcourt, Brace, 1970), pp. 48-49.

16. A. M. Hocart, *Social Origins* (London: Watts, 1954), p. 35.

17. *Slave Ship* (New York: Ballantine, 1957), p. 147.

18. Reproduced in Brian Aldiss, *Science Fiction Art* (New York: Bounty, 1975), p. 85.

19. Springfield, Ill.: Charles C. Thomas, 1968, p. 85.

20. "First Contact," in *The Science Fiction Hall of Fame,* Vol. I, ed. Robert Silverberg (Garden City, N.J.: Doubleday, 1970), p. 254. Future references are to this edition.

21. Quoted in Sam Moskowitz, *Seekers of Tomorrow* (New York: Ballantine, 1967), p. 70.

22. "Scientific Method" in Chad Oliver, *Another Kind* (New York: Ballantine, 1955), p. 62.

23. New York: New American Library, 1957, p. 43. Future references are to this edition.

24. Walter Evans, "Monster Movies: A Sexual Theory," *Journal of Popular Film,* 3 (1974), pp. 353-65.

25. New York: Ballantine, 1971, p. 210.

26. Blish, *Seedling Stars,* p. 7.

27. Personal communication, 1974.

28. New York: Ace, 1952, p. 114.

29. "Ancient Myths and Modern Man," in *Man and His Symbols,* ed. C. G. Jung and M.-L. von Franz (Garden City, N.J.: Doubleday, 1964), pp. 149-51.

30. *ESPer* (New York: Avon, 1958), p. 139.

31. *More Than Human* (New York: Ballantine, 1953), p. 4. Future references are to this edition.

32. *The Fantastic in Literature* (Princeton: Princeton University Press, 1976), p. 125.

33. Rabkin, *Fantastic in Literature,* p. 126.

34. *Odd John* in *The Portable Novels of Science,* ed. Donald A. Wollheim (New York: Viking, 1945), p. 509. Future references are to this edition.

35. New York: Harper Torchbooks, 1960, p. 52. Future references will be made in the text.

index

Ackerman, Forrest, 21, 198
Alas, Babylon, see Frank
Aldiss, Brian, 6, 61, 95, 105, 121, 126, 156, 166, 228; "But Who Can Replace a Man?" 177, 179; *The Primal Urge,* 29; *Starship (Non-Stop),* 66-67, 72
Allen, L. David, 138, 140
Allen, Walter, 6
"Alley Man, The," *see* Farmer
Amazing Stories, 9, 86, 117, 198
Amis, Kingsley, 94
And All the Stars a Stage, see Blish
Anderson, Poul *Brain Wave,* 204; *Shield,* 32; *Tau Zero,* 104
Andromeda Strain, The, see Crichton
". . . And Searching Mind," *see* Williamson
"Answer," *see* Brown
Anthony, Piers, *Macroscope,* 28
Aquinas, St. Thomas, 23
Arcologies, 90, 98, 116-20
"Arena," *see* Brown
Arnold, Jack, 187, 189, 198, 201
Around the Moon, see Verne
Asimov, Isaac, 9, 88, 181; *The Caves of Steel,* 89, 94, 102; "The Foundation of S.F. Success," 129; *Foundation* trilogy, 62, 105, 163, 221; *The Gods Themselves,* 33; "Hell-Fire," 125; *I, Robot,* 153, 157-64; "The Last Question," 155, 175-76, 178; laws of robotics, 158-59, 168; "Liar!" 159; "Little Lost Robot," 159, 162; "Nightfall," 24-26; "Robby," 154; "Runaround," 159, 160-61, 164
Astounding, 61, 126, 153, 166

Atlantis, 228
Auden, W. H., 89
"Automata," *see* Wright, S. Fowler

"Baby is Three," *see* Sturgeon
Bachelard, Gaston, 55, 59
Bacon, Sir Francis, *The New Atlantis,* 28
Ballard, J. G., 93, 127; "Chronopolis," 104; *The Crystal World,* 189; *The Drowned World,* 127, 146; "The Impossible Man," 184; "The Overloaded Man," 184; "The Subliminal Man," 184
Balmer, Edwin, and Philip Wylie, *When Worlds Collide,* 127, 146-47
Barbour, Ian, 5
"Barrier," *see* Boucher
"Barrier of Dread," *see* Merril
Barriers, 17, 18, 30-51
Barthell, Robert, 9
Barthes, Roland, 55
Bates, Harry, "Farewell to the Master," 155
Baxter, John, 198
Beast with a Million Eyes, The (film), 204
Being There, see Kosinski
Beneath the Planet of the Apes (film), 93
Berger, Peter, 85
Bergonzi, Bernard, 94
Bermuda triangle, 228
Bernanos, Michel, *The Other Side of the Mountain,* 188
Berry, Adrian, 33
Bester, Alfred, *The Demolished Man,* 184, 216, 217; *The Stars My Destination,* 27
Beyond the Barrier, see Knight, Damon

Beyond 30, see Burroughs
Big Eye, The, see Ehrlich
Binder, Eando, "Queen of the Skies," 121
Bionics, 185
Bixby, Jerome, "It's a *Good* Life," 48
Black Cloud, The, see Hoyle
Blake, William, 27
Blish, James, *And All the Stars a Stage*, 72, 84; *Cities in Flight*, 59, 84, 104, 109, 121, 129; "Common Time," 78, 83; *The Duplicated Man*, 184; *Jack of Eagles (ESPer)*, 216; *A Life for the Stars*, 121-23; "Seeding Program" ("A Time to Survive"), 211-12; *The Seedling Stars*, 84, 208-14; "Surface Tension," 32, 210, 212-13; "The Thing in the Attic," 212-13, 214; *The Triumph of Time*, 104, 123-24; "Watershed," 213-14; and Norman Knight, *A Torrent of Faces*, 93
Blob, The (film), 201
"Bloodless Peril, The," *see* Kuttner
Body Snatchers, The, see Finney
Bosch, Hieronymous, 191
Boucher, Anthony, "Barrier," 31, 45-47; "The Greatest Tertian," 138
"Boy and His Dog, A," *see* Ellison
Brackett, Leigh, *The Long Tomorrow*, 93, 128, 134-37, 145
Bradbury, Ray, *Fahrenheit 451*, 89, 139; *The Illustrated Man*, 184; "I, Rocket," 79; "I Sing the Body Electric!," 155; *The Martian Chronicles*, 74, 84, 91; "The Million Year Picnic," 74
Bradshaw, William, *The Goddess of Atvatabar*, 191
Brain Wave, see Anderson
Bretnor, Reginald, 23
Brown, Fredric, "Answer," 175; "Arena," 32, 35-38; "Etaoin Shrdlu," 151
Brown, Norman O., 91
Brunner, John, *Stand on Zanzibar*, 90, 93, 102; *The Whole Man*, 184
"Bulkhead," *see* Sturgeon
Burroughs, Edgar Rice, *Beyond 30*, 45; *Pellucidar*, 44
"But Who Can Replace a Man?," *see* Aldiss

Caidin, Martin, 155; *The God Machine*, 175

Campbell, John W., Jr., 153, 166, 169; "Who Goes There?," 191
Campbell, Joseph, 71
Canary, Robert, 129
Canticle for Leibowitz, A, see Miller
Capek, Karel, *R.U.R.*, 141, 156
Captive Universe, see Harrison
Car, The (film), 152
Caves of Steel, The, see Asimov
Cawelti, John, 58-59, 229
Childhood's End, see Clarke
"Chlorophyll," *see* Tall
Christopher, John, 93, 127; *The City of Gold and Lead*, 94; *The Long Winter*, 146; *No Blade of Grass (The Death of Grass)*, 146
"Chronopolis," *see* Ballard
Chrysalids, The, see Wyndham
Cirlot, J. E., 186
Cities, 20, 86-124
Cities in Flight, see Blish
"Cities in the Air," *see* Hamilton
City, see Simak
City and Stars, The, see Clarke
City of a Thousand Suns, The, see Delany
City of Gold and Lead, The, see Christopher
Clareson, Thomas, 44, 227
Clarke, Arthur C., *Against the Fall of Night*, 235-36 n; *Childhood's End*, 4, 20, 35, 50, 137, 173-74, 210, 216, 223; *The City and the Stars*, 89, 90, 92, 94, 101, 103, 104, 109, 110-16, 120, 124, 129, 172, 204, 205; "History Lesson," 138; *Rendezvous with Rama*, 28, 205
Clement, Hal, 199, 209; "The Creation of Imaginary Beings," 199, 201
Close Encounters of the Third Kind (film), 16, 19, 121, 228
Colossus, see Jones
Columbus of Space, A, see Serviss
"Common Sense," *see* Heinlein
"Common Time," *see* Blish
Conklin, Groff, 237 n
Coon, Horace, *43,000 Years Later*, 138
Cooper, Edmund, *The Overman Culture*, 62, 90, 109; *Seed of Light*, 65, 71-72, 73, 74, 109, 125
Cooper, Merian C., 187

Corman, Roger, 126
Costigan's Needle, see Sohl
"Country of the Kind, The," *see* Knight,
Damon
Crane, Robert, *Hero's Walk,* 93
"Creator, The," *see* Simak
Creature from the Black Lagoon, The
(film), 21, 187, 198
"Creeping Terror, The," *see* Matheson
Crichton, Michael, *The Andromeda
Strain,* 189, 201; *The Terminal Man,* 184
"Crystal Egg, The," *see* Wells
Crystal World, The, see Ballard

Dark Universe, see Galouye
Darwin, Erasmus, 6
"Daughters of Earth," *see* Merril
Daulton, George, "The Death Trap," 95
Day of the Dolphin, The, see Merle
Day of the Triffids, The, see Wyndham
Day of the Triffids, The (film), 189
Day the World Ended, The (film), 126
Deadly Mantis, The (film), 198
Death of Grass, The, see Christopher
"Death-Trap, The," *see* Daulton
de Camp, L. Sprague, "The Gnarly Man,"
184
Delany, Samuel, 18, 129; *The City of a
Thousand Suns,* 108-9; *Dhalgren,* 93;
The Fall of the Towers, 105-9, 120
del Rey, Lester, 228; "For I am a Jealous
People!" 13, 174; "Helen O'Loy," 154;
"Instinct," 155, 176-77, 179
Demolished Man, The, see Bester
Destination Moon (film), 60
Destination: Void, see Herbert
Dhalgren, see Delany
Dick, Philip K., 29; "The Variable Man,"
184
Dickens, Charles, 95; *A Tale of Two Cities,*
27
Disch, Thomas M., 93, 334
Dispossessed, The, see Le Guin
Disraeli, Benjamin, 95
*Dr. Strangelove, or How I Learned to Stop
Worrying and Love the Bomb* (film), 126
Douglas, Mary, 156
Doyle, Arthur Conan, 8; *The Lost World,*
44; *The Poison Belt,* 127; "When the
World Screamed," 190
Dreaming Jewels, The, see Sturgeon
Dream Millennium, The, see White, James
Drowned World, The, see Ballard
Duel (film), 152
Duncan, David, *Occam's Razor,* 33
Dune, see Herbert
Duplicated Man, The, see Blish
Dyson sphere, 28

Earth Abides, see Stewart, George R.
Earthquake (film), 93
Ehrlich, Max, *The Big Eye,* 127
Eisenstein, Alex, 235 n
Eliade, Mircea, 4, 88
Ellison, Harlan, "A Boy and His Dog," 204
Ellul, Jacques, *The Technological Society
(La Technique),* 12, 160, 168, 173
Emerson, Ralph Waldo, 25
"End, The," *see* Leinster
ESPer, see Blish
"Etaoin Shrdlu," *see* Brown
Evolution Man, The, see Lewis, Roy
Extrapolation, 48

Fagg, Ken, 121
Fahrenheit 451, see Bradbury
Fail-Safe (film), 126
Fall of the Towers, The, see Delany
Famous Monsters of Filmland, 21, 198
Fantastic Adventures, 202
Fantasy, 5
"Farewell to the Master," *see* Bates
Farmer, Philip José, "The Alley Man,"
184; *Inside Outside,* 65; *The Lovers,* 186;
Riverworld series, 29; *To Your
Scattered Bodies Go,* 3
Ferkiss, Victor, *Technological Man,* 12,
169, 173
Finney, Jack, *The Body Snatchers,* 49, 188,
191, 203
"First Contact," *see* Leinster
First Men in the Moon, The, see Wells
Five, (film), 126
"Flowering of the Strange Orchid, The,"
see Wells
"For a Breath I Tarry," *see* Zelazny
Forbidden Area, see Frank
Forbidden Planet (film), 20, 32, 199-200

Force fields, 32-33
"For I am a Jealous People!" *see* del Rey
Forster, E. M., "The Machine Stops," 101-5, 109, 118, 156
Foundation trilogy, *see* Asimov
Frank, Pat, *Alas, Babylon,* 126; *Forbidden Area,* 126
Frankenstein, see Shelley
Frankfort, H. A., 185
Frankfort, Henri, 5
Franklin, H. Bruce, 227
Frazer, Sir James, 194
Freas, Frank Kelly, 228
Fresco, Robert, 189
Freud, Sigmund, *Moses and Monotheism,* 20
Friend, Beverly, 234 n
From the Earth to the Moon, see Verne
"From *The London Times* of 1904," *see* Twain
Frye, Northrop, 88
Fuller, Buckminster, 59
Fury, see Kuttner
Future history, 8, 129-30

Galileo, 63, 213, 233 n
Galouye, Daniel, *Dark Universe,* 84, 128; *The Infinite Man,* 184
Galvani, Luigi, 6
Gantz, Kenneth, *Not in Solitude,* 191.
Gernsback, Hugo, 45, 89; *Ralph 124C41+,* 17, 28, 86, 87
Gerrold, David, *Star Trek* scripts, 204; *When Harlie was One,* 175
Giedion, Siegfried, *Mechanization Takes Command,* 12
Gilgamesh, 186
Gillon, Diana and Meir, 29
Gissing, George, 95
Glicksohn, Susan, 88
"Gnarly Man, The," *see* de Camp
Goddess of Atvatabar, The, see Bradshaw
Gods Themselves, The, see Asimov
Gog (film), 152
Gothic novel, 6
"Grand Central Terminal," *see* Szilard
"Greatest Tertian, The," *see* Boucher
Greenberg, Martin, 237 n
Greener Than You Think, see Moore, Ward

Green Rain, The, see Tabori
Griffin, Russell, 139, 142
Grimal, Pierre, 3, 5
Guénon, René, 92
Gunn, James, 8, 10, 12; *Alternate Worlds,* 12

Haggard, H. Rider, *She,* 44
Hamilton, Edmond, "Cities in the Air," 121
"Hands Across Space," *see* Oliver
Harris, John Beynon, *see* Wyndham
Harrison, Harry, 61; *Captive Universe,* 67, 69-71, 72, 74, 84; *Make Room! Make Room!,* 93
"Heart of the Serpent, The," *see* Yefremov
Heinlein, Robert, 5, 8, 89; "Common Sense," 61, 64; "Life-Line," 233 n; *Methuselah's Children,* 59, 74; *Orphans of the Sky,* 61-65, 72; *The Puppet Masters,* 203; "The Roads Must Roll," 104; *Stranger in a Strange Land,* 4, 27; "Universe," 17, 59, 61-65, 72, 84, 129; "Waldo," 154
Heisenberg, Werner, 43
"Helen O'Loy," *see* del Rey
"Hell-Fire," *see* Asimov
Henderson, Joseph L., 215
Herbert, Frank, *Destination: Void,* 79, 175; *Dune,* 4, 105; *The Santaroga Barrier,* 44, 45, 47-50
Hiroshima, 22
"History Lesson," *see* Clarke
Hocart, A. M., 200
Holberg, Lewis, *The Journey of Niels Klim to the World Underground,* 191
Housman, A. E., *A Shropshire Lad,* 180, 182
Hoyle, Fred, *The Black Cloud,* 19, 127
Hubbard, L. Ron, 166, 228
"Huddling Place," *see* Simak
Humanoids, The, see Williamson
Huntington, John, 15
Huxley, Aldous, 101; *Island,* 44
Huxley, Julian, 11

Icons, 16-29 and passim
If, 121

Illustrated Man, The, see Bradbury
I Married a Monster from Outer Space
  (film), 203
"Impacted Man, The," *see* Sheckley
"Impossible Man, The," *see* Ballard
Incredible Shrinking Man, The (film), 201
Infinite Man, The, see Galouye
Inside Outside, see Farmer
"Instinct," *see* del Rey
Invaders from Mars (film), 203
Invasion of the Body Snatchers (film), 49,
  203, *see also* Finney
Invisible Man, The, see Wells
I, Robot, see Asimov
"I, Rocket," *see* Bradbury
"I Sing the Body Electric!," *see* Bradbury
Island, see Huxley, Aldous
Island of Dr. Moreau, The, see Wells
Isotope Man, The, see Maine
"It," *see* Sturgeon
"It's a *Good* Life," *see* Bixby

Jack of Eagles, see Blish
Jaspers, Karl, 48
"Jesting Pilot," *see* Kuttner
"Jigsaw Man, The," *see* Niven
Johannesson, Olof, *The Tale of the Big
  Computer,* 175
Johnson, George Clayton, and William
  Nolan, *Logan's Run,* 90
Jones, D. F., *Colossus,* 155, 174-75
Jones, Robert L., 92
*Journey of Niels Klim to the World
  Underground, The, see* Holberg
Jung, Carl Gustav, 19-20
Just Imagine (film), 86

Kael, Pauline, 93
Kafka, Franz, *The Trial,* 30, 32
Kelley, R. Gordon, 13
Kennedy, John F., 21
Kepler, Johannes, *Somnium,* 10
Kesey, Ken, 4
Ketterer, David, 87
"Killdozer!," *see* Sturgeon
King Kong (film), 187
Kingsley, Charles, *Yeast,* 95
Kneale, Nigel, *The Quatermass
  Experiment,* 192

Knight, Damon, *Beyond the Barrier,* 31;
  "The Country of the Kind," 90
Knight, Norman, and James Blish, *A
  Torrent of Faces,* 93
Kosinski, Jerzy, *Being There,* 238 n
Kramer, Stanley, 126
Krupa, Julian, 117
Kubrick, Stanley, 22, 60, 80, 126, 155
Kuhn, Thomas, 14-15
Kuttner, Henry, "The Bloodless Peril,"
  191; *Fury,* 128; "Jesting Pilot," 31, 32;
  Mutant, 185, 186, 216, 217; "Raider of
  the Spaceways," 191; and C. L. Moore,
  "The Proud Robot," 157-58

Lang, Fritz, 11, 17, 87, 95, 103, 105
Laplace, Pierre, 14
"Last Question, The," *see* Asimov
Last Man, The, see Shelley
Leach, Edmund, 179
Le Guin, Ursula, 9, 29, 208, 227; *The
  Dispossessed,* 44; Hainish stories, 105
Leiber, Fritz, *The Wanderer,* 127
Leibniz, Gottfried Wilhelm, 222-23
Leinster, Murray, "The End," 104; "First
  Contact," 59, 206-7; "Mad Planet," 198;
  The Monster from Earth's End, 191;
  "The Plants," 195; "Proxima Centauri,"
  191
Lem, Stanislaw, 9-10, 23, 34, 158, 227; *The
  Invincible,* 189
Lévi-Strauss, Claude, 110
Lewis, C. S., *Out of the Silent Planet,* 58;
  Perelandra, 204-5
Lewis, Roy, *The Evolution Man,* 184
"Liar!," *see* Asimov
Life for the Stars, A, see Blish
Limbo, see Wolfe
Lindsay, David, *A Voyage to Arcturus,*
  189, 210
Linebarger, Paul, *see* Smith, Cordwainer
Little Fuzzy, see Piper
"Little Lost Robot," *see* Asimov
"Living Galaxy, The," *see* Manning
Loeb, Jacques, 190
Logan's Run, see Nolan
Logan's Run (film), 93
London, Jack, "The Scarlet Plague," 127;
  "An Unparalleled Invasion," 186

Long, Frank Belknap, "The Robot Empire," 155
Long Loud Silence, The, see Tucker
Long Tomorrow, The, see Brackett
Long Winter, The, see Christopher
Lord of Light, see Zelazny
Lost World, The, see Doyle
"Lotus Eaters, The," *see* Weinbaum
Lovecraft, H. P., 194, 198-99
Lovejoy, Arthur O., *The Great Chain of Being,* 222-23, 225
Lovers, The, see Farmer
Lucas, George, 43, 228, 237 n
Lucifer's Hammer, see Niven
Luckmann, Thomas, 85
"Lulu," *see* Simak
Lundwall, Sam, 23, 158

McCaffrey, Anne, *The Ship Who Sang,* 59, 78, 80-84
MacDougall, Ranald, 126
McGowan, Roger A., 151
McIlwaine, David, *see* Maine
McIntosh, J. T., 61; *The Million Cities,* 94
Macroscope, see Anthony
"Mad Planet," *see* Leinster
Magazine of Fantasy and Science Fiction, The, 47
Maine, Charles Eric, *The Isotope Man,* 184; *The Tide Went Out,* 146; *World Without Men,* 20
"Mainstream" literature, 9, 126-27
Make Room! Make Room!, see Harrison
Manning, Laurence, "The Living Galaxy," 61, 69
Manson, Charles, 4
Man Who Fell to Earth, The, see Tevis
Martian Chronicles, The, see Bradbury
"Martian Odyssey, A," *see* Weinbaum
Matheson, Richard, "The Creeping Terror," 90; "Duel," 152; "Shipshape Home," 121; *The Shrinking Man,* 184, 201
Merle, Robert, *The Day of the Dolphin,* 204
Merril, Judith, "Barrier of Dread," 31, 34; "Daughters of Earth," 75
Merritt, Abraham, *The Metal Monster,* 190

Metal Monster, The, see Merritt
Methuselah's Children, see Heinlein
Metropolis (film), 11, 17, 22, 87, 89, 95, 99, 103, 105
Metropolis (novel), *see* von Harbou
"Microcosmic God," *see* Sturgeon
Midwich Cuckoos, The, see Wyndham
Milland, Ray, 126
Miller, Walter M., Jr., *A Canticle for Leibowitz,* 62, 128, 137-46
Million Cities, The, see McIntosh
"Million Year Picnic, The," *see* Bradbury
"Minimum Man, The," *see* Sheckley
Modern Utopia, A, see Wells
Monolith Monsters, The (film), 189
"Monster, The," *see* van Vogt
Monster from Earth's End, The, see Leinster
Monster from Green Hell, The (film), 198
Monsters, 21, 184-224
Moore, C. L., and Henry Kuttner, "The Proud Robot," 157-58
Moore, Maxine, 158, 175, 176
Moore, Ward, *Greener Than You Think,* 191
More Than Human, see Sturgeon
Morris, William, *News from Nowhere,* 97
Moskowitz, Sam, 165
Mullen, Richard D., 129
Mumford, Lewis, 59, 86, 87, 88, 97, 193, 200, 222; *The Pentagon of Power,* 10-11; *Technics and Human Development,* 10
Mutant, see Kuttner
Mutants, 17-18, 22, 185-86, 209, 216-22
Myth, and science fiction, 3-6, 10, 13-16; and speculation, 3-6

Nabokov, Vladimir, 26
Navy vs. the Night Monsters, The (film), 191
New Atlantis, The, see Bacon
News from Nowhere, see Morris
Nielsen, Leslie, 199
"Nightfall," *see* Asimov
Niven, Larry, "The Jigsaw Man," 184; *Ringworld,* 28; *World Out of Time,* 20, 60; and Jerry Pournelle, *Lucifer's Hammer,* 146
No Blade of Grass, see Christopher

Nolan, William, and George Clayton Johnson, *Logan's Run*, 90
Non-Stop, see Aldiss
Not in Solitude, see Gantz
"Null-P," *see* Tenn

Oboler, Arch, 126
Occam's Razor, see Duncan
Oliver, Chad, 61; "Scientific Method" ("Hands Across Space"), 206, 207-8; *Shadows in the Sun*, 203; "Stardust," 67
Omega Man, The (film), 184
"Once a Greech," *see* Smith, Evelyn A.
On the Beach, see Shute
Orbitsville, see Shaw
Ordway, Frederick I., 151
Orphans of the Sky, see Heinlein
Other Days, Other Eyes, see Shaw
Other Side of the Mountain, The, see Bernanos
Outer Limits, The (TV), 21
Out of the Silent Planet, see Lewis, C. S.
Outward Urge, The, see Wyndham
"Overloaded Man, The," *see* Ballard
Overman Culture, The, see Cooper

Padgett, Lewis, *see* Kuttner
Pal, George, 200
Panic in Year Zero (film), 126
Panshin, Alexei, *Rite of Passage*, 77, 84
Parkes, Lucas, *see* Wyndham
Paul, Frank R., 86, 87, 89, 116-17, 202
Pearson's Magazine, 95
Pellucidar, see Burroughs
Perelandra, see Lewis, C. S.
Piper, H. Beam, *Little Fuzzy*, 204
Planet of the Apes (film), 93
Plank, Robert, *The Emotional Significance of Imaginary Beings*, 205
"Plants, The," *see* Leinster
"Pod in the Barrier, The," *see* Sturgeon
Poe, Edgar Allan, 127, 194; Dupin stories, 8; "The Gold Bug," 7-8, 34, 158; "Mellonta Tauta," 7; "The Narrative of Arthur Gordon Pym," 7
Pohl, Frederik, *Man Plus*, 185; *Slave Ship*, 200, 204
Poison Belt, The, see Doyle
Polanyi, Michael, 12-13, 14

"Pork-Chop Tree, The," *see* Schmitz
Pournelle, Jerry, and Larry Niven, *Lucifer's Hammer*, 146
Power, The, see Robinson
Powys, John Cowper, 26
Primal Urge, The, see Aldiss
"Proud Robot, The," *see* Kuttner
"Proxima Centauri," *see* Leinster
Puppet Masters, The, see Heinlein
Purple Cloud, The, see Shiel

Quatermass Experiment, The (TV), 192
"Queen of the Skies," *see* Binder

Rabkin, Eric, S., 139, 220, 237 n
Radcliffe, Ann, 6
"Raider of the Spaceways, The," *see* Kuttner
Ralph 124C 41+, see Gernsback
Re-Birth, see Wyndham
Rendezvous with Rama, see Clarke
Ringworld, see Niven
Rite of Passage, see Panshin
Riverworld series, *see* Farmer
"Roads Must Roll, The," *see* Heinlein
"Robby," *see* Asimov
Robinson, Frank, *The Power*, 43
"Robot Empire, The," *see* Long
Robots, 20, 21, 151-83
"Robot's Return," *see* Williams
Robur the Conqueror, see Verne
Rockets, *see* spaceships
Roeg, Nicholas, 203
Roszak, Theodore, *Where the Wasteland Ends*, 12, 86, 87, 91
Rottensteiner, Franz, 23, 24, 237 n
"Runaround," *see* Asimov
R.U.R., see Čapek
Russ, Joanna, 18
Russell, Eric Frank, "Sinister Barrier," 31, 34

Saberhagen, Fred, 84
Samuelson, David, 145
Santaroga Barrier, The, see Herbert
"Scanners Live in Vain," *see* Smith, Cordwainer
"Scarlet Plague, The," *see* London

Schmitz, James H., "The Pork-Chop Tree," 196
Scholes, Robert, 139, 237 n
Schopenhauer, Arthur, 157, 189-90
Science fiction, and myth, 3-6, 10, 13-16; readership, 3-4, 17, 64, 225, 227
Science-fiction art, 86, 116-17, 121, 202, 228; *see also* individual artists
Science-fiction commercials, 228
Science-fiction film, 11, 16, 21, 22, 30, 60, 74, 93, 126, 152, 187, 189, 198, 200-1, 202-4, 206, 228; *see also* individual films
Science Fiction Hall of Fame, The, see Silverberg
Science-fiction television, 21, 32, 61, 152, 155, 228; *see also* individual programs
Science Wonder Stories, 117
Scientific method, 4, 8-9, 15, 189
"Scientific Method," *see* Oliver
Scientology, 228
"Seeding Program," *see* Blish
Seedling Stars, The, see Blish
Seed of Light, see Cooper
"Sentinel, The," *see* Clarke
Serling, Rod, "A Thing About Machines," 152
Serviss, Garrett P., 127; *A Columbus of Space,* 57-58, 60
Sexism, in science fiction, 73-75, 234 n
Shadows in the Sun, see Oliver
Shakespeare, William, *The Tempest,* 20, 199
Shaver, Richard, 228
Shaw, Bob, *Orbitsville,* 28; *Other Days, Other Eyes,* 29
She, see Haggard
Sheckley, Robert, "The Impacted Man," 184; "The Minimum Man," 184; "Specialist," 79
Shelley, Mary, *Frankenstein,* 6-7, 153; *The Last Man,* 184
Sherwood, John, 189
Shiel, M. P., 186; *The Purple Cloud,* 93, 127, 186
Shield, see Anderson
"Shipshape Home," *see* Matheson
Ship Who Sang, The, see McCaffrey
Shrinking Man, The, see Matheson
Shute, Nevil, *On the Beach,* 93, 126

Silverberg, Robert, 227; *The Science Fiction Hall of Fame,* 31; *Son of Man,* 210; *The Stochastic Man,* 184; *The World Inside,* 90, 91-92, 98, 102, 116-20, 121
Simak, Clifford, 61; *All Flesh is Grass,* 32; *City,* 32, 88, 124, 204, 214-15; "The Creator," 174; "Huddling Place," 32; "Lulu," 78, 80-81; "Skirmish," 152, 204; "Target Generation," 65-66, 84; *Time and Again,* 32, 33-34
Singer, June, 15
"Sinister Barrier," *see* Russell
Sirius, see Stapledon
Six Million Dollar Man, The (TV), 155, 184
Skinner, B. F., *Walden Two,* 163
"Skirmish," *see* Simak
Skylab, 17
Slan, see van Vogt
Slave Ship, see Pohl
Smith, Clark Ashton, "Marooned on Andromeda," 191
Smith, Cordwainer, 20; "The Burning of the Brain," 75-77; Instrumentality stories, 105, 204; "The Lady Who Sailed The Soul," 77; "Scanners Live in Vain," 185, 215; "Three to a Given Star," 80
Smith, Evelyn E., "Once a Greech," 79
Socrates, 24
Sohl, Jerry, *Costigan's Needle,* 33; *The Transcendent Man,* 184
Soleri, Paolo, 116
Son of Man, see Silverberg
Sontag, Susan, 198
Space-Born, The, see Tubb
Space: 1999 (TV), 190
Spaceships, 17, 19, 20, 21, 55-85
Space shuttle, 17, 21
"Specialist," *see* Sheckley
Speculation, and myth, 3-6
Spengler, Oswald, 90, 129
Spielberg, Steven, 121, 152, 228
Stand on Zanzibar, see Brunner
Stapledon, William Olaf, 88, 223; *Last and First Men,* 221; *Odd John,* 221-22; *Sirius,* 204; *Star Maker,* 192-93, 221, 222
"Stardust," *see* Oliver
Starlost, The (TV), 61

Starship, see Aldiss
Stars My Destination, The, see Bester
Star Trek (TV), 32, 190, 204
Star Wars (film), 16, 43, 60, 228, 237 n
Stevens, Wallace, 184
Stewart, Alfred, 172
Stewart, George R., *Earth Abides,* 127
Stochastic Man, The, see Silverberg
"Story of the Days to Come, A," *see* Wells
Stover, Leon, 48, 50
Stranger in a Strange Land, see Heinlein
Sturgeon, Theodore, "Baby is Three," 217;
   "Bulkhead," 17; *The Dreaming Jewels
   (The Synthetic Man),* 184, 190; "It," 218;
   "Killdozer!," 152, 169; "Microcosmic
   God," 31, 32; *More Than Human,* 44, 50,
   79, 169, 216, 217-22; "Pod in the Barrier,
   The," 32, 35, 38-44; "Tiny and the
   Monster," 204
"Subliminal Man, The," *see* Ballard
Super Science Fiction, 198
"Surface Tension," *see* Blish
Swift, Jonathan, 121
Synthetic Man, The, see Sturgeon
Szilard, Leo, "Grand Central Terminal,"
   138

Tabori, Paul, *The Green Rain,* 191-92
Tale of the Big Computer, The, see
   Johannesson
Tall, Stephen, "Chlorophyll," 194-95
"Target Generation," *see* Simak
Tau Zero, see Anderson
Telepaths, 216-22
Tempest, The, see Shakespeare
Tenn, William, "Null-P," 133
Terminal Man, The, see Crichton
Tevis, Walter, *The Man Who Fell to Earth,*
   203
Them! (film), 198
Thing, The (film), 191, 201
"Thing in the Attic, The," *see* Blish
"Three to a Given Star," *see* Smith,
   Cordwainer
Tide Went Out, The, see Maine
Time and Again, see Simak
Time Machine, The, see Wells
Time machines, 18
"Time to Survive, A," *see* Blish

"Tiny and the Monster," *see* Sturgeon
Tomorrow!, see Wylie
Torrent of Faces, A, see Blish
Tors, Ivan, 152
To Your Scattered Bodies Go, see Farmer
Transcendent Man, The, see Sohl
Trial, The, see Kafka
Triumph, see Wylie
Triumph of Time, The, see Blish
Trumbull, Douglas, 121
Tubb, E. C., *The Space-Born,* 60, 61, 67-69
Tucker, Wilson, *The Long Loud Silence,*
   93, 128
Twain, Mark, "From *The London Times
   of* 1904," 28
Twilight Zone, The (TV), 152
2001: A Space Odyssey (film), 22, 60, 80,
   114, 155, 161, 204

"Universe," *see* Heinlein
"Unparalleled Invasion, An," *see* London
van Vogt, A. E., 14, 61, 129; "The
   Monster," 223-24; *Slan,* 185, 186, 216,
   217
"Variable Man, The," *see* Dick
Verhoeven, Cornelius, *The Philosophy of
   Wonder,* 24
Verne, Jules, 55-56, 59; *Around the Moon,*
   55-56; *From the Earth to the Moon,* 55;
   Robur the Conqueror, 55
Vernier, Jean-Pierre, 94
Vinci, Leonardo da, 127
von Harbou, Thea, *Metropolis,* 87, 105
Voyage to Arcturus, A, see Lindsay
Voyage to the Bottom of the Sea (TV), 21

Walden Two, see Skinner
"Waldo," *see* Heinlein
Wanderer, The, see Leiber
War Game, The (film), 126
War of the Worlds, The, see Wells
War of the Worlds, The (film), 200
Wasteland, 22, 127-47
"Watershed," *see* Blish
Watkins, Peter, 126
Watson, Ian, 29
Weinbaum, Stanley, "The Lotus Eaters,"
   193; "A Martian Odyssey," 205

Wells, H. G., "The Crystal Egg," 27; *The First Men in the Moon*, 56-57, 59, 60; "The Flowering of the Strange Orchid," 191; *The Invisible Man*, 184; *The Island of Dr. Moreau*, 200; *A Modern Utopia*, 101; "A Story of the Days to Come," 97-99, 117; *The Time Machine*, 10, 94-98, 100, 102, 104, 117, 118, 156, 202; *The War of the Worlds*, 57, 63, 93, 189, 202, 206, 219; *When the Sleeper Wakes*, 95, 99-101, 103, 117

When Harlie Was One, see Gerrold

When the Sleeper Wakes, see Wells

"When the World Screamed," *see* Doyle

When Worlds Collide, see Wylie

White, James, 61; *The Dream Millennium*, 78

White, Ted, 9

White, William A., *see* Boucher

"Who Goes There?," *see* Campbell

Whole Man, The, see Brunner

Wiener, Norbert, 22, 152

Wilcoxon, Fred, 199

Williams, Raymond, 95

Williams, Robert Moore, "Robot's Return," 177-78

Williamson, Jack, 157; ". . . And Searching Mind," 166; *The Humanoids*, 20, 27, 129, 159, 164-74, 177; "With Folded Hands," 159, 164-74

Wilson, Edmund, 198-99

Winner, Langdon, *Autonomous Technology*, 13

"With Folded Hands," *see* Williamson

Wolfe, Bernard, *Limbo*, 155

Wollheim, Donald, *The Universe Makers*, 12, 13

Wonder, sense of, 23-27

World Almanac, 159

World Inside, The, see Silverberg

World Out of Time, see Niven

World, the Flesh, and the Devil, The (film), 126, 186

World Without Men, see Maine

Wright, Frank Lloyd, 116

Wright, S. Fowler, 127; "Automata," 156, 160, 162, 169, 174

Wylie, Philip, *Tomorrow!*, 93, 125; *Triumph*, 126; and Edwin Balmer, *When Worlds Collide*, 127, 146-47

Wymer, Thomas, 213

Wyndham, John, *Day of the Triffids*, 188, 191-97; *The Midwich Cuckoos*, 19; *The Outward Urge*, 75; *Re-Birth (The Chrysalids)*, 62, 128, 131-34, 135, 137

Yefremov, Ivan, "The Heart of the Serpent," 207

Zamiatin, Eugene, 101

Zelazny, Roger, "For a Breath I Tarry," 155, 178-83; *Lord of Light*, 92

GARY K. WOLFE received his doctorate from The University of Chicago and is now Associate Professor of Humanities at Roosevelt University. His numerous writings on science-fiction topics and adult education include a chapter in *Many Futures, Many Worlds* (Kent State University Press, 1977).